P9-AOJ-628

EUGENE O'NEILL

THE GREAT GOD BROWN
THE FOUNTAIN
THE MOON OF THE CARIBBEES
And Other Plays

PLAYS OF
EUGENE O'NEILL

Uniform with this edition

THE EMPEROR JONES
GOLD
THE FIRST MAN
THE DREAMY KID
In one volume

BEYOND THE HORIZON
THE STRAW
BEFORE BREAKFAST
In one volume

ANNA CHRISTIE
ALL GOD'S CHILLUN GOT WINGS
and DIFF'RENT
In one volume

DESIRE UNDER THE ELMS
THE HAIRY APE, and
WELDED
In one volume

EUGENE O'NEILL

THE GREAT GOD BROWN
THE FOUNTAIN
THE MOON OF THE CARIBBEES
And Other Plays

NEW YORK
BONI & LIVERIGHT
1 9 2 6

PLAYS OF EUGENE O'NEILL

Printed in the United States of America

First printing, March, 1926
Second printing, June, 1926
Third printing, September, 1926
Fourth printing, January, 1927

NOTE

CONTENTS

THE GREAT GOD BROWN

(1925)

CHARACTERS

William A. Brown
His Father, *a contractor*
His Mother
Dion Anthony
His Father, *a builder*
His Mother
Margaret
Her Three Sons
Cybel
Two Draftsmen } *in Brown's office*
A Stenographer }

SCENES

PROLOGUE

The Pier of the Casino. Moonlight in middle June.

ACT ONE

SCENE I: Sitting room, Margaret Anthony's apartment. Afternoon, seven years later.

SCENE II: Billy Brown's office. The same afternoon.

SCENE III: Cybel's parlor. That night.

ACT TWO

SCENE I: Cybel's parlor. Seven years later. Dusk.

SCENE II: Drafting room, William A. Brown's office. That evening.

SCENE III: Library, William A. Brown's home. That night.

ACT THREE

SCENE I: Brown's office, a month later. Morning.

SCENE II: Library, Brown's home. That evening.

SCENE III: Sitting room, Margaret's home. That night.

ACT FOUR

SCENE I: Brown's office, weeks later. Late afternoon.

SCENE II: Library, Brown's house, hours later. The same night.

EPILOGUE

The Pier of the Casino. Four years later.

THE GREAT GOD BROWN

PROLOGUE

SCENE. *A cross section of the pier of the Casino. In the rear, built out beyond the edge, is a rectangular space with benches on the three sides. A rail encloses the entire wharf at the back.*

It is a moonlight night in mid-June. From the Casino comes the sound of the school quartet rendering "Sweet Adeline" with many ultra-sentimental barber-shop quavers. There is a faint echo of the ensuing hand-clapping—then nothing but the lapping of ripples against the piles and their swishing on the beach—then footsteps on the boards and BILLY BROWN *walks along from right with his* MOTHER *and* FATHER. *The* MOTHER *is a dumpy woman of forty-five, overdressed in black lace and spangles. The* FATHER *is fifty or more, the type of bustling, genial, successful, provincial business man, stout and hearty in his evening dress.*

BILLY BROWN *is a handsome, tall and athletic boy of nearly eighteen. He is blond and blue-eyed, with a likeable smile and a frank good-humored face, its expression already indicating a disciplined restraint. His manner has the easy self-assurance of a normal intelligence. He is in evening dress.*

They walk arm in arm, the MOTHER *between.*

MOTHER. (*always addressing the* FATHER) This Commencement dance is badly managed. Such singing! Such poor voices! Why doesn't Billy sing?

BILLY. (*to her*) Mine is a regular fog horn! (*He laughs*)

MOTHER. (*to the air*) I had a pretty voice, when I was a girl. (*Then, to the* FATHER, *caustically*) Did you see young Anthony strutting around the ballroom in dirty flannel pants?

FATHER. He's just showing off.

MOTHER. Such impudence! He's as ignorant as his father.

FATHER. The old man's all right. My only kick against him is he's been too damned conservative to let me branch out.

MOTHER. (*bitterly*) He has kept you down to his level—out of pure jealousy.

FATHER. But he took me into partnership, don't forget——

MOTHER. (*sharply*) Because you were the brains! Because he was afraid of losing you! (*A pause*)

BILLY. (*admiringly*) Dion came in his old clothes on a bet with me. He's a real sport. He wouldn't have been afraid to appear in his pajamas! (*He grins with appreciation*)

MOTHER. Isn't the moonlight clear! (*She goes and sits on the center bench.* BILLY *stands at the left corner, forward, his hand on the rail, like a prisoner at the bar, facing the judge. His* FATHER *stands in front of the bench on right. The* MOTHER *announces, with finality*) After he's through college, Billy must study for a profession of some sort, I'm determined on that! (*She turns to her husband, defiantly, as if expecting opposition*)

FATHER. (*eagerly and placatingly*) Just what I've been thinking, my dear. Architecture! How's that? Billy a first-rate, number-one architect! That's my proposition! What I've always wished I could have been myself! Only I never had the opportunity. But Billy—we'll make him a partner in the firm after. Anthony, Brown *and Son, architects* and builders—instead of *contractors* and builders!

MOTHER. (*yearning for the realization of a dream*) And we won't lay sidewalks—or dig sewers—ever again?

FATHER. (*a bit ruffled*) I and Anthony can build anything your pet can draw—even if it's a church! (*Then, selling his idea*) It's a great chance for him! He'll design—expand us—make the firm famous.

MOTHER. (*to the air—musingly*) When you proposed, I thought your future promised success—my future—(*with a sigh*)—Well, I suppose we've been comfortable. Now, it's his future. How would Billy like to be an architect? (*She does not look at him*)

BILLY (*to her*) All right, Mother. (*Then sheepishly*) I guess I've never bothered much about what I'd like to do after college—but architecture sounds all right to me, I guess.

MOTHER. (*to the air—proudly*) Billy used to draw houses when he was little.

FATHER. (*jubilantly*) Billy's got the stuff in him to win, if he'll only work hard enough.

BILLY. (*dutifully*) I'll work hard, Dad.

MOTHER. Billy can do anything!

BILLY. (*embarrassed*) I'll try, Mother. (*There is a pause*)

MOTHER. (*with a sudden shiver*) The nights are so much colder than they used to be! Think of it, I once went moonlight bathing in June when I was a girl—but the moonlight was so warm and beautiful in those days, do you remember, Father?

FATHER. (*puts his arm around her affectionately*) You bet I do, Mother. (*He kisses her. The orchestra at the Casino strikes up a waltz*) There's the music. Let's go back and watch the young folks dance. (*They start off, leaving* BILLY *standing there*)

MOTHER. (*suddenly calls back over her shoulder*) I want to watch Billy dance.

BILLY (*dutifully*) Yes, Mother! (*He follows them. For a moment the faint sound of the music and the lapping of waves is heard. Then footsteps again and the three* ANTHONYS *come in. First come the* FATHER *and* MOTHER, *who are not masked. The* FATHER *is a tall lean man of fifty-five or sixty with a grim, defensive face, obstinate to the point of stupid weakness. The* MOTHER *is a thin frail faded woman, her manner perpetually nervous and distraught, but with a sweet and gentle face that had once been beautiful. The* FATHER *wears an ill-fitting black suit, like a mourner. The* MOTHER *wears a cheap, plain, black dress. Following them, as if he were a stranger, walking alone, is their son,* DION. *He is about the same height as young* BROWN *but lean and wiry, without repose, continually in restless nervous movement. His face is masked. The mask is a fixed forcing of his own face—dark, spiritual, poetic, passionately super-sensitive, helplessly unprotected in its childlike, religious faith in life—into the expression of a mocking, reckless, defiant, gayly scoffing and sensual young Pan. He is dressed in a gray flannel shirt, open at the neck, sneakers over bare feet, and soiled white flannel trousers. The* FATHER *strides to the center bench and sits down. The* MOTHER, *who has been holding to his arm, lets go and stands by the bench at the right. They both stare at* DION, *who, with a studied carelessness, takes his place at the rail, where young* BROWN *had stood. They watch him, with queer, puzzled eyes*)

MOTHER. (*suddenly—pleading*) You simply must send him to college!

FATHER. I won't. I don't believe in it. Colleges turn out lazy loafers to sponge on their poor old fathers! Let him slave like I had to! That'll teach him the value of a dollar! College'll only make him a bigger fool than he is already! I never got above grammar school but I've made money and established a sound business. Let him make a man out of himself like I made of myself!

DION. (*mockingly—to the air*) This Mr. Anthony is my father, but he only imagines he is God the Father. (*They both stare at him*)

FATHER. (*with angry bewilderment*) What—what—what's that?

MOTHER. (*gently remonstrating to her son*) Dion, dear! (*Then to her husband—tauntingly*) Brown takes all the credit! He tells everyone the success is all due to his energy—that you're only an old stick-in-the-mud!

FATHER. (*stung, harshly*) The damn fool! He knows better'n anyone if I hadn't held him down to common sense, with his crazy wild-cat notions, he'd have had us ruined long ago!

MOTHER. He's sending Billy to college—Mrs. Brown just told me—going to have him study architecture afterwards, too, so's he can help expand your firm!

FATHER. (*angrily*) What's that? (*Suddenly turns on* DION *furiously*) Then you can make up your mind to go, too!

And you'll learn to be a better architect than Brown's boy or I'll turn you out in the gutter without a penny! You hear?

DION. (*mockingly—to the air*) It's difficult to choose—but architecture sounds less laborious.

MOTHER (*fondly*) You ought to make a wonderful architect, Dion. You've always painted pictures so well——

DION. (*with a start—resentfully*) Why must she lie? Is it my fault? She knows I only try to paint. (*Passionately*) But I will, some day! (*Then quickly, mocking again*) On to college! Well, it won't be home, anyway, will it? (*He laughs queerly and approaches them. His* FATHER *gets up defensively.* DION *bows to him*). I thank Mr. Anthony for this splendid opportunity to create myself—— (*He kisses his mother, who bows with a strange humility as if she were a servant being saluted by the young master—then adds lightly*)—in my mother's image, so she may feel her life comfortably concluded. (*He sits in his* FATHER'*s place at center and his mask stares with a frozen mockery before him. They stand on each side, looking dumbly at him*)

MOTHER. (*at last, with a shiver*) It's cold. June didn't use to be cold. I remember the June when I was carrying you, Dion—three months before you were born. (*She stares up at the sky*) The moonlight was warm, then. I could feel the night wrapped around me like a gray velvet gown lined with warm sky and trimmed with silver leaves!

FATHER. (*gruffly—but with a certain awe*) My mother used to believe the full of the moon was the time to sow. She was terrible old-fashioned. (*With a grunt*) I can feel it's bringing on my rheumatism. Let's go back indoors.

DION. (*with intense bitterness*) Hide! Be ashamed! (*They both start and stare at him*)

FATHER. (*with bitter hopelessness. To his wife—indicating their son*) Who is he? You bore him!

MOTHER. (*proudly*) He's my boy! He's Dion!

DION. (*bitterly resentful*) What else, indeed! The identical son! (*Then mockingly*) Are Mr. Anthony and his wife going in to dance? The nights grow cold! The days are dimmer than they used to be! Let's play hide-and-seek! Seek the monkey in the moon! (*He suddenly cuts a grotesque caper, like a harlequin and darts off, laughing with forced abandon. They stare after him—then slowly follow. Again there is silence except for the sound of the lapping waves. Then* MARGARET *comes in, followed by the humbly worshiping* BILLY BROWN. *She is almost seventeen, pretty and vivacious, blonde, with big romantic eyes, her figure lithe and strong, her facial expression intelligent but youthfully dreamy, especially now in the moonlight. She is in a simple white dress. On her entrance, her face is masked with an exact, almost transparent reproduction of her own features, but giving her the abstract quality of a Girl instead of the individual* MARGARET)

MARGARET. (*looking upward at the moon and singing in low tone as they enter*) "Ah, moon of my delight that knowest no wane!"

BILLY. (*eagerly*) I've got that record—John McCormack. It's a peach! Sing some more. (*She looks upward in silence. He keeps standing respectfully in back of her, glancing embarrassedly toward her averted face. He tries to make conversation*) I think the *Rubáiyát's* great stuff, don't you? I never could memorize poetry worth a darn. Dion can recite lots of Shelley's poems by heart.

MARGARET. (*slowly takes off her mask—to the moon*) Dion! (*A pause*)

BILLY (*fidgeting*) Margaret!

MARGARET (*to the moon*) Dion is so wonderful!

BILLY (*blunderingly*) I asked you to come out here because I wanted to tell you something.

MARGARET. (*to the moon*) Why did Dion look at me like that? It made me feel so crazy!

BILLY. I wanted to ask you something, too.

MARGARET. That one time he kissed me—I can't forget it! He was only joking—but I felt—and he saw and just laughed!

BILLY. Because that's the uncertain part. My end of it is a sure thing, and has been for a long time, and I guess everybody in town knows it—they're always kidding me—so it's a cinch you must know—how I feel about you.

MARGARET. Dion's so different from all the others. He can paint beautifully and write poetry and he plays and sings and dances so marvelously. But he's sad and shy, too, just like a baby sometimes, and he understands what I'm really like inside —and—and I'd love to run my fingers through his hair—and I love him! Yes, I love him! (*She stretches out her arms to the moon*) Oh, Dion, I love you!

BILLY. I love you, Margaret.

MARGARET. I wonder if Dion—— I saw him looking at me again tonight—— Oh, I wonder. . . . !

BILLY. (*takes her hand and blurts out*) Can't you love me? Won't you marry me—after college——

MARGARET. Where is Dion now, I wonder?

BILLY. (*shaking her hand in an agony of uncertainty*) Margaret! Please answer me!

MARGARET. (*her dream broken, puts on her mask and turns to him—matter-of-factly*) It's getting chilly. Let's go back and dance, Billy.

BILLY. (*desperately*) I love you! (*He tries clumsily to kiss her*)

MARGARET. (*with an amused laugh*) Like a brother! You can kiss me if you like. (*She kisses him*) A big-brother kiss. It doesn't count. (*He steps back crushed, with head bowed. She turns away and takes off her mask—to the moon*) I wish Dion would kiss me again!

BILLY. (*painfully*) I'm a poor boob. I ought to know better. I'll bet I know. You're in love with Dion. I've seen you look at him. Isn't that it?

MARGARET. Dion! I love the sound of it!

BILLY. (*huskily*) Well—he's always been my best friend—I'm glad it's him—and I guess I know how to lose—— (*He takes her hand and shakes it*)—so here's wishing you all the success and happiness in the world, Margaret—and remember I'll always be your best friend! (*He gives her hand a final shake—swallows hard—then manfully*) Let's go back in!

MARGARET. (*To the moon—faintly annoyed*) What is Billy Brown doing here? I'll go down to the end of the dock and wait. Dion is the moon and I'm the sea. I want to feel the moon kissing the sea. I want Dion to leave the sky to me. I want the tides of my blood to leave my heart and follow him! (*She whispers like a little girl*) Dion! Margaret! Peggy! Peggy is Dion's girl—Peggy is Dion's little girl—— (*She sings *laughingly, elfishly)* Dion is my Daddy-O! *(She is walking toward the end of the dock, off left)*

BILLY. *(who has turned away)* I'm going. I'll tell Dion you're here.

MARGARET. *(more and more strongly and assertively, until at the end she is a wife and a mother)* And I'll be Mrs. Dion—Dion's wife—and he'll be my Dion—my own Dion—my little boy—my baby! The moon is drowned in the tides of my heart, and peace sinks deep through the sea! *(She disappears off left, her upturned unmasked face like that of a rapturous visionary. There is silence again, in which the dance music is heard. Then this stops and* DION *comes in. He walks quickly to the bench at center and throws himself on it, hiding his masked face in his hands. After a moment, he lifts his head, peers about, listens huntedly, then slowly takes off his mask. His real face is revealed in the bright moonlight, shrinking, shy and gentle, full of a deep sadness)*

DION. *(with a suffering bewilderment)* Why am I afraid to dance, I who love music and rhythm and grace and song and laughter? Why am I afraid to live, I who love life and the beauty of flesh and the living colors of earth and sky and sea? Why am I afraid of love, I who love love? Why am I afraid, I who am not afraid? Why must I pretend to scorn in order to pity? Why must I hide myself in self-contempt in order to understand? Why must I be so ashamed of my strength, so proud of my weakness? Why must I live in a cage like a criminal, defying and hating, I who love peace and friendship? *(Clasping his hands above in supplication)* Why was I born without a skin, O God, that I must wear armor in order to touch or to be touched? *(A second's pause of wait-*

ing silence—then he suddenly claps his mask over his face again, with a gesture of despair and his voice becomes bitter and sardonic) Or rather, Old Graybeard, why the devil was I ever born at all? *(Steps are heard from the right.* DION *stiffens and his mask stares straight ahead.* BILLY *comes in from the right. He is shuffling along disconsolately. When he sees* DION, *he stops abruptly and glowers resentfully—but at once the "good loser" in him conquers this)*

BILLY. *(embarrassedly)* Hello, Dion. I've been looking all over for you. *(He sits down on the bench at right, forcing a joking tone)* What are you sitting here for, you nut—trying to get more moonstruck? *(A pause—awkwardly)* I just left Margaret——

DION. *(gives a start—immediately defensively mocking)* Bless you, my children!

BILLY. *(gruffly and slangily)* I'm out of it—she gave me the gate. You're the original white-haired boy. Go on in and win! We've been chums ever since we were kids, haven't we? —and—I'm glad it's you, Dion. *(This huskily—he fumbles for* DION's *hand and gives it a shake)*

DION. *(letting his hand fall back—bitterly)* Chums? Oh no, Billy Brown would despise me!

BILLY. She's waiting for you now, down at the end of the dock.

DION. For me? Which? Who? Oh no, girls only allow themselves to look at what is seen!

BILLY. She's in love with you.

DION. *(moved—a pause—stammers)* Miracle? I'm afraid! *(He chants flippantly)* I love, thou lovest, he loves, she loves! She loves, she loves—what?

BILLY. And I know damn well, underneath your nuttiness, you're gone on her.

DION. (*moved*) Underneath? I love love! I'd love to be loved! But I'm afraid! (*Then aggressively*) *Was* afraid! Not now! Now I can make love—to anyone! Yes, I love Peggy! Why not? Who is she? Who am I? We love, you love, they love, one loves! No one loves! All the world loves a lover, God loves us all and we love Him! Love is a word—a shameless ragged ghost of a word—begging at all doors for life at any price!

BILLY. (*always as if he hadn't listened to what the other said*) Say, let's you and me room together at college——

DION. Billy wants to remain by her side!

BILLY. It's a bet, then! (*Forcing a grin*) You can tell her I'll see that you behave! (*Turns away*) So long. Remember she's waiting. (*He goes*)

DION. (*dazedly, to himself*) Waiting—waiting for me! (*He slowly removes his mask. His face is torn and transfigured by joy. He stares at the sky raptly*) O God in the moon, did you hear? She loves me! I am not afraid! I am strong! I can love! She protects me! Her arms are softly around me! She is warmly around me! She is my skin! She is my armor! Now I am born—I—the I!—one and indivisible—I who love Margaret! (*He glances at his mask triumphantly—in tones of deliverance*) You are outgrown! I am beyond you! (*He stretches out his arms to the sky*) O God, now I believe! (*From the end of the wharf, her voice is heard*)

MARGARET. Dion!

DION. (*raptly*) Margaret!

MARGARET. (*nearer*) Dion!

DION. Margaret!

MARGARET. Dion! (*She comes running in, her mask in her hands. He springs toward her with outstretched arms but she shrinks away with a frightened shriek and hastily puts on her mask.* DION *starts back. She speaks coldly and angrily*) Who are you? Why are you calling me? I don't know you!

DION. (*heart-brokenly*) I love you!

MARGARET (*freezingly*) Is this a joke—or are you drunk?

DION. (*with a final pleading whisper*) Margaret! (*But she only glares at him contemptuously. Then with a sudden gesture he claps his mask on and laughs wildly and bitterly*) Ha-ha-ha! That's one on you, Peg!

MARGARET. (*with delight, pulling off her mask*) Dion! How did you ever—— Why, I never knew you!

DION. (*puts his arm around her boldly*) How? It's the moon—the crazy moon—the monkey in the moon—playing jokes on us! (*He kisses her with his masked face with a romantic actor's passion again and again*) You love me! You know you do! Say it! Tell me! I want to hear! I want to feel! I want to know! I want to want! To want you as you want me!

MARGARET. (*in ecstasy*) Oh, Dion, I do! I do love you!

DION. (*with ironic mastery—rhetorically*) And I love you! Oh, madly! Oh, forever and ever, amen! You are my evening star and all my Pleiades! Your eyes are blue pools in which gold dreams glide, your body is a young white birch leaning backward beneath the lips of spring. So! (*He has bent her back, his arms supporting her, his face above hers*) So! (*He kisses her*)

MARGARET. (*with overpowering passionate languor*) Oh, Dion! Dion! I love you!

DION. (*with more and more mastery in his tone*) I love, you love, we love! Come! Rest! Relax! Let go your clutch on the world! Dim and dimmer! Fading out in the past behind! Gone! Death! Now! Be born! Awake! Live! Dissolve into dew—into silence—into night—into earth—into space—into peace—into meaning—into joy—into God—into the Great God Pan! (*While he has been speaking, the moon has passed gradually behind a black cloud, its light fading out. There is a moment of intense blackness and silence. Then the light gradually comes on again. Dion's voice, at first in a whisper, then increasing in volume with the light, is heard*) Wake up! Time to get up! Time to exist! Time for school! Time to learn! Learn to pretend! Cover your nakedness! Learn to lie! Learn to keep step! Join the procession! Great Pan is dead! Be ashamed!

MARGARET. (*with a sob*) Oh, Dion, I am ashamed!

DION. (*mockingly*) Sssshh! Watch the monkey in the moon! See him dance! His tail is a piece of string that was left when he broke loose from Jehovah and ran away to join Charley Darwin's circus!

MARGARET. I know you must hate me now! (*She throws her arms around him and hides her head on his shoulder*).

DION. (*deeply moved*) Don't cry! Don't——! (*He suddenly tears off his mask—in a passionate agony*) Hate you? I love you with all my soul! Love me! Why can't you love me, Margaret? (*He tries to kiss her but she jumps to her feet with a frightened cry holding up her mask before her face protectingly*)

MARGARET. Don't! Please! I don't know you! You frighten me!

DION. (*puts on his mask again—quietly and bitterly*) All's well. I'll never let you see again. (*He puts his arm around her —gently mocking*) By proxy, I love you. There! Don't cry! Don't be afraid! Dion Anthony will marry you some day. (*He kisses her*) "I take this woman——" (*Tenderly joking*) Hello, woman! Do you feel older by æons? Mrs. Dion Anthony, shall we go in and may I have the next dance?

MARGARET. (*tenderly*) You crazy child! (*Then, laughing with joy*) Mrs. Dion Anthony! It sounds wonderful, doesn't it? (*They go out as*

The Curtain Falls)

ACT ONE

SCENE ONE

SCENE. *Seven years later.*

The sitting room of MRS. DION ANTHONY'S *half of a two-family house in the homes section of the town—one of those one-design districts that daze the eye with multiplied ugliness. The four pieces of furniture shown are in keeping—an armchair at left, a table with a chair in back of it at center, a sofa at right. The same court-room effect of the arrangement of benches in Act One is held to here. The background is a backdrop on which the rear wall is painted with the intolerable lifeless realistic detail of the stereotyped paintings which usually adorn the sitting rooms of such houses. It is late afternoon of a gray day in winter.*

DION *is sitting behind the table, staring before him. The mask hangs on his breast below his neck, giving the effect of two faces. His real face has aged greatly, grown more strained and tortured, but at the same time, in some queer way, more selfless and ascetic, more fixed in its resolute withdrawal from life. The mask, too, has changed. It is older, more defiant and mocking, its sneer more forced and bitter, its Pan quality becoming Mephistophelean. It has already begun to show the ravages of dissipation.*

DION. (*suddenly reaches out and takes up a copy of the New Testament which is on the table and, putting a finger in at random, opens and reads aloud the text at which it points*) "Come unto me all ye who are heavy laden and I will give you rest." (*He stares before him in a sort of trance, his face lighted up from within but painfully confused—in an uncertain whisper*) I will come—but where are you, Savior? (*The noise of the outer door shutting is heard.* DION *starts and claps the mocking mask on his face again. He tosses the Testament aside contemptuously*) Blah! Fixation on old Mama Christianity! You infant blubbering in the dark, you! (*He laughs, with a bitter self-contempt. Footsteps approach. He picks up a newspaper and hides behind it hurriedly.* MARGARET *enters. She is dressed in stylish, expensive clothes and a fur coat, which look as if they had been remodeled and seen service. She has grown mature and maternal, in spite of her youth. Her pretty face is still fresh and healthy but there is the beginning of a permanently worried, apprehensive expression about the nose and mouth—an uncomprehending hurt in her eyes.* DION *pretends to be engrossed in his paper. She bends down and kisses him*)

MARGARET. (*with a forced gayety*) Good morning—at four in the afternoon! You were snoring when I left!

DION. (*puts his arms around her with a negligent, accustomed gesture—mockingly*) The Ideal Husband!

MARGARET. (*already preoccupied with another thought—comes and sits in chair on left*) I was afraid the children would disturb you, so I took them over to Mrs. Young's to play. (*A pause. He picks up the paper again. She asks anxiously*) I suppose they'll be all right over there, don't you? (*He doesn't answer. She is more hurt than offended)* I wish you'd try to take more interest in the children, Dion.

DION. *(mockingly)* Become a father — before breakfast? I'm in too delicate a condition. *(She turns away, hurt. Penitently he pats her hand—vaguely)* All right. I'll try.

MARGARET. *(squeezing his hand—with possessive tenderness)* Play with them. You're a bigger kid than they are—underneath.

DION. *(self-mockingly—flipping the Bible)* Underneath—I'm becoming downright infantile! "Suffer these little ones!"

MARGARET. *(keeping to her certainty)* You're my oldest.

DION. *(with mocking appreciation)* She puts the Kingdom of Heaven in its place!

MARGARET. *(withdrawing her hand)* I was serious.

DION. So was I—about something or other. *(He laughs)* This domestic diplomacy! We communicate in code—when neither has the other's key!

MARGARET. *(frowns confusedly—then forcing a playful tone)* I want to have a serious talk with you, young man! In spite of your promises, you've kept up the hard drinking and gambling you started the last year abroad.

DION. From the time I realized it wasn't in me to be an artist—except in living—and not even in that! *(He laughs bitterly)*

MARGARET. *(with conviction)* But you *can* paint, Dion—beautifully!

DION. *(with deep pain)* No! *(He suddenly takes her hand and kisses it gratefully)* I love Margaret! Her blindness surpasseth all understanding! *(Then bitterly)*—or is it pity?

MARGARET. We've only got about one hundred dollars left in the bank.

DION. (*with dazed surprise*) What! Is all the money from the sale of the house gone?

MARGARET. (*wearily*) Every day or so you've been cashing checks. You've been drinking—you haven't counted——

DION. (*irritably*) I know! (*A pause—soberly*) No more estate to fall back on, eh? Well, for five years it kept us living abroad in peace. It bought us a little happiness—of a kind—didn't it?—living and loving and having children—— (*A slight pause—bitterly*)—thinking one was creating before one discovered one couldn't!

MARGARET. (*this time with forced conviction*) But you *can* paint—beautifully!

DION. (*angrily*) Shut up! (*A pause—then jeeringly*) So my wife thinks it behooves me to settle down and support my family in the meager style to which they'll have to become accustomed?

MARGARET. (*shamefacedly*) I didn't say—still—something's got to be done.

DION. (*harshly*) Will Mrs. Anthony helpfully suggest what?

MARGARET. I met Billy Brown on the street. He said you'd have made a good architect, if you'd stuck to it.

DION. Flatterer! Instead of leaving college when my Old Man died? Instead of marrying Peggy and going abroad and being happy?

MARGARET. (*as if she hadn't heard*) He spoke of how well you used to draw.

DION. Billy was in love with Margaret at one time.

MARGARET. He wanted to know why you've never been in to see him.

DION. He's bound heaven-bent for success. It's the will of Mammon! Anthony and Brown, contractors and builders—death subtracts Anthony and I sell out—Billy graduates—Brown and Son, architects and builders—old man Brown perishes of paternal pride—and now we have William A. Brown, architect! Why his career itself already has an architectural design! One of God's mud pies!

MARGARET. He particularly told me to ask you to drop in.

DION. (*springs to his feet—assertively*) No! Pride! I have been alive!

MARGARET. Why don't you have a talk with him?

DION. Pride in my failure!

MARGARET. You were always such close friends.

DION. (*more and more desperately*) The pride which came after man's fall—by which he laughs as a creator at his self-defeats!

MARGARET. Not for my sake—but for your own—and, above all, for the children's!

DION. (*with terrible despair*) Pride! Pride without which the Gods are worms!

MARGARET. (*after a pause, meekly and humbly*) You don't want to? It would hurt you? All right, dear. Never mind. We'll manage somehow—you mustn't worry—you must start your beautiful painting again—and I can get that position in the library—it would be such fun for me working there! . . . (*She reaches out and takes his hand—tenderly*) I love you, dear. I understand.

DION. (*Slumps down into his chair, crushed, his face averted from hers, as hers is from him, although their hands are still clasped—in a trembling, expiring voice*) Pride is dying! (*As if he were suffocating, he pulls the mask from his resigned, pale, suffering face. He prays like a Saint in the desert, exorcizing a demon*) Pride is dead! Blessed are the meek! Blessed are the poor in spirit!

MARGARET. (*without looking at him—in a comforting, motherly tone*) My poor boy!

DION. (*resentfully—clapping on his mask again and springing to his feet—derisively*) Blessed are the meek for they shall inherit graves! Blessed are the poor in spirit for they are blind! (*Then with tortured bitterness*) All right! Then I ask my wife to go and ask Billy Brown—that's more deadly than if I went myself! (*With wild mockery*) Ask him if he can't find an opening for a talented young man who is only honest when he isn't sober—implore him, beg him in the name of old love, old friendship—to be a generous hero and save the woman and her children! (*He laughs with a sort of diabolical, ironical glee now, and starts to go out*)

MARGARET. (*meekly*) Are you going up street, Dion?

DION. Yes.

MARGARET. Will you stop at the butchers' and have them send two pounds of pork chops?

DION. Yes.

MARGARET. And stop at Mrs. Young's and ask the children hurry right home?

DION. Yes.

MARGARET. Will you be back for dinner, Dion?

DION. No. (*He goes, the outer door slams.* MARGARET *sighs with a tired incomprehension and goes to the window and stares out*)

MARGARET. (*worriedly*) I hope they'll watch out, crossing the street.

(*Curtain*)

ACT ONE

SCENE TWO

SCENE. BILLY BROWN'S *Office, at five in the afternoon. At center, a fine mahogany desk with a swivel chair in back of it. To the left of desk, an office armchair. To the right of desk, an office lounge. The background is a backdrop of an office wall, treated similarly to that of Scene One in its over-meticulous representation of detail.*

BILLY BROWN *is seated at the desk looking over a blue print by the light of a desk lamp. He has grown into a fine-looking, well-dressed, capable, college-bred American business man, boyish still and with the same engaging personality.*

The telephone rings.

BROWN. (*answering it*) Yes? Who? (*This in surprise—then with eager pleasure*) Let her come right in. (*He gets up and goes to the door, expectant and curious.* MARGARET *enters. Her face is concealed behind the mask of the pretty young matron, still hardly a woman, who cultivates a naïvely innocent and bravely hopeful attitude toward things and acknowledges no wound to the world. She is dressed as in Scene One but with an added touch of effective primping here and there*)

MARGARET. (*very gayly*) Hello, Billy Brown!

BROWN. (*awkward in her presence, shakes her hand*) Come in. Sit down. This is a pleasant surprise, Margaret. (*She sits down on the lounge. He sits in his chair behind the desk, as before*)

MARGARET. (*looking around*) What lovely offices! My, but Billy Brown is getting grand!

BROWN. (*pleased*) I've just moved in. The old place was too stuffy.

MARGARET. It looks so prosperous—but then, Billy is doing so wonderfully well, everyone says.

BROWN. (*modestly*) Well, to be frank, it's been mostly luck. Things have come my way without my doing much about it. (*Then, with an abashed pride*) Still—I have done a little something myself. (*He picks the plan from the desk*) See this? It's my design for the new Municipal Building. It's just been accepted—provisionally—by the Committee.

MARGARET. (*taking it—vaguely*) Oh? (*She looks at it abstractedly. There is a pause. Suddenly*) You mentioned the other day how well Dion used to draw——

BROWN. (*a bit stiffly*) Yes, he certainly did. (*He takes the drawing from her and at once becomes interested and squints at it frowningly*) Did you notice that anything seemed lacking in this?

MARGARET. (*indifferently*) Not at all.

BROWN. (*with a cheerful grin*) The Committee want it made a little more American. It's too much of a conventional Greco-Roman tomb, they say. (*Laughs*) They want an original touch of modern novelty stuck in to liven it up and make it look different from other town halls. (*Putting the drawing back on his desk*) And I've been figuring out how to give it to them but my mind doesn't seem to run that way. Have you any suggestion?

MARGARET. (*as if she hadn't heard*) Dion certainly draws well, Billy Brown was saying?

BROWN. (*trying not to show his annoyance*) Why, yes—he did—and still can, I expect. (*A pause. He masters what he feels to be an unworthy pique and turns to her generously*) Dion would have made a cracking good architect.

MARGARET. (*proudly*) I know. He could be anything he wanted to.

BROWN. (*a pause—embarrassedly*) Is he working at anything these days?

MARGARET. (*defensively*) Oh, yes! He's painting wonderfully! But he's just like a child, he's so impractical. He doesn't try to have an exhibition anywhere, or anything.

BROWN. (*surprised*) The one time I ran into him, I thought he told me he'd destroyed all his pictures—that he'd gotten sick of painting and completely given it up.

MARGARET. (*quickly*) He always tells people that. He doesn't want anyone even to look at his things, imagine! He keeps saying they're rotten—when they're really too beautiful! He's too modest for his own good, don't you think? But it is true he hasn't done so much lately since we've been back. You see the children take up such a lot of his time. He just worships them! I'm afraid he's becoming a hopeless family man, just the opposite of what anyone would expect who knew him in the old days.

BROWN. (*painfully embarrassed by her loyalty and his*

knowledge of the facts) Yes, I know. (*He coughs self-consciously*)

MARGARET. (*aroused by something in his manner*) But I suppose the gossips are telling the same silly stories about him they always did. (*She forces a laugh*) Poor Dion! Give a dog a bad name! (*Her voice breaks a little in spite of herself*)

BROWN. (*hastily*) I haven't heard any stories—(*he stops uncertainly, then decides to plunge in*)—except about money matters.

MARGARET. (*forcing a laugh*) Oh, perhaps they're true enough. Dion is such a generous fool with his money, like all artists.

BROWN. (*with a certain doggedness*) There's a rumor that you've applied for a position at the Library.

MARGARET. (*forcing a gay tone*) Yes, indeed! Won't it be fun! Maybe it'll improve my mind! And one of us has got to be practical, so why not me? (*She forces a gay, girlish laugh*)

BROWN. (*impulsively reaches out and takes her hand—awkwardly*) Listen, Margaret. Let's be perfectly frank, will you? I'm such an old friend, and I want like the deuce to. . . . You know darn well I'd do anything in the world to help you—or Dion.

MARGARET. (*withdrawing her hand, coldly*) I'm afraid I—don't understand, Billy Brown.

BROWN. (*acutely embarrassed*) Well, I—I just meant—you know, if you needed—— (*A pause. He looks questioningly at her averted face—then ventures on another tack, matter-of-*

factly) I've got a proposition to make to Dion—if I could ever get hold of him. It's this way: business has been piling up on me—a run of luck—but I'm short-handed. I need a crack chief draftsman darn badly—or I'm liable to lose out. Do you think Dion would consider it—as a temporary stop-gap—until he felt in the painting mood again?

MARGARET. (*striving to conceal her eagerness and relief—judicially*) Yes—I really do. He's such a good sport and Billy and he were such pals once. I know he'd be only too tickled to help him out.

BROWN. (*diffidently*) I thought he might be sensitive about working for—I mean, with me—when, if he hadn't sold out to Dad he'd be my partner now—(*earnestly*)—and, by jingo, I wish he was! (*Then, abruptly*) Let's try to nail him down right away, Margaret. Is he home now? (*He reaches for the phone*)

MARGARET. (*hurriedly*) No, he—he went out for a long walk.

BROWN. Perhaps I can locate him later around town somewhere.

MARGARET. (*with a note of pleading*) Please don't trouble. It isn't necessary. I'm sure when I talk to him—he's coming home to dinner—— (*Getting up*) Then it's all settled, isn't it? Dion will be so glad to be able to help an old friend—he's so terribly loyal, and he's always liked Billy Brown so much! (*Holding out her hand*) I really must go now!

BROWN. (*shakes her hand*) Good-by, Margaret. I hope you'll be dropping in on us a lot when Dion gets here.

MARGARET. Yes. (*She goes*)

BROWN. (*sits at his desk again, looking ahead in a not unsatisfying melancholy reverie. He mutters admiringly but pityingly*) Poor Margaret! She's a game sport, but it's pretty damn tough on her! (*Indignantly*) By God, I'm going to give Dion a good talking-to one of these days!

(*Curtain*)

ACT ONE

SCENE THREE

SCENE. *Cybel's parlor. An automatic, nickel-in-the-slot player-piano is at center, rear. On its right is a dirty gilt second-hand sofa. At the left is a bald-spotted crimson plush chair. The backdrop for the rear wall is cheap wall-paper of a dull yellow-brown, resembling a blurred impression of a fallow field in early spring. There is a cheap alarm clock on top of the piano. Beside it her mask is lying.*

DION *is sprawled on his back, fast asleep on the sofa. His mask has fallen down on his chest. His pale face is singularly pure, spiritual and sad.*

The player-piano is groggily banging out a sentimental medley of "Mother—Mammy" tunes.

CYBEL *is seated on the stool in front of the piano. She is a strong, calm, sensual, blonde girl of twenty or so, her complexion fresh and healthy, her figure full-breasted and wide-hipped, her movements slow and solidly languorous like an animal's, her large eyes dreamy with the reflected stirring of profound instincts. She chews gum like a sacred cow forgetting time with an eternal end. Her eyes are fixed, incuriously, on* DION*'s pale face.*

CYBEL. (*as the tune runs out, glances at the clock, which indicates midnight, then goes slowly over to* DION *and puts her hand gently on his forehead*) Wake up!

DION. (*stirs, sighs and murmurs dreamily*) "And He laid his hands on them and healed them." (*Then with a start he opens his eyes and, half sitting up, stares at her bewilderedly*) What—where—who are you? (*He reaches for his mask and claps it on defensively*)

CYBEL. (*placidly*) Only another female. You was camping on my steps, sound asleep. I didn't want to run any risk getting into more trouble with the cops pinching you there and blaming me, so I took you in to sleep it off.

DION. (*mockingly*) Blessed are the pitiful, Sister! I'm broke—but you will be rewarded in Heaven!

CYBEL. (*calmly*) I wasn't wasting my pity. Why should I? You were happy, weren't you?

DION. (*approvingly*) Excellent! You're not a moralist, I see.

CYBEL. (*going on*) And you look like a good boy, too—when you're asleep. Say, you better beat it home to bed or you'll be locked out.

DION. (*mockingly*) Now you're becoming maternal, Miss Earth. Is that the only answer—to pin my soul into every vacant diaper? (*She stares down at his mask, her face growing hard. He laughs*) But please don't stop stroking my aching brow. Your hand is a cool mud poultice on the sting of thought!

CYBEL. (*calmly*) Stop acting. I hate ham fats. (*She looks at him as if waiting for him to remove his mask—then turns her back indifferently and goes to the piano*) Well, if you simply got to be a regular devil like all the other visiting sports, I s'pose I got to play with you. (*She takes her mask and puts it on—then turns. The mask is the rouged and eye-blackened *countenance of the hardened prostitute. In a coarse, harsh voice*) Kindly state your dishonorable intentions, if any! I can't sit up all night keeping company! Let's have some music! (*She puts a plug in the machine. The same sentimental medley begins to play. The two masks stare at each other. She laughs*) Shoot! I'm all set! It's your play, Kid Lucifer!

DION. (*slowly removes his mask. She stops the music with a jerk. His face is gentle and sad—humbly*) I'm sorry. It has always been such agony for me to be touched!

CYBEL. (*taking off her mask—sympathetically as she comes back and sits down on her stool*) Poor kid! I've never had one, but I can guess. They hug and kiss you and take you on their laps and pinch you and want to see you getting dressed and undressed—as if they owned you—— I bet you I'd never let them treat one of mine that way!

DION. (*turning to her*) You're lost in blind alleys, too. (*Suddenly holding out his hand to her*) But you're strong. Let's be friends.

CYBEL. (*with a strange sternness, searches his face*) And never nothing more?

DION. (*with a strange smile*) Let's say, never anything less! (*She takes his hand. There is a ring at the outside door bell. They stare at each other. There is another ring*)

CYBEL. (*puts on her mask,* DION *does likewise. Mockingly*) When you got to love to live it's hard to love living. I better join the A. F. of L. and soap-box for the eight-hour night! Got a nickel, baby? Play a tune. (*She goes out.* DION *puts a nickel in. The same sentimental tune starts.* CYBEL *returns, followed by* BILLY BROWN. *His face is rigidly composed, but his superior disgust for* DION *can be seen.* DION *jerks off the music and he and* BILLY *look at each other for a moment,* CYBEL *watching them both—then, bored, she yawns*) He's hunting for you. Put out the lights when you go. I'm going to sleep. (*She starts to go—then, as if reminded of something—to* DION) Life's all right, if you let it alone. (*Then mechanically flashing a trade smile at* BILLY) Now you know the way, Handsome, call again! (*She goes*)

BROWN. (*after an awkward pause*) Hello, Dion! I've been looking all over town for you. This place was the very last chance. . . . (*Another pause—embarrassedly*) Let's take a walk.

DION. (*mockingly*) I've given up exercise. They claim it lengthens your life.

BROWN. (*persuasively*) Come on, Dion, be a good fellow. You're certainly not staying here——

DION. Billy would like to think me taken in *flagrante delicto,* eh?

BROWN. Don't be a damn fool! Listen to me! I've been looking you up for purely selfish reasons. I need your help.

DION. (*astonished*) What?

BROWN. I've a proposition to make that I hope you'll consider favorably out of old friendship. To be frank, Dion, I need you to lend me a hand down at the office.

DION. (*with a harsh laugh*) So it's the job, is it? Then my poor wife did a-begging go!

BROWN. (*repelled—sharply*) On the contrary, I had to beg her to beg you to take it! (*More angrily*) Look here, Dion! I won't listen to you talk that way about Margaret! And you wouldn't if you weren't drunk! (*Suddenly shaking him*) What in hell has come over you, anyway! You didn't use to be like this! What the devil are you going to do with yourself—sink into the gutter and drag Margaret with you? If you'd heard her defend you, lie about you, tell me how hard you were working, what beautiful things you were painting, how you stayed at home and idolized the children!—when everyone knows you've been out every night sousing and gambling away the last of your estate. . . . (*He stops, ashamed, controlling himself*)

DION. (*wearily*) She was lying about her husband, not me, you fool! But it's no use explaining. (*Then, in a sudden, excitable passion*) What do you want? I agree to anything—except the humiliation of yelling secrets at the deaf!

BROWN. (*trying a bullying tone—roughly*) Bunk! Don't try to crawl out! There's no excuse and you know it. (*Then as* DION *doesn't reply—penitently*) But I know I shouldn't talk this way, old man! It's only because we're such old pals—and I hate to see you wasting yourself—you who had more brains than any of us! But, damn it, I suppose you're too much of a rotten cynic to believe I mean what I've just said!

DION. (*touched*) I know Billy was always Dion Anthony's friend.

BROWN. You're damn right I am—and I'd have proved it long ago if you'd only given me half a chance! After all, I couldn't keep chasing after you and be snubbed every time. A man has some pride!

DION. (*bitterly mocking*) Dead wrong! Never more! None whatever! It's unmoral! Blessed are the poor in spirit, Brother! When shall I report?

BROWN. (*eagerly*) Then you'll take the—you'll help me?

DION. (*wearily bitter*) I'll take the job. One must do something to pass away the time, while one is waiting—for one's next incarnation.

BROWN. (*jokingly*) I'd say it was a bit early to be worrying about that. (*Trying to get* DION *started*) Come along, now. It's pretty late.

DION. (*shakes his hand off his shoulder and walks away from him—after a pause*) Is my father's chair still there?

BROWN. (*turns away—embarrassed*) I—I don't really remember, Dion—I'll look it up.

DION. (*taking off his mask—slowly*) I'd like to sit where he spun what I have spent. What aliens we were to each other! When he lay dead, his face looked so familiar that I wondered where I had met that man before. Only at the second of my conception. After that, we grew hostile with concealed shame. And my mother? I remember a sweet, strange girl, with affectionate, bewildered eyes as if God had locked her in a dark closet without any explanation. I was the sole doll our ogre, her husband, allowed her and she played mother and child with me for many years in that house until at last through two tears I watched her die with the shy pride of one who has lengthened her dress and put up her hair. And I felt like a forsaken toy and cried to be buried with her, because her hands alone had caressed without clawing. She lived long and aged greatly in the two days before they closed her coffin. The last time I looked, her purity had forgotten me, she was stainless and imperishable, and I knew my sobs were ugly and meaningless to her virginity; so I shrank away, back into life, with naked nerves jumping like fleas, and in due course of nature another girl called me her boy in the moon and married me and became three mothers in one person, while I got paint on my paws in an endeavor to see God! (*He laughs wildly—claps on his mask*) But that Ancient Humorist had given me weak eyes, so now I'll have to foreswear my quest for Him and go in for the Omnipresent Successful Serious One, the Great God Mr. Brown, instead! (*He makes him a sweeping, mocking bow*)

BROWN. (*Repelled but cajolingly*) Shut up, you nut! You're still drunk. Come on! Let's start! (*He grabs* DION *by the arm and switches off the light*)

DION. (*from the darkness—mockingly*) I am thy shorn, bald, nude sheep! Lead on, Almighty Brown, thou Kindly Light!

(*Curtain*)

ACT TWO

SCENE ONE

SCENE. CYBEL'S *parlor—about sunset in spring seven years later. The arrangement of furniture is the same but the chair and sofa are new, bright-colored, costly pieces. The old automatic piano at center looks exactly the same. The cheap alarm clock is still on top of it. On either side of the clock, the masks of* DION *and* CYBEL *are lying. The background backdrop is brilliant, stunning wall-paper, on which crimson and purple flowers and fruits tumble over one another in a riotously profane lack of any apparent design.*

DION *sits in the chair on left,* CYBEL *on the sofa. A card-table is between them. Both are playing solitaire.* DION *is now prematurely gray. His face is that of an ascetic, a martyr, furrowed by pain and self-torture, yet lighted from within by a spiritual calm and human kindliness.*

CYBEL *has grown stouter and more voluptuous, but her face is still unmarked and fresh, her calm more profound. She is like an unmoved idol of Mother Earth.*

The piano is whining out its same old sentimental medley. They play their cards intently and contentedly. The music stops.

CYBEL. (*musingly*) I love those rotten old sob tunes. They make me wise to people. That's what's inside them—what makes them love and murder their neighbor—crying jags set to music!

DION. (*compassionately*) Every song is a hymn. They keep trying to find the Word in the Beginning.

CYBEL. They try to know too much. It makes them weak. I never puzzled them with myself. I gave them a Tart. They understood her and knew their parts and acted naturally. And on both sides we were able to keep our real virtue, if you get me. (*She plays her last card—indifferently*) I've made it again.

DION. (*smiling*) Your luck is uncanny. It never comes out for me.

CYBEL. You keep getting closer, but it knows you still want to win—a little bit—and it's wise all I care about is playing. (*She lays out another game*) Speaking of my canned music, our Mr. Brown hates that old box. (*At the mention of* BROWN, DION *trembles as if suddenly possessed, has a terrible struggle with himself, then while she continues to speak, gets up like an automaton and puts on his mask. The mask is now terribly ravaged. All of its Pan quality has changed into a diabolical Mephistophelean cruelty and irony*) He doesn't mind the music inside. That gets him somehow. But he thinks the case looks shabby and he wants it junked. But I told him that just because he's been keeping me so long, he needn't start bossing like a husband or I'll—— (*She looks up and sees the masked* DION *standing by the piano—calmly*) Hello! Getting jealous again?

DION. (*jeeringly*) Are you falling in love with your keeper, old Sacred Cow?

CYBEL. (*without taking offense*) Cut it! You've been asking me that for years. Be yourself! He's healthy and handsome—but he's too guilty. What makes you pretend you think love is so important, anyway? It's just one of a lot of things you do to keep life living.

DION. (*in same tone*) Then you've lied when you've said you loved me, have you, Old Filth?

CYBEL. (*affectionately*) You'll never grow up! We've been friends, haven't we, for seven years? I've never let myself want you nor you me. Yes, I love you. It takes all kinds of love to make a world! Ours is the living cream, I say, living rich and high! (*A pause. Coaxingly*) Stop hiding. I know you.

DION. (*taking off his mask, wearily comes and sits down at her feet and lays his head in her lap—with a grateful smile*) You're strong. You always give. You've given my weakness strength to live.

CYBEL. (*tenderly, stroking his hair maternally*) You're not weak. You were born with ghosts in your eyes and you were brave enough to go looking into your own dark—and you got afraid. (*After a pause*) I don't blame your being jealous of Mr. Brown sometimes. I'm jealous of your wife, even though I know you do love her.

DION. (*slowly*) I love Margaret. I don't know who my wife is.

CYBEL. (*after a pause—with a queer broken laugh*) Oh, God, sometimes the truth hits me such a sock between the eyes I can see the stars!—and then I'm so damn sorry for the lot of you, every damn mother's son-of-a-gun of you, that I'd like to run out naked into the street and love the whole mob to death like I was bringing you all a new brand of dope that'd make you forget everything that ever was for good! (*Then, with a twisted smile*) But they wouldn't see me, any more than they see each other. And they keep right on moving along and dying without my help anyway.

DION. (*sadly*) You've given me strength to die.

CYBEL. You may be important but your life's not. There's millions of it born every second. Life can cost too much even for a sucker to afford it—like everything else. And it's not sacred—only the you inside is. The rest is earth.

DION. (*gets to his knees and with clasped hands looks up raptly and prays with an ascetic fervor*) "Into thy hands, O Lord," . . . (*Then suddenly, with a look of horror*) Nothing! To feel one's life blown out like the flame of a cheap match . . . ! (*He claps on his mask and laughs harshly*) To fall asleep and know you'll never, never be called to get on the job of existence again! "Swift be thine approaching flight! Come soon—soon!" (*He quotes this last with a mocking longing*)

CYBEL. (*pats his head maternally*) There, don't be scared. It's born in the blood. When the time comes, you'll find it's easy.

DION. (*jumps to his feet and walks about excitedly*) It won't be long. My wife dragged in a doctor the day before yesterday. He says my heart is gone—booze—— He warned me, never another drop or—— (*Mockingly*) What say? Shall we have a drink?

CYBEL. (*like an idol*) Suit yourself. It's in the pantry. (*Then, as he hesitates*) What set you off on this bat? You were raving on about some cathedral plans. . . .

DION. (*wildly mocking*) They've been accepted—Mr. Brown's designs! My designs really! You don't need to be told that. He hands me one mathematically correct barn after another and I doctor them up with cute allurements so that fools will desire to buy, sell, breed, sleep, love, hate, curse and pray in them! I do this with devilish cleverness to their entire delight! Once I dreamed of painting wind on the sea and the skimming flight of cloud shadows over the tops of trees! Now . . . (*He laughs*) But pride is a sin—even in a memory of the long deceased! Blessed are the poor in spirit! (*He subsides weakly on his chair, his hand pressed to his heart*)

CYBEL. (*like an idol*) Go home and sleep. Your wife'll be worried.

DION. She knows—but she'll never admit to herself that her husband ever entered your door. (*Mocking*) Aren't women loyal—to their vanity and their other things!

CYBEL. Brown is coming soon, don't forget.

DION. He knows too and can't admit. Perhaps he needs me here—unknown. What first aroused his passion to possess you exclusively, do you think? Because he knew you loved me and he felt himself cheated. He wanted what he thought was my love of the flesh! He feels I have no right to love. He'd like to steal it as he steals my ideas—complacently—righteously. Oh, the good Brown!

CYBEL. But you like him, too! You're brothers, I guess, somehow. Well, remember he's paying, he'll pay—in some way or other.

DION. (*raises his head as if starting to remove the mask*) I know. Poor Billy! God forgive me the evil I've done him!

CYBEL. (*reaches out and takes his hand*) Poor boy!

DION. (*presses her convulsively—then with forced harshness*) Well, homeward Christian Soldier! I'm off! By-bye, Mother Earth! (*He starts to go off right. She seems about to let him go*)

CYBEL. *(suddenly starts and calls with deep grief)* Dion! *(He looks at her. A pause. He comes slowly back. She speaks strangely in a deep, far-off voice—and yet like a mother talking to her little son)* You mustn't forget to kiss me before you go, Dion. *(She removes his mask)* Haven't I told you to take off your mask in the house? Look at me, Dion. I've—just—seen—something. I'm afraid you're going away a long, long ways. I'm afraid I won't see you again for a long, long time. So it's good-by, dear. *(She kisses him gently. He begins to sob. She hands him back his mask)* Here you are. Don't get hurt. Remember, it's all a game, and after you're asleep I'll tuck you in.

DION. *(in a choking, heart-broken cry)* Mother! *(Then he claps on his mask with a terrible effort of will—mockingly)* Go to the devil, you sentimental old pig! See you tomorrow! *(He goes, whistling, slamming the door)*

CYBEL. *(like an idol again)* What's the good of bearing children? What's the use of giving birth to death? *(She sighs wearily, turns, puts a plug in the piano, which starts up its old sentimental tune. At the same moment* BROWN *enters quietly from the left. He is the ideal of the still youthful, good-looking, well-groomed, successful provincial American of forty. Just now, he is plainly perturbed. He is not able to see either* CYBEL'S *face or her mask)*

BROWN. Cybel! *(She starts, jams off the music and reaches for her mask but has no time to put it on)* Wasn't that Dion I just saw going out—after all your promises never to see him! *(She turns like an idol, holding the mask behind her. He stares, bewildered—stammers)* I—I beg your pardon—I thought——

CYBEL. (*in her strange voice*) Cybel's gone out to dig in the earth and pray.

BROWN. (*with more assurance*) But—aren't those her clothes?

CYBEL. Cybel doesn't want people to see me naked. I'm her sister. Dion came to see me.

BROWN. (*relieved*) So that's what he's up to, is it? (*Then with a pitying sigh*) Poor Margaret! (*Then with playful reproof*) You really shouldn't encourage him. He's married and got three big sons.

CYBEL. And you haven't.

BROWN. (*stung*) No, I'm not married.

CYBEL. He and I were friends.

BROWN. (*with a playful wink*) Yes, I can imagine how the platonic must appeal to Dion's pure, innocent type! It's no good your kidding me about Dion. We've been friends since we were kids. I know him in and out. I've always stood up for him whatever he's done—so you can be perfectly frank. I only spoke as I did on account of Margaret—his wife—it's pretty tough on her.

CYBEL. You love his wife.

BROWN. (*scandalized*) What? What are you talking about? (*Then uncertainly*) Don't be a fool! (*A pause—then as if impelled by an intense curiosity*) So Dion is your lover, eh? That's very interesting. (*He pulls his chair closer to hers*) Sit down. Let's talk. (*She continues to stand, the mask held behind her*) Tell me—I've always been curious—what is it that makes Dion so attractive to women—especially certain types of women, if you'll pardon me? He always has been and yet I never could see exactly what they saw in him. Is it his looks

—or because he's such a violent sensualist—or because he poses as artistic and temperamental—or because he's so wild—or just what is it?

CYBEL. He's alive!

BROWN. (*suddenly takes one of her hands and kisses it—insinuatingly*) Well, don't you think I'm alive, too? (*Eagerly*) Listen. Would you consider giving up Dion—and letting me take care of you under a similar arrangement to the one I've made with Cybel? I like you, you can see that. I won't bother you much—I'm much too busy—you can do what you like—lead your own life—except for seeing him. (*He stops. A pause. She stares ahead unmoved as if she hadn't heard. He pleads*) Well—what do you say? Please do!

CYBEL. (*her voice very weary*) Cybel said to tell you she'd be back next week, Mr. Brown.

BROWN. (*with queer agony*) You mean you won't? Don't be so cruel! I love you! (*She walks away. He clutches at her, pleadingly*) At least—I'll give you anything you ask!—please promise me you won't see Dion Anthony again!

CYBEL. (*with deep grief*) He will never see me again, I promise you. Good-by!

BROWN. (*jubilantly, kissing her hand—politely*) Thank you! Thank you! I'm exceedingly grateful. (*Tactfully*) I won't disturb you any further. Please forgive my intrusion, and remember me to Cybel when you write. (*He bows, turns, and goes off left*)

(*Curtain*)

ACT TWO

SCENE TWO

SCENE. *The drafting room in* BROWN'S *office.* DION'S *drafting table with a high stool in front is at center. Another stool is to the left of it. At the right is a bench. It is in the evening of the same day. The black wall drop has windows painted on it with a dim, street-lighted view of black houses across the way.*

DION *is sitting on the stool in back of the table, reading aloud from the "Imitation of Christ" by Thomas à Kempis to his mask, which is on the table before him. His own face is gentler, more spiritual, more saintlike and ascetic than ever before.*

DION. (*like a priest, offering up prayers for the dying*) "Quickly must thou be gone from hence, see then how matters stand with thee. Ah, fool—learn now to die to the world that thou mayst begin to live with Christ! Do now, beloved, do now all thou canst because thou knowst not when thou shalt die; nor dost thou know what shall befall thee after death. Keep thyself as a pilgrim, and a stranger upon earth, to whom the affairs of this world do not—belong! Keep thy heart free and raised upwards to God because thou hast not here a lasting abode. 'Because at what hour you know not the Son of Man will come!'" Amen. (*He raises his hand over the mask as if he were blessing it, closes the book and puts it back in his pocket. He raises the mask in his hands and stares at it with a pitying tenderness*) Peace, poor tortured one, brave pitiful pride of man, the hour of our deliverance comes. Tomorrow we may be with Him in Paradise! (*He kisses it on the lips and sets it down again. There is the noise of footsteps climbing the stairs in the hallway. He grabs up the mask in a sudden panic and, as a knock comes on the door, he claps it on and calls mockingly*) Come in, Mrs. Anthony, come in! (MARGARET *enters. In one hand behind her, hidden from him, is the mask of the brave face she puts on before the world to hide her suffering and disillusionment, and which she has just taken off. Her own face is still sweet and pretty but lined, drawn and careworn for its years, sad, resigned, but a bit querulous*)

MARGARET. (*wearily reproving*) Thank goodness I've found you! Why haven't you been home the last two days? It's bad enough your drinking again without your staying away and worrying us to death!

DION. (*bitterly*) My ears knew her footsteps. One gets to recognize everything—and to see nothing!

MARGARET. I finally sent the boys out looking for you and came myself. (*With tired solicitude*) I suppose you haven't eaten a thing, as usual. Won't you come home and let me fry you a chop?

DION. (*wonderingly*) Can Margaret still love Dion Anthony? Is it possible she does?

MARGARET. (*forcing a tired smile*) I suppose so, Dion. I certainly oughtn't to, had I?

DION. (*in same tone*) And I love Margaret! What haunted, haunting ghosts we are! We dimly remember so much it will take us so many million years to forget! (*He comes forward, putting one arm around her bowed shoulders, and they kiss*)

MARGARET. (*patting his hand affectionately*) No, you certainly don't deserve it. When I stop to think of all you've made me go through in the years since we settled down here. . . ! I really don't believe I could ever have stood it if it weren't for the boys! (*Forcing a smile*) But perhaps I would, I've always been such a big fool about you.

DION. (*a bit mockingly*) The boys! Three strong sons! Margaret can afford to be magnanimous!

MARGARET. If they didn't find you, they were coming to meet me here.

DION. (*with sudden wildness—torturedly, sinking on his knees beside her*) Margaret! Margaret! I'm lonely! I'm frightened! I'm going away! I've got to say good-by!

MARGARET. (*patting his hair*) Poor boy! Poor Dion! Come home and sleep.

DION. (*springs up frantically*) No! I'm a man! I'm a lonely man! I can't go back! I have conceived myself! (*Then with desperate mockery*) Look at me, Mrs. Anthony! It's the last chance! Tomorrow I'll have moved on to the next hell! Behold your man—the sniveling, cringing, life-denying Christian slave you have so nobly ignored in the father of your sons! Look! (*He tears the mask from his face, which is radiant with a great pure love for her and a great sympathy and tenderness*) O woman—my love—that I have sinned against in my sick pride and cruelty—forgive my sins—forgive my solitude—forgive my sickness—forgive me! (*He kneels and kisses the hem of her dress*)

MARGARET. (*who has been staring at him with terror, raising her mask to ward off his face*) Dion! Don't! I can't bear it! You're like a ghost! You're dead! Oh, my God! Help! Help! (*She falls back fainting on the bench. He looks at her—then takes her hand which holds her mask and looks at that face—gently*) And now I am permitted to understand and love you, too! (*He kisses the mask first—then kisses her face, murmuring*) And you, sweetheart! Blessed, thrice blessed are the meek! (*There is a sound of heavy, hurrying footsteps on the stairs. He puts on his mask in haste. The* THREE SONS *rush into the room. The Eldest is about fourteen, the two others thirteen and twelve. They look healthy, normal likeable boys, with much the same quality as* BILLY BROWN'S *in Act One, Scene One. They stop short and stiffen all in a row, staring from the woman on the bench to their father, accusingly*)

ELDEST. We heard someone yell. It sounded like Mother.

DION. (*defensively*) No. It was this lady—my wife.

ELDEST. But hasn't Mother come yet?

DION. (*going to* MARGARET) Yes. Your Mother is here. (*He stands between them and puts her mask over* MARGARET'S *face—then steps back*) She has fainted. You'd better bring her to.

BOYS. Mother! (*They run to her side, kneel and rub her wrists. The* ELDEST *smooths back her hair*)

DION. (*watching them*) At least I am leaving her well provided for. (*He addresses them directly*) Tell your mother she'll get word from Mr. Brown's house. I must pay him a farewell call. I am going. Good-by. (*They stop, staring at him fixedly, with eyes a mixture of bewilderment, distrust and hurt*)

ELDEST. (*awkwardly and shamefacedly*) Honest, I think you ought to have . . .

SECOND. Yes, honest you ought . . .

YOUNGEST. Yes, honest . . .

DION. (*in a friendly tone*) I know. But I couldn't. That's for you who can. You must inherit the earth for her. Don't forget now, boys. Good-by.

BOYS. (*in the same awkward, self-conscious tone, one after another*) Good-by—good-by—good-by. (DION *goes*)

(*Curtain*)

ACT TWO

SCENE THREE

SCENE. *The library of* WILLIAM BROWN'S *home—night of the same day. A backdrop of carefully painted, prosperous, bourgeois culture, bookcases filled with sets, etc. The heavy table at center is expensive. The leather armchair at left of it and the couch at right are opulently comfortable. The reading lamp on the table is the only light.*

BROWN *sits in the chair at left reading an architectural periodical. His expression is composed and gravely receptive. In outline, his face suggests a Roman consul on an old coin. There is an incongruous distinction about it, the quality of unquestioning faith in the finality of its achievement.*

There is a sudden loud thumping on the front door and the ringing of the bell. BROWN *frowns and listens as a servant answers.* DION'S *voice can be heard, raised mockingly.*

DION. Tell him it's the devil come to conclude a bargain.

BROWN. (*suppressing annoyance, calls out with forced good nature*) Come on in, Dion. (DION *enters. He is in a wild state. His clothes are disheveled, his masked face has a terrible deathlike intensity, its mocking irony becomes so cruelly malignant as to give him the appearance of a real demon, tortured into torturing others*) Sit down.

DION. (*stands and sings*) William Brown's soul lies moldering in the crib but his body goes marching on!

BROWN. (*maintaining the same indulgent, big-brotherly tone, which he tries to hold throughout the scene*) Not so loud, for Pete's sake! I don't mind—but I've got neighbors.

DION. Hate them! Fear thy neighbor as thyself! That's the leaden rule for the safe and sane. (*Then advancing to the table with a sort of deadly calm*) Listen! One day when I was four years old, a boy sneaked up behind when I was drawing a picture in the sand he couldn't draw and hit me on the head with a stick and kicked out my picture and laughed when I cried. It wasn't what he'd done that made me cry, but him! I had loved and trusted him and suddenly the good God was disproved in his person and the evil and injustice of Man was born! Everyone called me cry-baby, so I became silent for life and designed a mask of the Bad Boy Pan in which to live and rebel against that other boy's God and protect myself from His cruelty. And that other boy, secretly he felt ashamed but he couldn't acknowledge it; so from that day he instinctively developed into the good boy, the good friend, the good man, William Brown!

BROWN. (*shamefacedly*) I remember now. It was a dirty trick. (*Then with a trace of resentment*) Sit down. You know where the booze is. Have a drink, if you like. But I guess you've had enough already.

DION. (*looks at him fixedly for a moment—then strangely*) Thanks be to Brown for reminding me. I must drink. (*He goes and gets a bottle of whisky and a glass*)

BROWN. (*with a good-humored shrug*) All right. It's your funeral.

DION. (*returning and pouring out a big drink in the tumbler*)

And William Brown's! When I die, he goes to hell! Shöal! (*He drinks and stares malevolently. In spite of himself,* BROWN *is uneasy. A pause*)

BROWN. (*with forced casualness*) You've been on this toot for a week now.

DION. (*tauntingly*) I've been celebrating the acceptance of *my* design for the cathedral.

BROWN. (*humorously*) You certainly helped me a lot on it.

DION. (*with a harsh laugh*) O perfect Brown! Never mind! I'll make him look in my mirror yet—and drown in it! (*He pours out another big drink*)

BROWN. (*rather tauntingly*) Go easy. I don't want your corpse on my hands.

DION. But I do. (*He drinks*) Brown will still need me—to reassure him he's alive! I've loved, lusted, won and lost, sang and wept! I've been life's lover! I've fulfilled her will and if she's through with me now it's only because I was too weak to dominate her in turn. It isn't enough to be her creature, you've got to create her or she requests you to destroy yourself.

BROWN. (*good-naturedly*) Nonsense. Go home and get some sleep.

DION. (*as if he hadn't heard—bitingly*) But to be neither creature nor creator! To exist only in her indifference! To be unloved by life! (BROWN *stirs uneasily*) To be merely a successful freak, the result of some snide neutralizing of life forces—a spineless cactus—a wild boar of the mountains altered into a packer's hog eating to become food—a Don Juan inspired to romance by a monkey's glands—and to have Life not even think you funny enough to see!

BROWN. (*stung—angrily*) Bosh!

DION. Consider Mr. Brown. His parents bore him on earth as if they were thereby entering him in a baby parade with prizes for the fattest—and he's still being wheeled along in the procession, too fat now to learn to walk, let alone to dance or run, and he'll never live until his liberated dust quickens into earth!

BROWN. (*gruffly*) Rave on! (*Then with forced good-nature*) Well, Dion, at any rate, I'm satisfied.

DION. (*quickly and malevolently*) No! Brown isn't satisfied! He's piled on layers of protective fat, but vaguely, deeply he feels at his heart the gnawing of a doubt! And I'm interested in that germ which wriggles like a question mark of insecurity in his blood, because it's part of the creative life Brown's stolen from me!

BROWN. (*forcing a sour grin*) Steal germs? I thought you caught them.

DION. (*as if he hadn't heard*) It's mine—and I'm interested in seeing it thrive and breed and become multitudes and eat until Brown is consumed!

BROWN. (*cannot restrain a shudder*) Sometimes when you're drunk, you're positively evil, do you know it?

DION. (*somberly*) When Pan was forbidden the light and warmth of the sun he grew sensitive and self-conscious and proud and revengeful—and became Prince of Darkness.

BROWN. (*jocularly*) You don't fit the rôle of Pan, Dion. It sounds to me like Bacchus, alias the Demon Rum, doing the talking. (DION *recovers from his spasm with a start and stares at* BROWN *with terrible hatred. There is a pause. In spite of himself,* BROWN *squirms and adopts a placating tone*) Go home.

Be a good scout. It's all well enough celebrating our design being accepted but——

DION. (*in a steely voice*) I've been the brains! I've been the design! I've designed even his success—drunk and laughing at him—laughing at his career! Not proud! Sick! Sick of myself and him! Designing and getting drunk! Saving my woman and children! (*He laughs*) Ha! And this cathedral is my masterpiece! It will make Brown the most eminent architect in this state of God's Country. I put a lot into it—what was left of my life! It's one vivid blasphemy from sidewalk to the tips of its spires!—but so concealed that the fools will never know. They'll kneel and worship the ironic Silenus who tells them the best good is never to be born! (*He laughs triumphantly*) Well, blasphemy is faith, isn't it? In self-preservation the devil must believe! But Mr. Brown, the Great Brown, has no faith! He couldn't design a cathedral without it looking like the First Supernatural Bank! He only believes in the immortality of the moral belly! (*He laughs wildly—then sinks down in his chair, gasping, his hands pressed to his heart. Then suddenly becomes deadly calm and pronounces like a cruel malignant condemnation*) From now on, Brown will never design anything. He will devote his life to renovating the house of my Cybel into a home for my Margaret!

BROWN. (*springing to his feet, his face convulsed with strange agony*) I've stood enough! How dare you. . . !

DION. (*his voice like a probe*) Why has no woman ever loved him? Why has he always been the Big Brother, the Friend? Isn't their trust—a contempt?

BROWN. You lie!

DION. Why has he never been able to love—since my Margaret? Why has he never married? Why has he tried to steal Cybel, as he once tried to steal Margaret? Isn't it out of revenge—and envy?

BROWN. (*violently*) Rot! I wanted Cybel, and I bought her!

DION. Brown bought her for me! She has loved me more than he will ever know!

BROWN. You lie! (*Then furiously*) I'll throw her back on the street!

DION. To me! To her fellow creature! Why hasn't Brown had children—he who loves children—he who loves *my* children—he who envies me *my* children?

BROWN. (*brokenly*) I'm not ashamed to envy you them!

DION. They like Brown, too—as a friend—as an equal—as Margaret has always liked him——

BROWN. (*brokenly*) And as I've liked her!

DION. How many million times Brown has thought how much better for her it would have been if she'd chosen him instead!

BROWN. (*torturedly*) You lie! (*Then with sudden frenzied defiance*) All right! If you force me to say it, I do love Margaret! I always have loved her and you've always known I did!

DION. (*with a terrible composure*) No! That is merely the appearance, not the truth! Brown loves me! He loves me because I have always possessed the power he needed for love, because I am love!

BROWN. (*frenziedly*) You drunken bum! (*He leaps on* DION *and grabs him by the throat*)

DION. (*triumphantly, staring into his eyes*) Ah! Now he

looks into the mirror! Now he sees his face! (BROWN *lets go of him and staggers back to his chair, pale and trembling*)

BROWN. (*humbly*) Stop, for God's sake! You're mad!

DION. (*sinking in his chair, more and more weakly*) I'm done. My heart, not Brown—— (*Mockingly*) My last will and testament! I leave Dion Anthony to William Brown—for him to love and obey—for him to become me—then my Margaret will love me—my children will love me—Mr. and Mrs. Brown and sons, happily ever after! (*Staggering to his full height and looking upward defiantly*) Nothing more—but Man's last gesture—by which he conquers—to laugh! Ha—— (*He begins, stops as if paralyzed, and drops on his knees by* BROWN'*s chair, his mask falling off, his Christian Martyr's face at the point of death*) Forgive me, Billy. Bury me, hide me, forget me for your own happiness! May Margaret love you! May you design the Temple of Man's Soul! Blessed are the meek and the poor in spirit! (*He kisses* BROWN'*s feet—then more and more weakly and childishly*) What was the prayer, Billy? I'm getting so sleepy. . . .

BROWN. (*in a trancelike tone*) "Our Father who art in Heaven."

DION. (*drowsily*) "Our Father." . . . (*He dies. A pause.* BROWN *remains in a stupor for a moment—then stirs himself, puts his hand on* DION'*s breast*)

BROWN. (*dully*) He's dead—at last. (*He says this mechanically but the last two words awaken him—wonderingly*) At last? (*Then with triumph*) At last! (*He stares at* DION'*s real face contemptuously*) So that's the poor weakling you really were! No wonder you hid! And I've always been afraid of you—yes, I'll confess it now, in awe of you! Paugh! (*He picks up the mask from the floor*) No, not of you! Of this! Say what you like, it's strong if it is bad! And this is what Margaret loved, not you! Not you! This man!—this man who willed himself to me! (*Struck by an idea, he jumps to his feet*) By God! (*He slowly starts to put the mask on. A knocking comes on the street door. He starts guiltily, laying the mask on the table. Then he picks it up again quickly, takes the dead body and carries it off left. He reappears immediately and goes to the front door as the knocking recommences—gruffly*) Hello! Who's there?

MARGARET. It's Margaret, Billy. I'm looking for Dion.

BROWN. (*uncertainly*) Oh—all right—— (*Unfastening door*) Come in. Hello, Margaret. Hello, Boys! He's here. He's asleep. I—I was just dozing off too. (MARGARET *enters. She is wearing her mask. The* THREE SONS *are with her*)

MARGARET. (*seeing the bottle, forcing a laugh*) Has he been celebrating?

BROWN. (*with strange glibness now*) No. I was. He wasn't. He said he'd sworn off tonight—forever—for your sake—and the kids!

MARGARET. (*with amazed joy*) Dion said that? (*Then hastily defensive*) But of course he never does drink much. Where is he?

BROWN. Upstairs. I'll wake him. He felt bad. He took off his clothes to take a bath before he lay down. You just wait here. (*She sits in the chair where* DION *had sat and stares straight before her. The* SONS *group around her, as if for a family photo.* BROWN *hurries out left*)

MARGARET. It's late to keep you boys up. Aren't you sleepy?

BOYS. No, Mother.

MARGARET. (*proudly*) I'm glad to have three such strong boys to protect me.

ELDEST. (*boastingly*) We'd kill anyone that touched you, wouldn't we?

NEXT. You bet! We'd make him wish he hadn't!

YOUNGEST. You bet!

MARGARET. You're Mother's brave boys! (*She laughs fondly —then curiously*) Do you like Mr. Brown?

ELDEST. Sure thing! He's a regular fellow.

NEXT. He's all right!

YOUNGEST. Sure thing!

MARGARET. (*half to herself*) Your father claims he steals his ideas.

ELDEST. (*with a sheepish grin*) I'll bet father said that when he was—just talking.

NEXT. Mr. Brown doesn't have to steal, does he?

YOUNGEST. I should say not! He's awful rich.

MARGARET. Do you love your father?

ELDEST. (*scuffling—embarrassed*) Why—of course——

NEXT. (*ditto*) Sure thing!

YOUNGEST. Sure I do.

MARGARET. (*with a sigh*) I think you'd better start on before—right now—before your father comes—— He'll be very sick and nervous and he'll want to be quiet. So run along!

BOYS. All right. (*They file out and close the front door as* BROWN, *dressed in* DION'*s clothes and wearing his mask, appears at left*)

MARGARET. (*taking off her mask, gladly*) Dion! (*She stares wonderingly at him and he at her; goes to him and puts an arm around him*) Poor dear, do you feel sick? (*He nods*)

But you look—(*squeezing his arms*)—why, you actually feel stronger and better already! Is it true what Billy told me—about your swearing off forever? (*He nods. She exclaims intensely*) Oh, if you'll only—and get well—we can still be so happy! Give Mother a kiss. (*They kiss. A shudder passes through both of them. She breaks away laughing with aroused desire*) Why, Dion? Aren't you ashamed? You haven't kissed me like that in ages!

BROWN. (*his voice imitating* DION's *and muffled by the mask*) I've wanted to, Margaret!

MARGARET. (*gayly and coquettishly now*) Were you afraid I'd spurn you? Why, Dion, something has happened. It's like a miracle! Even your voice is changed! It actually sounds younger, do you know it? (*Then, solicitously*) But you must be worn out. Let's go home. (*With an impulsive movement she flings her arms wide open, throwing her mask away from her as if suddenly no longer needing it*) Oh, I'm beginning to feel so happy, Dion—so happy!

BROWN. (*stifledly*) Let's go home. (*She puts her arm around him. They walk to the door*)

(*Curtain*)

ACT THREE

SCENE ONE

SCENE. *The drafting room and private office of* BROWN *are both shown. The former is at left, the latter at right of a dividing wall at center. The arrangement of furniture in each room is the same as in previous scenes. It is ten in the morning of a day about a month later. The backdrop for both rooms is of plain wall with a few tacked-up designs and blue prints painted on it.*

TWO DRAFTSMEN, *a middle-aged and a young man, both stoop-shouldered, are sitting on stools behind what was formerly* DION'S *table. They are tracing plans. They talk as they work.*

OLDER DRAFTSMAN. W. B. is late again.

YOUNGER DRAFTSMAN. Wonder what's got into him the last month? (*A pause. They work silently*)

OLDER DRAFTSMAN. Yes, ever since he fired Dion. . . .

YOUNGER DRAFTSMAN. Funny his firing him all of a sudden like that. (*A pause. They work*)

OLDER DRAFTSMAN. I haven't seen Dion around town since then. Have you?

YOUNGER DRAFTSMAN. No, not since Brown told us he'd canned him. I suppose he's off drowning his sorrow!

OLDER DRAFTSMAN. I heard someone had seen him at home and he was sober and looking fine. (*A pause. They work*)

YOUNGER DRAFTSMAN. What got into Brown? They say he fired all his old servants that same day and only uses his house to sleep in.

OLDER DRAFTSMAN. (*with a sneer*) Artistic temperament, maybe—the real name of which is swelled head! (*There is a noise of footsteps from the hall. Warningly*) Ssstt! (*They bend over their table.* MARGARET *enters. She does not need to wear a mask now. Her face has regained the self-confident spirit of its youth, her eyes shine with happiness*)

MARGARET. (*heartily*) Good morning! What a lovely day!

BOTH. (*perfunctorily*) Good morning, Mrs. Anthony.

MARGARET. (*looking around*) You've been changing around in here, haven't you? Where is Dion? (*They stare at her*) I forgot to tell him something important this morning and our phone's out of order. So if you'll tell him I'm here—— (*They don't move. A pause.* MARGARET *says stiffly*) Oh, I realize Mr. Brown has given strict orders Dion is not to be disturbed, but surely. . . . (*Sharply*) Where is my husband, please?

OLDER DRAFTSMAN. We don't know.

MARGARET. You don't know?

YOUNGER DRAFTSMAN. We haven't seen him.

MARGARET. Why, he left home at eight-thirty!

OLDER DRAFTSMAN. To come here?

YOUNGER DRAFTSMAN. This morning?

MARGARET. (*provoked*) Why, of course, to come here—as he does every day! (*They stare at her. A pause*)

OLDER DRAFTSMAN. (*evasively*) We haven't seen him.

MARGARET. (*with asperity*) Where is Mr. Brown?

YOUNGER DRAFTSMAN. (*at a noise of footsteps from the hall*

—sulkily) Coming now. (BROWN *enters. He is now wearing a mask which is an exact likeness of his face as it was in the last scene—the self-assured success. When he sees* MARGARET, *he starts back apprehensively*)

BROWN. (*immediately controlling himself—breezily*) Hello, Margaret! This is a pleasant surprise! (*He holds out his hand*)

MARGARET. (*hardly taking it—reservedly*) Good morning.

BROWN. (*turning quickly to the* DRAFTSMEN) I hope you explained to Mrs. Anthony how busy Dion . . .

MARGARET. (*interrupting him—stiffly*) I certainly can't understand——

BROWN. (*hastily*) I'll explain. Come in here and be comfortable. (*He throws open the door and ushers her into his private office*)

OLDER DRAFTSMAN. Dion must be putting over some bluff on her.

YOUNGER DRAFTSMAN. Pretending he's still here — and Brown's helping him. . . .

OLDER DRAFTSMAN. But why should Brown, after he . . . ?

YOUNGER DRAFTSMAN. Well, I suppose—— Search me. (*They work*)

BROWN. Have a chair, Margaret. (*She sits on the chair stiffly. He sits behind the desk*)

MARGARET. (*coldly*) I'd like some explanation. . . .

BROWN. (*coaxingly*) Now, don't get angry, Margaret! Dion is hard at work on his design for the new State Capitol, and I don't want him disturbed, not even by you! So be a good sport! It's for his own good, remember! I asked him to explain to you.

MARGARET. (*relenting*) He told me you'd agreed to ask me and the boys not to come here—but then, we hardly ever did.

BROWN. But you might! (*Then with confidential friendliness*) This is for his sake, Margaret. I know Dion. He's got to be able to work without distractions. He's not the ordinary man, you appreciate that. And this design means his whole future! He's to get full credit for it, and as soon as it's accepted, I take him into partnership. It's all agreed. And after that I'm going to take a long vacation—go to Europe for a couple of years—and leave everything here in Dion's hands! Hasn't he told you all this?

MARGARET. (*jubilant now*) Yes—but I could hardly believe . . . (*Proudly*) I'm sure he can do it. He's been like a new man lately, so full of ambition and energy! It's made me so happy! (*She stops in confusion*)

BROWN. (*deeply moved, takes her hand impulsively*) And it has made me happy, too!

MARGARET. (*confused—with an amused laugh*) Why, Billy Brown! For a moment, I thought it was Dion, your voice sounded so much . . . !

BROWN. (*with sudden desperation*) Margaret, I've got to tell you! I can't go on like this any longer! I've got to confess. . . ! There's something. . . !

MARGARET. (*alarmed*) Not—not about Dion?

BROWN. (*harshly*) To hell with Dion! To hell with Billy Brown! (*He tears off his mask and reveals a suffering face that is ravaged and haggard, his own face tortured and distorted by the demon of Dion's mask*) Think of me! I love you, Margaret! Leave him! I've always loved you! Come away with me! I'll sell out here! We'll go abroad and be happy!

MARGARET. (*amazed*) Billy Brown, do you realize what you're saying? (*With a shudder*) Are you crazy? Your face —is terrible. You're sick! Shall I phone for a doctor?

BROWN. (*turning away slowly and putting on his mask—dully*) No. I've been on the verge—of a breakdown—for some time. I get spells. . . . I'm better now. (*He turns back to her*) Forgive me! Forget what I said! But, for all our sakes, don't come here again.

MARGARET. (*coldly*) After this—I assure you. . . ! (*Then looking at him with pained incredulity*) Why, Billy—I simply won't believe—after all these years. . . !

BROWN. It will never happen again. Good-by.

MARGARET. Good-by. (*Then, wishing to leave on a pleasant change of subject—forcing a smile*) Don't work Dion to death! He's never home for dinner any more. (*She goes out past the* DRAFTSMEN *and off right, rear.* BROWN *sits down at his desk, taking off the mask again. He stares at it with bitter, cynical amusement*)

BROWN. You're dead, William Brown, dead beyond hope of resurrection! It's the Dion you buried in your garden who killed you, not you him! It's Margaret's husband who . . . (*He laughs harshly*) Paradise by proxy! Love by mistaken identity! God! (*This is almost a prayer—then fiercely defiant*) But it *is* paradise! I *do* love! (*As he is speaking, a well-dressed, important, stout man enters the drafting room. He is carrying a rolled-up plan in his hand. He nods condescendingly and goes directly to* BROWN'*s door, on which he raps sharply, and, without waiting for an answer, turns the knob.* BROWN *has just time to turn his head and get his mask on*)

MAN. (*briskly*) Ah, good morning! I came right in. Hope I didn't disturb . . . ?

BROWN. (*the successful architect now—urbanely*) Not at all, sir. How are you? (*They shake hands*) Sit down. Have a cigar. And now what can I do for you this morning?

MAN. (*unrolling his plan*) It's your plan. My wife and I have been going over it again. We like it—and we don't—and when a man plans to lay out half a million, why he wants everything exactly right, eh? (BROWN *nods*) It's too cold, too spare, too like a tomb, if you'll pardon me, for a liveable home. Can't you liven it up, put in some decorations, make it fancier and warmer—you know what I mean. (*Looks at him a bit doubtfully*) People tell me you had an assistant, Anthony, who was a real shark on these details but that you've fired him——

BROWN. (*suavely*) Gossip! He's still with me but, for reasons of his own, doesn't wish it known. Yes, I trained him and he's very ingenious. I'll turn this right over to him and instruct him to carry out your wishes. . . .

(*Curtain*)

ACT THREE

SCENE TWO

SCENE. *The same as Act Two, Scene Three—the library of* BROWN'S *home about eight the same night. He can be heard feeling his way in through the dark. He switches on the reading lamp on the table. Directly under it on a sort of stand is the mask of* DION, *its empty eyes staring front.*

BROWN *takes off his own mask and lays it on the table before* DION'S. *He flings himself down in the chair and stares without moving into the eyes of* DION'S *mask. Finally, he begins to talk to it in a bitter, mocking tone*)

BROWN. Listen! Today was a narrow escape—for us! We can't avoid discovery much longer. We must get our plot to working! We've already made William Brown's will, leaving you his money and business. We must hustle off to Europe now—and murder him there! (*A bit tauntingly*) Then you—the I in you—*I* will live with Margaret happily ever after. (*More tauntingly*) She will have children by me! (*He seems to hear some mocking denial from the mask. He bends toward it*) What? (*Then with a sneer*) Anyway, that doesn't matter! Your children already love me more than they ever loved you! And Margaret loves me more! You think you've won, do you—

that I've got to vanish into you in order to live? Not yet, my friend! Never! Wait! Gradually Margaret will love what is beneath—me! Little by little I'll teach her to know me, and then finally I'll reveal myself to her, and confess that I stole your place out of love for her, and she'll understand and forgive and love me! And you'll be forgotten! Ha! (*Again he bends down to the mask as if listening—torturedly*) What's that? She'll never believe? She'll never see? She'll never understand? You lie, devil! (*He reaches out his hands as if to take the mask by the throat, then shrinks back with a shudder of hopeless despair*) God have mercy! Let me believe! Blessed are the merciful! Let me obtain mercy! (*He waits, his face upturned—pleadingly*) Not yet? (*Despairingly*) Never? (*A pause. Then, in a sudden panic of dread, he reaches out for the mask of* DION *like a dope fiend after a drug. As soon as he holds it, he seems to gain strength and is able to force a sad laugh*) Now I am drinking your strength, Dion—strength to love in this world and die and sleep and become fertile earth, as you are becoming now in my garden—your weakness the strength of my flowers, your failure as an artist painting their petals with life! (*Then, with bravado*) Come with me while Margaret's bridegroom dresses in your clothes, Mr. Anthony! I need the devil when I'm in the dark! (*He goes off left, but can be heard talking*) Your clothes begin to fit me better than my own! Hurry, Brother! It's time we were home. Our wife is waiting! (*He reappears, having changed his coat and trousers*) Come with me and tell her again I love her! Come and hear her tell me how she loves you! (*He suddenly cannot help kissing the mask*) I love you because she loves you! My kisses on your lips are for her! (*He puts the mask over *his face and stands for a moment, seeming to grow tall and proud—then with a laugh of bold self-assurance)* Out by the back way! I mustn't forget I'm a desperate criminal, pursued by God, and by myself! (*He goes out right, laughing with amused satisfaction*)

(*Curtain*)

ACT THREE

SCENE THREE

SCENE. *Is the same as Scene One of Act One—the sitting-room of* MARGARET'S *home. It is about half an hour after the last scene.* MARGARET *sits on the sofa, waiting with the anxious, impatient expectancy of one deeply in love. She is dressed with a careful, subtle extra touch to attract the eye. She looks young and happy. She is trying to read a book. The front door is heard opening and closing. She leaps up and runs back to throw her arms around* BROWN *as he enters from right, rear. She kisses him passionately.*

MARGARET. (*as he recoils with a sort of guilt—laughingly*) Why, you hateful old thing, you! I really believe you were trying to avoid kissing me! Well, just for that, I'll never . . .

BROWN. (*with fierce, defiant passion, kisses her again and again*) Margaret!

MARGARET. Call me Peggy again. You used to when you really loved me. (*Softly*) Remember the school commencement dance—you and I on the dock in the moonlight?

BROWN. (*with pain*) No. (*He takes his arms from around her*)

MARGARET. (*still holding him—with a laugh*) Well, I like that! You old bear, you! Why not?

BROWN. (*sadly*) It was so long ago.

MARGARET. (*a bit melancholy*) You mean you don't want to be reminded that we're getting old?

BROWN. Yes. (*He kisses her gently*) I'm tired. Let's sit down. (*They sit on the sofa, his arm about her, her head on his shoulder*)

MARGARET. (*with a happy sigh*) I don't mind remembering—now I'm happy. It's only when I'm unhappy that it hurts—and I've been so happy lately, dear—and so grateful to you! (*He stirs uneasily. She goes on joyfully*) Everything's changed! I'd gotten pretty resigned to—and sad and hopeless, too—and then all at once you turn right around and everything is the same as when we were first married—much better even, for I was never sure of you then. You were always so strange and aloof and alone, it seemed I was never really touching you. But now I feel you've become quite human—like me—and I'm so happy, dear! (*She kisses him*)

BROWN. (*his voice trembling*) Then I have made you happy—happier than ever before—no matter what happens? (*She nods*) Then—that justifies everything! (*He forces a laugh*)

MARGARET. Of course it does! I've always known that. But you—you wouldn't be—or you couldn't be—and I could never help you—and all the time I knew you were so lonely! I could always hear you calling to me that you were lost, but I couldn't find the path to you because I was lost, too! That's an awful way for a wife to feel! (*She laughs—joyfully*) But now you're here! You're mine! You're my long-lost lover, and my husband, and my big boy, too!

BROWN. (*with a trace of jealousy*) Where are your other big boys tonight?

MARGARET. Out to a dance. They've all acquired girls, I'll have you know.

BROWN. (*mockingly*) Aren't you jealous?

MARGARET. (*gayly*) Of course! Terribly! But I'm diplomatic. I don't let them see. (*Changing the subject*) Believe me, they've noticed the change in you! The eldest was saying to me to-day: "It's great not to have Father so nervous, any more. Why, he's a regular sport when he gets started!" And the other two said very solemnly: "You bet!" (*She laughs*)

BROWN. (*brokenly*) I—I'm glad.

MARGARET. Dion! You're crying!

BROWN. (*stung by the name, gets up—harshly*) Nonsense! Did you ever know Dion to cry about anyone?

MARGARET. (*sadly*) You couldn't—then. You were too lonely. You had no one to cry to.

BROWN. (*goes and takes a rolled-up plan from the table drawer—dully*) I've got to do some work.

MARGARET. (*disappointedly*) What, has that old Billy Brown got you to work at home again, too?

BROWN. (*ironically*) It's for Dion's good, you know—and yours.

MARGARET. (*making the best of it—cheerfully*) All right. I won't be selfish. It really makes me proud to have you so ambitious. Let me help. (*She brings his drawing-board, which he puts on the table and pins his plan upon. She sits on sofa and picks up her book*)

BROWN. (*carefully casual*) I hear you were in to see me today?

MARGARET. Yes, and Billy wouldn't hear of it! I was quite furious until he convinced me it was all for the best. When is he going to take you into partnership?

BROWN. Very soon now.

MARGARET. And will he really give you full charge when h goes abroad?

BROWN. Yes.

MARGARET. (*practically*) I'd pin him down if I could. Promises are all right, but— (*she hesitates*) I don't trust him.

BROWN. (*with a start, sharply*) What makes you say that?

MARGARET. Oh, something that happened today.

BROWN. What?

MARGARET. I don't mean I blame him, but—to be frank, I think the Great God Brown, as you call him, is getting a bit queer and it's time he took a vacation. Don't you?

BROWN. (*his voice a bit excited—but guardedly*) But why? What did he do?

MARGARET. (*hesitatingly*) Well—it's really too silly—he suddenly got awfully strange. His face scared me. It was like a corpse. Then he raved on some nonsense about he'd always loved me. He went on like a perfect fool! (*She looks at* BROWN, *who is staring at her. She becomes uneasy*) Maybe I shouldn't tell you this. He simply wasn't responsible. Then he came to himself and was all right and begged my pardon and seemed dreadfully sorry, and I felt sorry for him. (*Then with a shudder*) But honestly, Dion, it was just too disgusting for words to hear him! (*With kind, devastating contempt*) Poor Billy!

BROWN (*with a show of tortured derision*) Poor Billy! Poor Billy the Goat! (*With mocking frenzy*) I'll kill him for you! I'll serve you his heart for breakfast!

MARGARET. (*jumping up—frightenedly*) Dion!

BROWN. (*waving his pencil knife with grotesque flourishes*) I tell you I'll murder this God-damned disgusting Great God

Brown who stands like a fatted calf in the way of our health and wealth and happiness!

MARGARET. (*bewilderedly, not knowing how much is pretending, puts an arm about him*) Don't, dear! You're being horrid and strange again. It makes me afraid you haven't really changed, after all.

BROWN. (*unheeding*) And then my wife can be happy! Ha! (*He laughs. She begins to cry. He controls himself—pats her head—gently*) All right, dear. Mr. Brown is now safely in hell. Forget him!

MARGARET. (*stops crying—but still worriedly*) I should never have told you—but I never imagined you'd take it seriously. I've never thought of Billy Brown except as a friend, and lately not even that! He's just a stupid old fool!

BROWN. Ha-ha! Didn't I say he was in hell? They're torturing him! (*Then controlling himself again—exhaustedly*) Please leave me alone now. I've got to work.

MARGARET. All right, dear. I'll go into the next room and anything you want, just call. (*She pats his face—cajolingly*) Is it all forgotten?

BROWN. Will you be happy?

MARGARET. Yes.

BROWN. Then it's dead, I promise! (*She kisses him and goes out. He stares ahead, then shakes off his thoughts and concentrates on his work—mockingly*) Our beautiful new Capitol calls you, Mr. Dion! To work! We'll adroitly hide old Silenus on the cupola! Let him dance over their law-making with his eternal leer! (*He bends over his work*)

(*Curtain*)

ACT FOUR

SCENE ONE

SCENE. *Same as Scene One of Act Three—the drafting room and* BROWN'S *office. It is dusk of a day about a month later.*

The TWO DRAFTSMEN *are bent over their table, working.*

BROWN. (*at his desk, is working feverishly over a plan. He is wearing the mask of* DION. *The mask of* WILLIAM BROWN *rests on the desk beside him. As he works, he chuckles with malicious glee—finally flings down his pencil with a flourish*)

BROWN. Done! In the name of the Almighty Brown, amen, amen! Here's a wondrous fair capitol! The design would do just as well for a Home for Criminal Imbeciles! Yet to them, such is my art, it will appear to possess a pure common-sense, a fat-bellied finality, as dignified as the suspenders of an assemblyman! Only to me will that pompous façade reveal itself as the wearily ironic grin of Pan as, his ears drowsy with the crumbling hum of past and future civilizations, he half-listens to the laws passed by his fleas to enslave him! Ha-ha-ha! (*He leaps grotesquely from behind his desk and cuts a few goatish capers, laughing with lustful merriment*) Long live Chief of Police Brown! District Attorney Brown! Alderman Brown! Assemblyman Brown! Mayor Brown! Congressn Brown! Governor Brown! Senator Brown! President Brown! (*He chants*) Oh, how many persons in one God make up the good God Brown? Hahahaha! (*The* TWO DRAFTSMEN *in the next room have stopped work and are listening*)

YOUNGER DRAFTSMAN. Drunk as a fool!

OLDER DRAFTSMAN. At least Dion used to have the decency to stay away from the office——

YOUNGER DRAFTSMAN. Funny how it's got hold of Brown so quick!

OLDER DRAFTSMAN. He was probably hitting it up on the Q.T. all the time.

BROWN. (*has come back to his desk, laughing to himself and out of breath*) Time to become respectable again! (*He takes off the* DION *mask and reaches out for the* WILLIAM BROWN *one —then stops, with a hand on each, staring down on the plan with fascinated loathing. His real face is now sick, ghastly, tortured, hollow-cheeked and feverish-eyed*) Ugly! Hideous! Despicable! Why must the demon in me pander to cheapness —then punish me with self-loathing and life-hatred? Why am I not strong enough to perish—or blind enough to be content? (*To heaven, bitterly but pleadingly*) Give me the strength to destroy this!—and myself!—and him!—and I will believe in Thee! (*While he has been speaking there has been a noise from the stairs. The* TWO DRAFTSMEN *have bent over their work.* MARGARET *enters, closing the door behind her. At this sound,* BROWN *starts. He immediately senses who it is—with alarm*) Margaret! (*He grabs up both masks and goes into room off right*)

MARGARET. (*she looks healthy and happy, but her face wears a worried, solicitous expression—pleasantly to the staring*

DRAFTSMEN) Good morning. Oh, you needn't look worried, it's Mr. Brown I want to see, not my husband.

YOUNGER D. (*hesitatingly*) He's locked himself in—but maybe if you'll knock——

MARGARET. (*knocks—somewhat embarrassedly*) Mr. Brown! (BROWN *enters his office, wearing the* WILLIAM BROWN *mask. He comes quickly to the other door and unlocks it*).

BROWN. (*with a hectic cordiality*) Come on, Margaret! Enter! This is delightful! Sit down! What can I do for you?

MARGARET. (*taken aback—a bit stiffly*) Nothing much.

BROWN. Something about Dion, of course. Well, your darling pet is all right—never better!

MARGARET. (*coldly*) That's a matter of opinion. I think you're working him to death.

BROWN. Oh, no, not him. It's Brown who is to die. We've agreed on that.

MARGARET. (*giving him a queer look*) I'm serious.

BROWN. So am I. Deadly serious! Hahaha!

MARGARET. (*checking her indignation*) That's what I came to see you about. Really, Dion has acted so hectic and on edge lately I'm sure he's on the verge of a breakdown.

BROWN. Well, it certainly isn't drink. He hasn't had a drop. He doesn't need it! Haha! And I haven't either, although the gossips are beginning to say I'm soused all the time! It's because I've started to laugh! Hahaha! They can't believe in joy in this town except by the bottle! What funny little people! Hahaha! When you're the Great God Brown, eh, Margaret? Hahaha!

MARGARET (*getting up—uneasily*) I'm afraid I——

BROWN. Don't be afraid, my dear! I won't make love to you

again! Honor bright! I'm too near the grave for such folly! But it must have been funny for you when you came here the last time—watching a disgusting old fool like me, eh?—too funny for words! Hahaha! (*Then with a sudden movement he flourishes the design before her*) Look! We've finished it! Dion has finished it! His fame is made!

MARGARET. (*tartly*) Really, Billy, I believe you are drunk!

BROWN. Nobody kisses me—so you can all believe the worst! Hahaha!

MARGARET. (*chillingly*) Then if Dion is through, why can't I see him?

BROWN. (*crazily*) See Dion? See Dion? Well, why not? It's an age of miracles. The streets are full of Lazaruses. Pray! I mean—wait a moment, if you please.

(BROWN *disappears into the room off right. A moment later he reappears in the mask of* DION. *He holds out his arms and* MARGARET *rushes into them. They kiss passionately. Finally he sits with her on the lounge*)

MARGARET. So you've finished it!

BROWN. Yes. The Committee is coming to see it soon. I've made all the changes they'll like, the fools!

MARGARET. (*lovingly*) And can we go on that second honeymoon, right away now?

BROWN. In a week or so, I hope—as soon as I've gotten Brown off to Europe.

MARGARET. Tell me—isn't he drinking hard?

BROWN. (*laughing as* BROWN *did*) Haha! Soused to the ears all the time! Soused on life! He can't stand it! It's burning his insides out!

MARGARET. (*alarmed*) Dear! I'm worried about you. You sound as crazy as he did—when you laugh! You must rest!

BROWN. (*controlling himself*) I'll rest in peace—when he's gone!

MARGARET. (*with a queer look*) Why Dion, that isn't your suit. It's just like——

BROWN. It's his! We're getting to be like twins. I'm inheriting his clothes already! (*Then calming himself as he sees how frightened she is*) Don't be worried, dear. I'm just a trifle elated, now the job's done. I guess I'm a bit soused on life, too! (*The* COMMITTEE, *three important-looking, average personages, come into the drafting room*)

MARGARET. (*forcing a smile*) Well, don't let it burn *your* insides out!

BROWN. No danger! Mine were tempered in hell! Hahaha!

MARGARET. (*kissing him, coaxingly*) Come home, dear—please!

OLDER DRAFTSMAN. (*knocks on the door*) The Committee is here, Mr. Brown.

BROWN. (*hurriedly to* MARGARET) You receive them. Hand them the design. I'll get Brown. (*He raises his voice*) Come right in, gentlemen. (*He goes off right, as the* COMMITTEE *enter the office. When they see* MARGARET, *they stop in surprise*)

MARGARET. (*embarrassedly*) Good afternoon. Mr. Brown will be right with you. (*They bow.* MARGARET *holds out the design to them*) This is my husband's design. He finished it today.

COMMITTEE. Ah! (*They crowd around to look at it—with enthusiasm*) Perfect! Splendid! Couldn't be better! Exactly what we suggested!

MARGARET. (*joyfully*) Then you accept it? Mr. Anthony will be so pleased!

MEMBER. Mr. Anthony?

ANOTHER. Is he working here again?

THIRD. Did I understand you to say this was your husband's design?

MARGARET. (*excitedly*) Yes! Entirely his! He's worked like a dog— (*Appalled*) You don't mean to say—Mr. Brown never told you? (*They shake their heads in solemn surprise*) Oh, the contemptible cad! I hate him!

BROWN. (*appearing at right—mockingly*) Hate me, Margaret? Hate Brown? How superfluous! (*Oratorically*) Gentlemen, I have been keeping a secret from you in order that you might be the more impressed when I revealed it. That design is entirely the inspiration of Mr. Dion Anthony's genius. I had nothing to do with it.

MARGARET. (*contritely*) Oh, Billy! I'm sorry! Forgive me!

BROWN. (*ignoring her, takes the plan from the* COMMITTEE *and begins unpinning it from the board—mockingly*) I can see by your faces you have approved this. You are delighted, aren't you? And why not, my dear sirs? Look at it, and look at you! Hahaha! It'll immortalize you, my good men! You'll be as death-defying a joke as any in Joe Miller! (*Then with a sudden complete change of tone—angrily*) You damn fools! Can't you see this is an insult—a terrible, blasphemous insult!—that this embittered failure Anthony is hurling in the teeth of our success—an insult to you, to me, to you, Margaret—and to Almighty God! (*In a frenzy of fury*) And if you are weak and cowardly enough to stand for it, I'm not! (*He *tears the plan into four pieces. The* COMMITTEE *stands aghast.* MARGARET *runs forward*)

MARGARET. (*in a scream*) You coward! Dion! Dion! (*She picks up the plan and hugs it to her bosom*)

BROWN. (*with a sudden goatish caper*) I'll tell him you're here. (*He disappears, but reappears almost immediately in the mask of* DION. *He is imposing a terrible discipline on himself to avoid dancing and laughing. He speaks suavely*) Everything is all right—all for the best—you mustn't get excited! A little paste, Margaret! A little paste, gentlemen! And all will be well! Life is imperfect, Brothers! Men have their faults, Sister! But with a few drops of glue much may be done! A little dab of pasty resignation here and there—and even broken hearts may be repaired to do yeoman service! (*He has edged toward the door. They are all staring at him with petrified bewilderment. He puts his finger to his lips*) Ssssh! This is Daddy's bedtime secret for today: Man is born broken. He lives by mending. The grace of God is glue! (*With a quick prancing movement, he has opened the door, gone through, and closed it after him silently, shaking with suppressed laughter. He springs lightly to the side of the petrified* DRAFTSMEN—*in a whisper*) They will find him in the little room. Mr. William Brown is dead! (*With light leaps he vanishes, his head thrown back, shaking with silent laughter. The sound of his feet leaping down the stairs, five at a time, can be heard. Then a pause of silence. The people in the two rooms stare. The* YOUNGER DRAFTSMAN *is the first to recover*)

YOUNGER DRAFTSMAN (*rushing into the next room, shouts in terrified tones*) Mr. Brown is dead!

COMMITTEE. He murdered him! (*They all run into the little*

room off right. MARGARET *remains, stunned with horror. They return in a moment, carrying the mask of* WILLIAM BROWN, *two on each side, as if they were carrying a body by the legs and shoulders. They solemnly lay him down on the couch and stand looking down at him)*

FIRST COMMITTEEMAN. (*with a frightened awe*) I can't believe he's gone.

SECOND COMMITTEEMAN. (*in same tone*) I can almost hear him talking. (*As if impelled, he clears his throat and addresses the mask importantly*) Mr. Brown— (*then stops short*)

THIRD COMMITTEEMAN. (*shrinking back*) No. Dead, all right! (*Then suddenly, hysterically angry and terrified*) We must take steps at once to run Anthony to earth!

MARGARET. (*with a heart-broken cry*) Dion's innocent!

YOUNGER DRAFTSMAN. I'll phone for the police, sir! (*He rushes to the phone*)

(*Curtain*)

ACT FOUR

SCENE TWO

SCENE. *The same as Scene Two of Act Three—the library of* WILLIAM BROWN'S *home. The mask of* DION *stands on the table beneath the light, facing front.*

On his knees beside the table, facing front, stripped naked except for a white cloth around his loins, is BROWN. *The clothes he has torn off in his agony are scattered on the floor. His eyes, his arms, his whole body strain upward, his muscles writhe with his lips as they pray silently in their agonized supplication. Finally a voice seems torn out of him.*

BROWN. Mercy, Compassionate Savior of Man! Out of my depths I cry to you! Mercy on thy poor clod, thy clot of unhallowed earth, thy clay, the Great God Brown! Mercy, Savior! (*He seems to wait for an answer—then leaping to his feet he puts out one hand to touch the mask like a frightened child reaching out for its nurse's hand—then with immediate mocking despair*) Bah! I am sorry, little children, but your kingdom is empty. God has become disgusted and moved away to some far ecstatic star where life is a dancing flame! We must die without him. (*Then—addressing the mask—harshly*) Together, my friend! You, too! Let Margaret suffer! Let the whole world suffer as I am suffering! (*There is a sound of a door being pushed violently open, padding feet in slippers, and* CYBEL, *wearing her mask, runs into the room. She stops short on seeing* BROWN *and the mask, and stares from one to the other for a second in confusion. She is dressed in a black kimono robe and wears slippers over her bare feet. Her yellow hair hangs down in a great mane over her shoulders. She has grown stouter, has more of the deep objective calm of an idol)*

BROWN. (*staring at her—fascinated—with great peace as if her presence comforted him*) Cybel! I was coming to you! How did you know?

CYBEL. (*takes off her mask and looks from* BROWN *to the* DION *mask, now with a great understanding*) So that's why you never came to me again! You are Dion Brown!

BROWN (*bitterly*) I am the remains of William Brown! (*He points to the mask of* DION) I am his murderer and his murdered!

CYBEL. (*with a laugh of exasperated pity*) Oh, why can't you ever learn to leave yourselves alone and leave me alone!

BROWN. (*boyishly and naïvely*) I am Billy.

CYBEL. (*immediately, with a motherly solicitude*) Then run, Billy, run! They are hunting for someone! They came to my place, hunting for a murderer, Dion! They must find a victim! They've got to quiet their fears, to cast out their devils, or they'll never sleep soundly again! They've got to absolve themselves by finding a guilty one! They've got to kill someone now, to live! You're naked! You must be Satan! Run, Billy, run! They'll come here! I ran here to warn—someone! So run away if you want to live!

BROWN. (*like a sulky child*) I'm too tired. I don't want to.

CYBEL. (*with motherly calm*) All right, you needn't, Bil Don't sulk. (*As a noise comes from outside*) Anyway, it's t late. I hear them in the garden now.

BROWN. (*listening, puts out his hand and takes the mask of* DION—*as he gains strength, mockingly*) Thanks for this one last favor, Dion! Listen! Your avengers! Standing on your grave in the garden! Hahaha! (*He puts on the mask and springs to the left and makes a gesture as if flinging French windows open. Gayly mocking*) Welcome, dumb worshippers! I am your great God Brown! I have been advised to run from you but it is my almighty whim to dance into escape over your prostrate souls! (*Shouts from the garden and a volley of shots.* BROWN *staggers back and falls on the floor by the couch, mortally wounded*)

CYBEL. (*runs to his side, lifts him on to the couch and takes off the mask of* DION) You can't take this to bed with you. You've got to go to sleep alone. (*She places the mask of* DION *back on its stand under the light and puts on her own, just as, after a banging of doors, crashing of glass, trampling of feet, a Squad of Police with drawn revolvers, led by a grizzly, brutal-faced Captain, run into the room. They are followed by* MARGARET, *still distractedly clutching the pieces of the plan to her breast*)

CAPTAIN. (*pointing to the mask of* DION—*triumphantly*) Got him! He's dead!

MARGARET. (*throws herself on her knees, takes the mask and kisses it—heart-brokenly*) Dion! Dion! (*Her face hidden in her arms, the mask in her hands above her bowed head, she remains, sobbing with deep, silent grief*)

CAPTAIN. (*noticing* CYBEL *and* BROWN—*startled*) Hey! Look at this! What're you doin' here? Who's he?

CYBEL. You ought to know. You croaked him!

CAPTAIN. (*with a defensive snarl—hastily*) It was Anthony! I saw his mug! This feller's an accomplice, I bet yuh! Serves him right! Who is he? Friend o' yours! Crook! What's his name? Tell me or I'll fix yuh!

CYBEL. Billy.

CAPTAIN. Billy what?

CYBEL. I don't know. He's dying. (*Then suddenly*) Leave me alone with him and maybe I'll get him to squeal it.

CAPTAIN. Yuh better! I got to have a clean report. I'll give yuh a couple o' minutes. (*He motions to the Policemen, who follow him off left.* CYBEL *takes off her mask and sits down by* BROWN'S *head. He makes an effort to raise himself toward her and she helps him, throwing her kimono over his bare body, drawing his head on to her shoulder*)

BROWN. (*snuggling against her—gratefully*) The earth is warm.

CYBEL. (*soothingly, looking before her like an idol*) Ssshh! Go to sleep, Billy.

BROWN. Yes, Mother. (*Then explainingly*) It was dark and I couldn't see where I was going and they all picked on me.

CYBEL. I know. You're tired.

BROWN. And when I wake up . . . ?

CYBEL. The sun will be rising again.

BROWN. To judge the living and the dead! (*Frightenedly*) I don't want justice. I want love.

There is only love.

BROWN. Thank you, Mother. (*Then feebly*) I'm getting sleepy. What's the prayer you taught me— Our Father——?

CYBEL. (*with calm exultance*) Our Father Who Art!

BROWN. (*taking her tone—exultantly*) Who art! Who art! (*Suddenly—with ecstasy*) I know! I have found Him! I hear Him speak! "Blessed are they that weep, for they shall laugh!" Only he that has wept can laugh! The laughter of Heaven sows earth with a rain of tears, and out of Earth's transfigured birth-pain the laughter of Man returns to bless and play again in innumerable dancing gales of flame upon the knees of God! (*He dies*)

CYBEL. (*gets up and fixes his body on the couch. She bends down and kisses him gently—she straightens up and looks into space—with a profound pain*) Always spring comes again bearing life! Always again! Always, always forever again!—Spring again!—life again!—summer and fall and death and peace again!—(*with agonized sorrow*)—but always, always, love and conception and birth and pain again—spring bearing the intolerable chalice of life again!—(*then with agonized exultance*)—bearing the glorious, blazing crown of life again! (*She stands like an idol of Earth, her eyes staring out over the world*)

MARGARET. (*lifting her head adoringly to the mask—triumphant tenderness mingled with her grief*) My lover! My husband! My boy! (*She kisses the mask*) Good-by. Thank you for happiness! And you're not dead, sweetheart! You can never die till my heart dies! You will live forever! You will sleep under my heart! I will feel you stirring in your sleep, forever under my heart! (*She kisses the mask again. There is a pause*)

CAPTAIN (*comes just into sight at left and speaks front without looking at them—gruffly*) Well, what's his name?

CYBEL. Man!

CAPTAIN. (*taking a grimy notebook and an inch-long pencil from his pocket*) How d'yuh spell it?

(*Curtain*)

EPILOGUE

SCENE. *Four years later.*

The same spot on the same dock as in Prologue on another moonlight night in June. The sound of the waves and of distant dance music.

MARGARET *and her* THREE SONS *appear from the right. The eldest is now eighteen. All are dressed in the height of correct Prep-school elegance. They are all tall, athletic, strong and handsome-looking. They loom up around the slight figure of their mother like protecting giants, giving her a strange aspect of lonely, detached, small femininity. She wears her mask of the proud, indulgent Mother. She has grown appreciably older. Her hair is now a beautiful gray. There is about her manner and voice the sad but contented feeling of one who knows her life-purpose well accomplished but is at the same time a bit empty and comfortless with the finality of it. She is wrapped in a gray cloak*)

ELDEST. Doesn't Bee look beautiful tonight, Mother?

NEXT. Don't you think Mabel's the best dancer in there, Mother?

YOUNGEST. Aw, Alice has them both beat, hasn't she, Mother?

MARGARET. (*with a sad little laugh*) Each of you is right. (*Then, with strange finality*) Good-by, boys.

BOYS. (*surprised*) Good-by.

MARGARET. It was here on a night just like this your father first—proposed to me. Did you ever know that?

BOYS. (*embarrassedly*) No.

MARGARET. (*yearningly*) But the nights now are so much colder than they used to be. Think of it, I went in moonlight-bathing in June when I was a girl. It was so warm and beautiful in those days. I remember the Junes when I was carrying you boys—— (*A pause. They fidget uneasily. She asks pleadingly*) Promise me faithfully never to forget your father!

BOYS. (*uncomfortably*) Yes, Mother.

MARGARET. (*forcing a joking tone*) But you mustn't waste June on an old woman like me! Go in and dance. (*As they hesitate dutifully*) Go on. I really want to be alone—with my Junes.

BOYS. (*unable to conceal their eagerness*) Yes, Mother. (*They go away*)

MARGARET. (*slowly removes her mask, laying it on the bench, and stares up at the moon with a wistful, resigned sweetness*) So long ago! And yet I'm still the same Margaret. It's only our lives that grow old. We *are* where centuries only count as seconds and after a thousand lives our eyes begin to open—(*she looks around her with a rapt smile*)—and the moon rests in the sea! I want to feel the moon at peace in the sea! I want Dion to leave the sky for me! I want him to sleep in the tides of my heart! (*She slowly takes from under her cloak, from her bosom, as if from her heart, the mask of* DION *as it was at the last and holds it before her face*) My lover! My husband! My boy! You can never die till my heart dies! You will live forever! You are sleeping under my heart! I feel you stirring in your sleep, forever under my heart. (*She kisses him on the lips with a timeless kiss*)

(*Curtain*)

THE FOUNTAIN

A Play in Eleven Scenes

(1921 - 22)

CHARACTERS

IBNU ASWAD, *a Moorish chieftain*

JUAN PONCE DE LEON

PEDRO, *his servant*

MARIA DE CORDOVA

LUIS DE ALVAREDO

YUSEF, *a Moorish minstrel*

DIEGO MENENDEZ, *a Franciscan*

VICENTE DE CORDOVA, *Maria's husband*

ALONZO DE OVIEDO
MANUEL DE CASTILLO
CRISTOVAL DE MENDOZA } *nobles*

A SOLDIER

FRIAR QUESADA, *a Franciscan*

BEATRIZ DE CORDOVA, *daughter of Maria and Vicente*

NANO, *an Indian chief*

A CHIEF OF THE INDIANS IN FLORIDA

A MEDICINE MAN

A FIGURE

A POET OF CATHAY

AN OLD INDIAN WOMAN OF THE BAHAMAS

A DOMINICAN MONK

FATHER SUPERIOR OF THE DOMINICANS IN CUBA

JUAN, *nephew of Juan Ponce de Leon*

Nobles, Monks, Soldiers, Sailors, Captive Indians of Porto Rico, Indians in Florida.

TIME: Late Fifteenth and early Sixteenth Centuries.

SCENES

Part One

Scene I: Courtyard of the house of Ibnu Aswad, Granada, Spain—the night of the Moorish capitulation, 1492.

Scene II: Columbus's flagship on the last day of his second voyage, 1493.

Part Two

Scene III: Courtyard of the Government House, Porto Rico, an afternoon twenty years or more later.

Scene IV: Cabinet of Bishop Menendez in the Government House—an evening three months later.

Scene V: A prisoner's cell in the Government House—the same time.

Scene VI: Same as Scene Three—immediately follows Scene Five.

Part Three

Scene VII: A strip of beach on the Florida coast—a night four months later.

Scene VIII: The same—noon the following day.

Scene IX: A clearing in the forest—that night.

Scene X: The same, some hours later.

Scene XI: Courtyard of a Dominican monastery in Cuba—several months later.

THE FOUNTAIN

SCENE ONE

SCENE. *Courtyard of* IBNU ASWAD'S *palace in Granada.*

The section forms a right triangle, its apex at the rear, right. In the left, center, a massive porte-cochère opens on the street. On the right, a door leading into the house itself. In the center of the courtyard, a large splendid fountain of green marble with human and animal figures in gilt bronze. The peristyle of the gallery running around the court is supported by slender columns of polished marble, partly gilded. The interspaces above the horseshoe arches springing from the columns are filled with arabesques, texts from the Koran, red, blue and gold in color. Above are the latticed windows of the women's apartments. Over the house-top a sky with stars can be seen. It is early night.

As the curtain rises, the court is empty and there is silence except for the splash of the fountain. Then a loud, imperious knocking, as of someone pounding with the hilt of a sword, is heard from the porte-cochère. IBNU ASWAD *enters from the right. He is an elderly, noble-looking Moor, the lower part of his face covered by a long, white beard. His expression is one of great pride borne down by sorrow and humiliation. He goes out through the porte-cochère, and returns ushering in* JUAN PONCE DE LEON *and his servant,* PEDRO. JUAN *is a tall, handsome Spanish noble of thirty-one, dressed in full uniform. His countenance is haughty, full of a romantic adventurousness and courage; yet he gives the impression of disciplined ability, of a confident self-mastery—a romantic dreamer governed by the ambitious thinker in him.* PEDRO *is a dull-looking young fellow.*

JUAN. (*as they enter*) (*To* ASWAD) Your pardon, Sir Moor.

ASWAD. (*haughtily*) You are quartered here? (JUAN *bows in affirmation*) Welcome then, since it is the will of Allah that you should conquer.

JUAN. (*graciously*) I am no conquerer here. I am a stranger grateful for hospitality.

ASWAD. (*unbending a bit*) You are kind. I have seen you in action on the field. You are brave. Defeat loses its bitterness when the foe is noble. (*Moodily and bitterly—staring at the fountain*) The waters of the fountain fall—but ever they rise again, Sir Spaniard. Such is the decree of destiny. (*With fervor*) Blessed be Allah who exalteth and debaseth the kings of the earth, according to his divine will, in whose fulfillment consists eternal justice. (*Fiercely and defiantly*) Whosoever the victor, there is no conqueror but Allah!

JUAN. (*stiffening—coldly*) Your fortitude does you honor. (*By way of dismissing the subject—abruptly*) I am expecting friends. Will that disturb your household? If so——

ASWAD. (*coldly*) My house is your house. It is decreed. (*He bows with stately grace and goes out, right*)

JUAN. (*makes a movement as if to detain him—then shrugs his shoulders*) What can I do for him? (*Ironically repeating* IBNU'S *inflection*) It is decreed by Spain if not by Allah. (*Seeing* PEDRO *lolling against the wall, drowsily staring at the fountain—amused*) Lazy lout! Does the fountain cause you, too, to dream? (*In a tone of command*) Bring the wine. They will be here soon.

PEDRO. Yes, sir. (*He goes.* JUAN *paces back and forth, humming to himself.* PEDRO *returns and approaches his master cautiously—in a mysterious whisper*) A lady, sir.

JUAN. (*frowning*) Is she alone? (PEDRO *nods,* JUAN *smiles cynically*) Surely you have mistaken her calling. Tell her I am not here. (*As* PEDRO *turns to go,* MARIA DE CORDOVA *appears in the arch of the porte-cochère. A heavy black veil is thrown over her face*)

MARIA. (*her voice forced and trembling*) Juan!

JUAN. (*immediately the gallant cavalier, makes a motion for* PEDRO *to leave, and bows low—mockery in his voice*) Beautiful lady, you do me an unmerited honor.

MARIA. (*wearily*) Spare me your mockery, Juan. (*She throws back her veil. She is a striking-looking woman of thirty-eight or forty, but discontent and sorrow have marked her age clearly on her face*)

JUAN. (*astonished*) Maria! (*Then with genuine alarm*) In God's name!

MARIA. (*her voice breaking*) Juan, I had to come.

JUAN. (*sternly*) Your husband is my brother in arms. To-night—here—he is to be among my guests. I feel that every word we speak now degrades me in my honor.

MARIA. (*in a tone of great grief*) You are cruel! I had to speak with you alone. This is my one chance. I leave the Court tomorrow.

JUAN. (*with evident relief*) Ah.

MARIA. (*stares at him with a pitiful appeal. He avoids her eyes*) Oh, what a fool I am—(*with a half-sob, as if the *confession were wrung from her*)—to love you, Juan! (*She makes a movement toward him, but he steps back, aloof and cold*)

JUAN. (*frowning*) That word—we have never uttered it before. You have always been—my friend. (*After a pause, with deep earnestness*) Why must you ruin our rare friendship for a word that every minstrel mouths? (*Then with irritation*) Love, love, love we chatter everlastingly. We pretend love alone is why we live! Bah! Life is nobler than the weak lies of poets—or it's nothing!

MARIA. (*wounded and indignant*) If you had had to fight for love as you have fought for glory!——

JUAN. (*struck by the pain in her tone, kneels and kisses her hand—remorsefully*) Forgive me! I would die rather than bring sorrow to a heart as kind as yours. Keep me forever in that heart, I beg—but as a friend—as it has always been.

MARIA. (*with a gasp of pain*) Ah! (*Taking her hand from his—with a deep sigh*) God give you knowledge of the heart!

JUAN. (*rises—plainly endeavoring to change the subject*) You are leaving the Court?

MARIA. The Queen has granted my wish to retire to Cordova. (*Passionately*) I'm sick of the Court! I long for simple things! I pray to become worthy again of that pure love of God I knew as a girl. I must seek peace in Him! (*After a pause*) Granada is ours. The Moors are driven from Spain. The wars are over. What will you do now, Juan?

JUAN. Peace means stagnation—a slack ease of cavaliers and songs and faded roses. I must go on.

MARIA. Where will you go?

JUAN. (*smiles half-whimsically at an idea*) Perhaps with

the Genoese, Christopher Columbus, when he sails to find the western passage to Cathay.

MARIA. (*disturbed*) But they say he is mad.

JUAN. (*seriously now*) Mad or not, he dreams of glory. I have heard he plans to conquer for Spain that immense realm of the Great Khan which Marco Polo saw.

MARIA. What! Abandon your career at Court now when your exploits have brought you in such favor? No one would ruin himself so senselessly save in despair! (*Jealously*) It must be from love you are fleeing! (*Fiercely mocking*) Is a woman avenging women? Tell me her name!

JUAN (*with a mocking laugh*) Love, love, and always love! Can no other motive exist for you? God pity women!

MARIA. (*after a pause—sadly*) God pity me—because pity is what you offer me. (*As* JUAN *seems about to protest wearily*) Don't deny it, Juan. It sneers at me in your pretended scorn of love—— You wish to comfort my humiliation! Am I a fool? Have you not loved others? I could name ten——

JUAN. Maria!

MARIA. Do you imagine I haven't guessed the truth? Those others had youth—while I—— And my love seems to you—pitiable!

JUAN (*kneeling and taking her hand—with passionate earnestness*) No, dear friend, no! I swear to you! (*After a pause*) What you call loves—they were merely moods—dreams of a night or two—lustful adventures—gestures of vanity, perhaps—but I have never loved. Spain is the mistress to whom I give my heart, Spain and my own ambitions, which are Spain's. Now do you understand?

MARIA. (*sadly*) No, Juan. (*He rises*) I understand that

I am growing old—that love has passed for me—and that I suffer in my loneliness. Perhaps if God had granted me a child—— But His justice punishes. He has seen my secret sin. I have loved you, Juan, for years. But it was only in the last year when my heart, feeling youth die, grew desperate that I dared let you see. And now, farewell, until God's will be done in death. We must not meet again.

JUAN. (*sternly*) No. (*Passionately*) I wish to God you had not told me this!

MARIA (*gently*) If you are still my friend you will not wish it. It was my final penance—that you should know. And, having told you, I am free, for my heart is dead. There is only my soul left that knows the love of God which blesses and does not torture. Farewell once more, Juan. (*He kneels and kisses her hand. She puts the other on his head as if blessing him*) You are noble, the soul of courage, a man of men. You will go far, soldier of iron—and dreamer. God pity you if those two selves should ever clash! You shall have all my prayers for your success—but I shall add, Dear Savior, let him know tenderness to recompense him when his hard youth dies! (*She turns quickly and goes out*)

JUAN. (*looks after her in melancholy thought for a while—then sighs deeply and shrugs his shoulders*) Time tarnishes even the pure, difficult things with common weakness. (LUIS DE ALVAREDO *enters through the porte-cochère. He is a dissipated-looking noble, a few years older than* JUAN. *His face is homely but extremely fetching in its nobility, its expression of mocking fun and raillery. He is dressed carelessly, is slightly drunk*)

LUIS. (*mockingly*) Lover of glory, beloved of women, hail!

(*He comes to the startled* JUAN *as voices are heard from the porte-cochère—in a hurried, cautioning whisper*) The devil, Juan! Have you lost your wits—or has she? I recognized her—and Vicente was only ten paces behind. (*Then again mockingly*) Discretion, my stainless knight, discretion!

JUAN. (*sternly*) Stop! You wrong her and me. (*Sounds of a loud, angry dispute are heard from without*) What is that brawling?

LUIS. My Moor. (*Explaining hurriedly to* JUAN) A fellow poet—a minstrel of their common folk. We found him running amuck about the streets declaiming to the stars that their king, Abdallah, had sold his soul to hell when he surrendered. (*With admiration*) By God, Juan, how he cursed! Oh, he's a precious songster, and as poet to poet I collared him and dragged him with us. Our friend, Diego, would have cut his throat for the Church's glory had I not interfered.

JUAN. (*smiling*) As madman for madman, eh? But why bring him here to howl?

LUIS. He has a lute. It is my whim he should sing some verses. (*With an amused grin*) The dog speaks only Arabic. If he is wily, he will chant such curses on our heads as will blight that fountain dry—and no one of us but me will understand. (*With great glee*) It will be sport, Juan! (*The clamor from outside grows more violent*) By God, Diego will murder my minstrel—after all my pains. (*Starts to hurry out—stops in the entrance*) Remember, Juan. Vicente may have recognized—the lady.

JUAN. (*nods, frowning*) The devil take all women! (LUIS *goes out.* PEDRO *enters, carrying two large baskets full of bottles and sets them down, rear*) Drink and forget sad nonsense.

Bring out cushions. We will sit beside the fountain. (PEDRO *goes into the house, right.* LUIS *reënters, holding* YUSEF *by the arm —a wizened old Moor dressed in the clothes of the common people, but wearing the turban signifying that he has made the pilgrimage to Mecca. His deep-set eyes smolder with hatred but physically he is so exhausted as to seem resigned to his fate. They are followed by* DIEGO MENENDEZ, *a Franciscan monk, about the same age as* JUAN *and* LUIS. *He has a pale, long face, the thin, cruel mouth, the cold, self-obsessed eyes of the fanatic. Just now he is full of helpless fury and indignation. Accompanying him is* VICENTE DE CORDOVA, *a gray-haired, stern, soldierly noble of forty-five. Following them are the three nobles,* OVIEDO, CASTILLO *and* MENDOZA. *They are the type of adventurous cavaliers of the day—cruel, courageous to recklessness, practically uneducated—knights of the true Cross, ignorant of and despising every first principle of real Christianity—yet carrying the whole off with a picturesque air*)

MENENDEZ. (*angrily*) I protest to you, Juan. It is heresy to suffer this dog's presence when we offer thanks to God for victory.

JUAN. (*stares at the Moor interestedly for a moment—then carelessly*) I see no desecration, Diego—if he will sing, not howl. (*Turning to* VICENTE, *scrutinizing his face keenly—carelessly*) What do you say, Vicente?

VICENTE. (*gives him a dark look of suspicion—coldly and meaningly*) I say nothing—now.

JUAN. Ah! (*He and* LUIS *exchange a look*)

OVIEDO. Well, I say let him remain. We may have sport with him.

CASTILLO. (*with a cruel smile*) Perhaps with a sword-point we can persuade him to sing where the townsfolk hid their gold.

MENDOZA. Your words are inspired, Manuel!

LUIS. (*scornfully*) Materialists! You would sack heaven and melt the moon for silver. Juan, where is your wine? (PEDRO *appears, bringing cushions and goblets for each. He uncorks the bottles and pours their goblets full. Scorning a goblet* LUIS *snatches a bottle from him and drinks from that*)

JUAN. (*keeping a wary eye on* VICENTE) Let us drink. (*Takes a goblet from* PEDRO) To our most Gracious Sovereigns and to Spain! (*He drinks*)

MENENDEZ. And to the Church! (*Angrily*) But I will not drink until that infidel is moved apart!

VICENTE. I agree.

JUAN. (*impatiently*) Let the Moor go, Luis—since Diego takes himself so seriously.

VICENTE. (*coldly resentful*) And I? (JUAN *is about to reply irritably when* LUIS *breaks in hurriedly*)

LUIS. Shhh! I'll sing a song for you. (*Releasing the Moor and pointing to the rear*) Go, brother bard, and take your ease. (*The Moor goes to the right, rear, and squats down in the shadow by the wall.* LUIS *sings*)

Love is a flower
Forever blooming.
Life is a fountain
Forever leaping
Upward to catch the golden sunlight,
Striving to reach the azure heaven;

Failing, falling,
Ever returning
To kiss the earth that the flower may live.

(*They all applaud as he finishes*)

JUAN. Charming, Sir Poet—but a lie. (*Mockingly*) Love, and love, and always love! The devil seize your flower! Do fountains flow only to nourish flowers that bloom a day and die?

LUIS. Roar, lion! You will not wake my dream that life is love!

JUAN. Listen to him, Diego! We know his only love is his old mother; and yet, to judge from his songs, you would think him a greater philanderer than—than——

VICENTE. (*interrupting sneeringly*) Than you, Don Juan?

JUAN. (*turning on him—coldly*) Gossip gives many a false name—but gossip only deludes old women.

VICENTE. (*growing pale*) Do you intend that insult? (*Their hands go to the hilt of their swords. The three nobles quicken to excited interest.* LUIS *leaps between them*)

LUIS. For God's sake! Is either of you a Moor? (*Raises his bottle*) Let us drink again to Spain!

OVIEDO. And to the next war!

CASTILLO. May it be soon!

MENDOZA. With a world to sack! Sing us a song of that, Luis!

LUIS. I am too thirsty. But come, I was forgetting our infidel. Let me use persuasion—— (*He goes back to the Moor, and can be heard talking to him in Arabic*)

JUAN. We were speaking of wars to come. With whom?

OVIEDO. With anyone!

JUAN. But guess. I think it will be in lands beyond strange seas—Cipango and Cathay—the cities of gold that Marco Polo saw.

OVIEDO. But who will lead us there?

JUAN. Why, Christopher Columbus. (*They all laugh*)

CASTILLO. That Genoese mongrel!—to lead Spaniards!

MENDOZA. He's mad. He claims the earth is round—like an egg! (*They all laugh*)

JUAN. (*impressively*) I saw him today. He was riding his flea-bitten mule as if he were a Cæsar in a triumph. His eyes were full of golden cities.

CASTILLO. Bah, Juan, you romance! The man's an idiot!

LUIS. (*coming back*) The more fool you to think so! He will yet find for Spain the Western Passage to the East.

CASTILLO. Or fall off the world's edge! I will wager you would not go with him for all the gold in Indies!

LUIS. You would lose!

JUAN. I'm planning to go. (*All are astonished*) But not on his first voyage. Before I pledge my sword I must have proof that it can serve Spain's glory. There is no profit in staking life for dreams.

LUIS. There is no profit in anything but that! You're from the East, Moor. Tell us of the Great Khan, of Cipango and Cathay and Cambuluc, of golden roofs and emerald-studded lintels to the doors. Your people must have heard these wonders.

MENDOZA. Yes, let him sing of treasure. (*But the Moor remains silent*)

LUIS. Wait, I'll talk to him. (*He goes back and speaks to the Moor in Arabic. The latter replies*)

MENENDEZ. (*furiously*) This is all treasonable. The dog had broken the peace. The punishment is death.

JUAN. (*mockingly*) Let him sing of treasure, Diego. Even the Church loves gold.

LUIS. (*coming back—exultantly*) He consents, Juan—because I am a colleague. He will sing of treasure in the East—a tale told to his father by some wandering poet who came from Cathay with a caravan. (*All except the outraged* DIEGO *and the sullen, preoccupied* VICENTE *quicken to interested attention. The Moor strikes a few notes on his lute*) Hush! (*The Moor begins a crooning chant of verses, accompanying himself on the lute. At first they are all held by its strange rhythm, then they begin to betray impatience*)

OVIEDO. By God, our wolf turns into a sick shepherd.

LUIS. Hush!

CASTILLO. (*impatiently*) What does he sing?

LUIS. (*enrapt—vaguely*) Hush, hush.

MENENDEZ. (*rising to his feet as the Moor's recitative abruptly ends—harshly*) This is the service in a devil's mass!

LUIS. (*passes his hand across his eyes, then stares into the fountain dreamily*) He sang of treasure—but strange to your longing. There is in some far country of the East—Cathay, Cipango, who knows—a spot that Nature has set apart from men and blessed with peace. It is a sacred grove where all things live in the old harmony they knew before man came. Beauty resides there and is articulate. Each sound is music, and every sight a vision. The trees bear golden fruit. And in the center of the grove, there is a fountain—beautiful beyond human dreams, in whose rainbows all of life is mirrored. In that fountain's waters, young maidens play and sing and tend it everlastingly for very joy in being one with it. This is the Fountain of Youth, he said. The wise men of that far-off land have known it many ages. They make it their last pilgrimage when sick with years and weary of their lives. Here they drink, and the years drop from them like a worn-out robe. Body and mind know youth again, and these young men, who had been old, leap up and join the handmaids' dance. Then they go back to life, but with hearts purified, and the old discords trouble them no more, but they are holy and the folk revere them. (*With a sigh*) That's his tale, my friends—but he added it is hard to find that fountain. Only to the chosen does it reveal itself.

MENENDEZ. (*furiously*) Idolatry!

OVIEDO. Is this his treasure? By God, he mocks us!

LUIS. Fools! Beauty is lost on you. Your souls clink like coppers. (MENENDEZ *slinks back step by step toward the Moor.* LUIS *grabs a bottle*) Come, let us drink! We'll all to Cathay with Don Christopher. You can burrow for dung there—but I will search for this fountain.

JUAN. (*drinking—a bit tipsily*) Drink and forget sad nonsense! The devil! His song beguiled me until you tricked it into that old woman's mumble. Youth! Is youth a treasure? Then are we all—except Vicente—priceless rich; and yet, God's blood, one has but to look to see how poor we are!

LUIS. Poor in spirit! I understand you, Juan.

JUAN. Fountain of youth, God help us, with love to boot! I wish he'd sung instead of the armies and power of the Great Khan! (*Then half-aside to* LUIS) The tale is always told to the wrong person. There was one here not long ago who would have given pearls for drops from that same fountain!

VICENTE. (*who has crept vengefully toward* JUAN *in time to hear these last words—with cold fury*) A moment ago you taunted me with age—and now you dare—— (*He slaps* JUAN *across the face. They draw their swords*)

LUIS. (*trying to intervene*) For God's sake, friends!

OVIEDO. (*with excited interest*) A duel! (*The others echo this. Suddenly there is a harsh shriek from the rear.* MENENDEZ *appears from the shadow, dagger in hand, a look of fanatical triumph on his face. Forgetting the duel, the others stand appalled*)

MENENDEZ. (*sheathing the dagger*) I have slain the dog. It was high time.

LUIS. Miserable bigot! (*Raging, he tries to throw himself at the monk, but* JUAN *grasps him and forces him down on a cushion. He breaks down, weeping*)

MENENDEZ. (*coldly scornful*) What! A soldier of Christ weep for an infidel!

JUAN. (*sternly*) Be still, Diego! (*Then frowning—curtly, in a tone of dismissal which silences all protest*) Our reveling is under an ill star. There is blood upon it. Good-night. (*Turning to* VICENTE) Until tomorrow.

(VICENTE *bows and goes, accompanied by* MENENDEZ. *The young nobles troop out behind, disputing noisily about the coming duel*)

JUAN. (*comes over and puts his hand on* LUIS' *shoulder—in a mocking, but comforting tone*) Come, Luis. Your brother romancer is dead. Tears will not help him. Perhaps even now he drinks of that Fountain of Youth in Dreamland—if he is not in hell.

LUIS. (*raising his head*) Juan, why do you always sneer at beauty—while your heart calls you liar?

JUAN. (*frowning*) I have Spain in my heart—and my ambition. All else is weakness. (*Changing his tone—carelessly*) Well, you were right. Vicente recognized—and so, a duel. I'll prick him in the thigh and send him home to bed. She will nurse and love him then—and hate me for a murderer. Thus, all works out for the best in this fair world! But—a rare thing dies—and I'm sad, Luis. (*Shaking himself and taking a goblet of wine*) Come, forget sad nonsense. We will drink to voyaging with Don Christopher—and to the battles before those golden cities of Cathay!

LUIS. (*recovering his spirits—grabbing a bottle*) Lucifer fire your cities! I drink to my fountain!

JUAN. Your health, Sir Lying Poet!

LUIS. And yours, Sir Glory-Glutton! (*They laugh, clink goblet and bottle, and drink as*

The Curtain Falls)

SCENE TWO

SCENE. *About a year later—Columbus's flagship on the last day of his second voyage. The section of the vessel shown reveals the main deck amidships, the mainmast, the mainsail with its Maltese Cross, the two higher decks of the poop, the lateen sail on the mizzenmast, etc. Wooden stairs on the starboard, near the bulwark, are the means of getting from one deck to another.*

It is the time just preceding the dawn. The ship is sailing steadily on a calm sea. There is a large lantern at center of the main deck, another low down in the rigging on the port side, another over the cross which hangs over the stern from the high poop. The ship is crowded with people. On the main deck are the nobles. They are dressed in rich uniforms, in armor. Most of them are asleep, lying sprawled on the deck, wrapped in their cloaks—or huddled in hunched attitudes, their backs propped against the mast or the bulwarks. But one small group has apparently been awake all night. They are sitting cross-legged, throwing dice by the light of the lantern. The faces of the gamesters are haggard and drawn, their eyes feverish. Prominent among them are OVIEDO, CASTILLO, MENDOZA *and* LUIS.

On the first deck of the poop, the monks, all Franciscans, are lying asleep. Here, also, are four of the converted Indians Columbus is bringing back. They are dressed in incongruous costumes, half savage and half civilized. They are huddled in the right corner, not asleep, but frozen in a helpless apathy.

On the highest deck JUAN *is seen standing by the pilot who tends the helm.*

LUIS. (*excitedly*) Double or quits!

OVIEDO. Done. (*They play.* LUIS *loses*)

LUIS. I am ruined again! (*With a comical groan of despair*) Fortune is a damned mercenary wench. She scorns the poor. (*Takes up the dice to throw*) Once more!

OVIEDO. (*grumblingly*) No. You owe me more than you can pay.

LUIS. I will soon be rich as Crœsus. Don Columbus says we will sight land today—the Indies, Isles of Spice, Cipango, Cathay, who knows what? I will stake my future wealth against yours. Come! One more cast for anything you wish.

OVIEDO. (*dryly*) For gold—gold I can see and touch.

LUIS. (*disgustedly*) The devil! I must borrow from Juan then. (*He gets to his feet*)

OVIEDO. He will not thank you to wake him on a beggar's errand.

LUIS. Do you imagine he sleeps with his Promised Land so near? He is astern on the Admiral's poop keeping a watch of his own—for fear the lookout will miss Cathay!

CASTILLO. Juan is over-eager. He will make the Genoese jealous.

MENDOZA. Has already. It is plain Columbus slights him.

OVIEDO. From policy. He knows Juan is in disgrace at Court since the duel. Our admiral trims his sails to the wind.

CASTILLO. Juan paid dearly for Vicente's wound—a pin-prick that hardly drew blood.

MENDOZA. It was the scandal.

LUIS. (*indignantly*) All false—the malice of envious tongues! Vicente himself apologized to Juan. As for the lady, when I was home in Cordova I saw her with Vicente. You could not find a more married pair. It was even rumored they were to have a child—— (JUAN *has come down from the Admiral's poop, passed through the sleeping monks and now appears by the light of the lamp in the rigging at the head of the stairs to the main deck.* LUIS *breaks off suddenly*) Is that you, Juan? Come, be a brother. This son of luck (*he indicates Oviedo*) has won everything but my skin.

JUAN. (*with a laugh*) Then stake the Fountain of Youth which you will find—tomorrow! Sold by the cask it should make you the richest man in Spain. (*The nobles laugh*)

LUIS. (*with real aversion*) What trader's scheming—from you! (*Then jokingly*) Take care! When the pox of old age is on you will come begging to me! (*Then rattling the dice*) But come, loan me gold for a last cast of revenge. (*Then with a sudden idea*) And you throw for me. My star is behind a cloud.

OVIEDO. Not fair. Juan always wins.

JUAN. (*frowning*) This is no time for gaming.

LUIS. (*insistently*) Just once, Juan.

JUAN. (*consenting unwillingly*) Only once. The stakes are yours. Let the cast be an augury for me. (*He takes gold from his purse. He and* OVIEDO *play.* OVIEDO *wins and there is a murmur of astonishment*)

OVIEDO. (*exultantly*) I win. The first time I have ever beat you, Juan.

JUAN. (*getting up*) A poor omen. (*Then mockingly*) But here on the under side of earth these signs must run by opposites.

MENDOZA. (*half frightenedly*) Can we be hanging head down and not know it?

CASTILLO. Bah! The Genoese made his first voyage safely. We cannot fall off, it seems.

OVIEDO. Columbus may be a liar.

MENDOZA. (*savagely*) A low-born braggart! He displayed his origin in the hoggish demands he made on the crown. What could the Sovereigns be thinking of—to make this foreign upstart an Admiral and a Viceroy?

JUAN. (*sternly rebuking*) It is not for us to question. (*He pauses—then adds*) His enterprise has served Spain well. He is our commander. That is enough to know. (*He turns his back on them and walks to the port side where he stands by the rigging looking out to sea. The nobles look after him for a moment in an abashed silence*)

CASTILLO. (*mockingly*) You are a perfect Christian, Juan—to love your enemy.

OVIEDO. (*yawns*) Put out the lantern. Let us sleep. The dawn will wake us. (MENDOZA *puts out the lantern. All except* LUIS *wrap themselves in their robes and lie down on the deck.* LUIS *comes over to* JUAN)

LUIS. (*scornfully*) Look at those clods. They would snore through the Last Judgment. (*Then as Juan is silent*) What are you dreaming of—Cathay and glory?

JUAN. No. (*Then suddenly*) When I came down I heard Vicente's name—and mention of a child. What were you saying?

LUIS. Gossip of Cordova. My mother told me Maria was

having masses said that she might bear an heir—and the rumor was her prayers were answered.

JUAN. (*with deep sincerity*) God grant it. She will be happy then. (*With an ironical laugh*) Did I not tell you that night our duel would reconcile them? (*Soberly*) But I pay. Well, what matter the cost if Maria wins happiness?

LUIS. (*reassuringly*) One exploit and the Court will be at your feet again.

JUAN. (*shaking his head*) We will be far from Spain—out of sight and mind. Columbus will be king here, and he and I are by nature antagonistic. (*There is a noise from the higher deck of the poop. A tall figure can be made out coming up on deck there from the companionway. He moves back until the light from the lantern above the cross reveals him. It is* COLUMBUS. *He is in full uniform but wears no hat on his long, white hair. A commanding figure of noble presence, the face full of the ardent, fixed enthusiasm of the religious devotee*)

LUIS. (*pulling* JUAN *back into the shadow*) Speak the devil's name! (*They stand, watching and listening, but hidden from the poop*)

COLUMBUS. (*to the helmsman*) Have you held the course?

HELMSMAN. Southwest by west, sir.

COLUMBUS. (*peering about him*) Will the dawn never come? (*He comes to the edge of the deck and calls down where the monks are—in a low voice*) Father Menendez. Are you awake?

MENENDEZ. (*gets up quickly from among the sleeping monks*) I am here, your Excellency. (*He mounts to the deck above and stands waiting respectfully*)

COLUMBUS. (*begins in a blunt, perfunctory tone*) Toscanelli's map must be in error. We should have sighted land before. (*A pause. He paces back and forth*) The sun will soon be up. It leaps from the darkness in these parts. (*A pause, then with evident irritation*) A weary voyage, Father! The spirit of these nobles is perverse. They look on this voyage as an escapade in search of easy riches, not as a crusade for the glory of God.

MENENDEZ. (*curtly*) They are brave. Many of them have proven their ability in war—Juan Ponce de Leon, for one.

COLUMBUS. (*resentfully*) A bravo! A duelist!

LUIS. (*in an indignant whisper*) The devil seize him!

JUAN. (*grimly*) Another aftermath of that cursed duel!

MENENDEZ. (*shortly*) You are unjust, Excellency.

COLUMBUS. Oh, I admit he possesses all the attributes but the one which alone gives them virtue—an humble piety. On this great quest there is no place for egotists who seek only selfish ends. We must all feel ourselves unworthy servants of God's Holy Will. (*Then breaking off—abruptly*) But I did not call you to speak of him. (*After a pause—despondently*) My soul is overburdened, Father.

MENENDEZ. (*dryly*) You wish to confess?

COLUMBUS. (*surprised*) Confess? (*Then in a loud, ringing tone*) Yes, to all men! Their mouths are full of lies against me. They say the demands I made for my share of discovery prove my low-minded avarice. Knaves! What can they know of my heart? Is it for myself I desire wealth? No! But as a chosen instrument of God, Who led me to His Indies, I need the power that wealth can give. I need it for God's glory, not my own! (*More and more exaltedly*) I have a dream, Father! Listen! From my earliest youth I have hated the infidel. I fought on the ships of Genoa against their corsairs and as I saw my city's commerce with the East cut off by their ruthlessness, I prayed for one glorious last Crusade that would reclaim the Mediterranean for Christendom and, most fervent prayer of all, regain from profanation the Holy Sepulchre of our Lord Jesus! (*He blesses himself.* MENENDEZ *also. Then he hurries on exultantly*) And now an answer is granted! With my share of the wealth from Indies, from Cipango and Cathay, I will fit out an army—the Last Crusade! I have promised it to His Holiness, the Pope—fifty thousand men, four thousand horse, with a like force to follow after five years. I shall reconquer the Blessed Tomb of Christ for the True Faith! And to that sacred end I devote my life and all my wealth and power! (*He stands looking up to heaven with the rapt gaze of a devotee*)

MENENDEZ. (*dryly*) Such a pious ambition does you honor.

JUAN. (*unable to restrain himself, calls mockingly*) The Crusades are dead—and the wealth of the East is still unwon.

COLUMBUS. (*stung—indignantly*) Who dares——?

JUAN. (*proudly*) A noble of Spain who thinks of her greatness while you dream of Genoa and Rome; a soldier of the present, not the ghost of a Crusader! (*Then with exasperated mockery*) God's blood, have all our leaders become half monk? There was a time for that when we fought the Moor, but now a new era of world empire dawns for Spain. By living in the past you will consecrate her future to fanaticism!

COLUMBUS. (*angrily*) Insolent!

JUAN. (*vehemently*) No. I respect you, Columbus—but I have my vision, too. Spain can become the mistress of the world, greater than ancient Rome, if she can find leaders who will weld conquest to her, who will dare to govern with tolerance. (*He laughs a bitter, mocking laugh*) But what a time to speak!

Look at the men of this fleet—now when the East dawns for them! I agree with you, Don Christopher—a weary voyage! Adventurers lusting for loot to be had by a murder or two; nobles of Spain dreaming greedy visions of wealth to be theirs by birthright; monks itching for the rack to torture useful subjects of the Crown into slaves of the Church! And for leader to have you, Don Christopher—you who will pillage to resurrect the Crusades! Looters of the land, one and all! There is not one who will see it as an end to build upon! We will loot and loot and, weakened by looting, be easy prey for stronger looters. God pity this land until all looters perish from the earth! (*While he is speaking it has grown perceptibly lighter*)

COLUMBUS. (*furiously*) Who are you? Stand forth! You dare not!

JUAN. (*jumps up to the lower level of the poop and advances to the ladder to the Admiral's poop—proudly*) It is I—Juan Ponce de Leon! Why should I not dare? Do you want men under your command—or lackeys?

COLUMBUS. (*striving to control his rage*) Silence! (*A wailing cry of "Land Ho" comes from the mainmast head. Immediately the same cry can be heard coming over the water from the other vessels of the fleet. Instantly all is confusion. Everyone jumps to their feet, half awake, peering about bewilderedly. The four Indians sense what has happened and hang over the bulwark, staring over the seas with intense longing. A crowd of half-dressed sailors and rabble pour up from below decks. There is a babble of excited shouts. Columbus looks upward to see where the lookout is pointing, then turns to the horizon off the starboard bow.* JUAN *leaps to the ratlines*)

THE CROWD. Land! Land! Where? I heard the call. He

shouted land! Is it Cathay? Where is he pointing? Look where the Admiral looks. When the sun comes—— (*Suddenly the ship is flooded by shafts of golden crimson light. They all cry*) The sun!

JUAN. (*pointing*) There! I see! In a haze of gold and purple—Greater Spain!

ALL. (*crowd to the starboard side and to the front. The Indians are pushed away, jostled, thrown aside contemptuously with imprecations until they are hunched disconsolately in the background in dumb terror and bewilderment*) Where? I see! Where? There! There! Cathay. Cipango. Is it Cathay? Where are the golden cities? Where are the golden roofs? Is it Cipango? The Indies! The Isles of Spice! Marco Polo's land! (*They all crowd, pushing and elbowing each other, craning their necks, the eyes of all, rabble, soldiers, nobles, priests, straining with the same greedy longing, the lust to loot*)

JUAN. (*exultantly*) Cathay or Cipango or the Isles of Spice, what difference? It shall be Greater Spain! (*The crowd cheers vociferously*)

COLUMBUS. (*trying to quell the tumult*) Silence, I say! (*Fixing his eyes sternly on* JUAN *with undisguised hostility—rebukingly*) The earth is God's! Give thanks to Him! Kneel, I command you! Raise the cross! (*The monks raise their cross. They kneel but the nobles and soldiers hesitate waiting for* JUAN *as if they saw in him their true commander*)

JUAN. (*leaps down from the rigging, drawing his sword—with fierce exultance*) This is a cross too, a soldier's cross—the cross of Spain! (*He sticks his sword-point into the deck before him. He kneels before it. All the nobles and soldiers do likewise with a great flourish of gestures and excited shouts. They are all kneeling with their quivering cross swords, hilts rising above their heads)*

COLUMBUS. *(from his knees—looking up to heaven devoutly)* Te Deum! *(The monks begin to chant. All join in, their pent-up excitement giving to the hymn a hectic, nervous quality.* JUAN *does not sing but stares at the land on the distant horizon)*

(The Curtain Falls)

SCENE THREE

SCENE. *Twenty years or so later—the courtyard of the Governor's palace, Porto Rico. Flowers, shrubs, a coco-palm, orange and banana trees. A large, handsome fountain closely resembling that of Scene One, is at center. Two marble benches are at front and rear of fountain. A narrow paved walk encircles the fountain basin, with other walks leading from it to the different entrances. Doors to the interior of the house are at left and right. The main entrance to the courtyard, opening on the road, is at rear center.*

It is in the late, languid hours of a torrid afternoon. The courtyard bakes in the heat, the fountain shimmering in the heat-waves.

JUAN *is seated on the stone bench in front of the basin. He is dressed in the full uniform of his authority as Governor. His face is aged, lined, drawn. His hair and beard are gray. His expression and attitude are full of great weariness. His eyes stare straight before him blankly in a disillusioned dream. The lines about his compressed lips are bitter.*

LUIS *enters from the left, rear. He is dressed in the robe of a Dominican monk. His face shows the years but it has achieved a calm, peaceful expression as if he were at last in harmony with himself. He comes down to* JUAN *and puts a hand on his shoulder.*

JUAN. (*starts—then greets his friend with a smile*) Ah, it's you, reverend Father. (*He accents this last mockingly*)

LUIS. (*good-naturedly*) Yes, illustrious Governor. (*He sits beside* JUAN—*with a laugh*) You are like a sulky child, Juan. Come, is it not time, after five years, you forgave me for being a Dominican?

JUAN. (*bitterly*) My friend deserting to my enemy!

LUIS. (*protestingly*) Come, come! (*Then after a pause, with a sigh*) You have always had the dream of Cathay. What had I? What had I done with life?—an aimless, posing rake, neither poet nor soldier, without place nor peace! I had no meaning even to myself until God awakened me to His Holy Will. Now I live in truth. You must renounce in order to possess.

JUAN. The world would be stale indeed if that were true! (*After a pause—irritably*) I fight the battles; you monks steal the spoils! I seek to construct; you bind my hands and destroy!

LUIS. (*remonstrating*) You speak of Diego and his kind.

JUAN. (*frowning*) Whether you convert by clemency or he by cruelty, the result is the same. All this baptizing of Indians, this cramming the cross down their throats has proved a ruinous error. It crushes their spirits and weakens their bodies. They become burdens for Spain instead of valuable servitors.

LUIS. Your army crushed them first——

JUAN. They had to be conquered, but there I would have stopped. (*Then irritably*) God's blood, here we are arguing about this same issue—for the thousandth time! It is too late. Talk is useless. (*With a weary sigh*) We do what we must—and sand covers our bodies and our deeds. (*With a smile*) And the afternoon is too hot, besides. Tell me some news. Will the fleet from Spain make port today?

LUIS. Just now I saw them rounding the point under full sail. They should anchor inside soon. (*They are interrupted by the noise of several people approaching from outside.* OVIEDO *and* FRIAR QUESADA, *a Franciscan, enter, followed by the Indian chief,* NANO, *who is guarded by two soldiers with drawn swords.* QUESADA *is a thin young monk with the sallow, gaunt face and burning eyes of a fanatic.* OVIEDO *is aged but gives no evidence of having changed in character.* NANO *is a tall, powerfully built Indian of fifty or so. Although loaded down with chains, he carries himself erect with an air of aloof, stoical dignity. He wears a headdress of feathers. His face and body are painted, ornaments are about his neck. He is naked except for a breech-clout and moccasins*)

QUESADA. (*fiercely and arrogantly*) I demand justice on this dog!

JUAN. (*freezing—proudly*) Demand?

QUESADA. (*with ill-concealed hatred but awed by* JUAN'S *manner*) Pardon my zeal in the service of God, Your Excellency. I ask justice. (*Then defiantly*) But it is not the Church's custom to be a suppliant.

JUAN. So much the worse—— (*Sternly*) What is this Indian's crime?

QUESADA. His tribe will not pay the tithes—and he himself has dared to refuse baptism!

JUAN. (*coldly*) I'll question him. (*Then as* QUESADA *hesitates, raging inwardly—sternly*) You may go.

QUESADA. (*controlling his rage, bows*) Yes, Your Excellency. (*He goes*)

JUAN. (*to* OVIEDO *with a certain contempt*) You also have a charge against this Indian?

OVIEDO. (*angrily*) A plea for justice! These dogs will not pay their taxes. And we who own estates cannot get them to work except by force, which you have arbitrarily curtailed. Then why not punish them by leasing their labor to us until their debt's wiped out? Thus the government will be paid, and we will have workers for our mines and fields.

JUAN. (*disgustedly*) Your brain is not inventive, Oviedo! You are well aware that is the same blunder which failed on Espaniola. It means slavery. It defeats its purpose. The Indians die under the lash—and your labor dies with them. (*Contemptuously*) Do you think I am Columbus that you ask this folly of me?

OVIEDO. (*haughtily*) You refuse? (*He goes to the rear where he turns—threateningly*) Take care, Juan! There will come a day of reckoning—when Diego returns from Spain. (*He goes out*)

JUAN. (*frowning*) Diego? What do you mean?

OVIEDO. (*with a revengeful smile*) Nothing. Adios, Don Juan. (*He goes out*)

JUAN. (*with a bitter laugh*) There you have it! Bah! What use——? (*He suddenly seems to see* NANO *for the first time. They stare at each other*) I was forgetting you. Are you not Nano, chief of the last tribe I conquered? (*As the Indian is silent—imperiously*) Speak!

NANO. The devils were with you. Our villages were burned. Women and children were killed—my wives, my children!

JUAN. (*frowning*) Contrary to my command. But, again, what use? The dead are dead. It is too late. (*After a pause*

—*with a sort of weary self-mockery*) Have you ever heard of Cathay—Cipango? Do you know of vast countries to the west —many peoples—great villages with high walls—much gold?

NANO. I have heard.

JUAN. (*surprised—eagerly*) Ah! Where are they? (*Nano points west*)

LUIS. (*amusedly*) Where the fountain of youth of my drunken days is located—in dreamland!

JUAN. (*with a certain seriousness*) Do you know, they say there is a similar fountain legend among these tribes. (*Then to* NANO *with a mocking smile*) My friend here is growing impatient waiting for immortality in heaven and would rather gain it here on earth——

LUIS. Juan!

JUAN. So tell him, O Mighty Chief, if there is not over there —a fountain—a spring—in which old men bathe or drink and become young warriors again?

NANO. (*to both their surprise*) The tale is told. Not here. In my home—a land that never ends. Our priests told the tale. I was young then. I was captured in war and brought here. I was adopted. I have never returned.

JUAN. (*lost in thought*) So? Where is this land, your home? (NANO *points as before*) Where Cathay is? And the fountain—the spring—is there?

NANO. (*after a moment's hesitation*) Yes. My people call it the Spring of Life.

LUIS. (*whimsically*) A pretty title, indeed. (*Sceptically*) But none can find it, I suppose?

NANO. Those the Gods love can find it.

JUAN. (*scornfully*) Aha, that old trick of poets—evasion of facts! (*Turning to* LUIS) Do you remember the Moor that night in Granada? "Only to the chosen." Here is the echo! Bah! What jugglery! (*Then thoughtfully*) But it is strange. Where there is so much smoke, there must be a spark of fire. The Moor traced his myth back to the East—Cathay—and now we discover it again—still in Cathay—circling the world—— (*Then, as if ashamed of himself for taking it so seriously—carelessly*) At all events, it is added evidence that Cathay is near. (*The boom of a cannon comes from the harbor*)

LUIS. The fleet has anchored. Diego will soon be here. If you can give this Indian into my keeping I will attempt his conversion.

JUAN. (*impatiently*) Until his case is investigated, he must go to prison. You may see him there. (*To* NANO, *sternly*) If it is proven you have encouraged rebellion against Spain, you will be hung. Against any other charge I will try to save you. (*Summoning the soldiers*) Guard. (*They salute and lead* NANO *out, left.* JUAN *paces up and down in frowning thought*) Diego! Did you hear Oviedo threaten me with him? What mischief will he bring from Spain this time, I wonder? The cursed spider! His intriguing will destroy all my work here—— (*With impotent anger*) And the fight is hopeless. His weapons are whispers. A man of honor stands disarmed. (*Intensely*) Would to God this fleet brought me the King's patent to discover new lands! I would sail tomorrow for Cathay—or for the moon!

LUIS. (*firmly*) Fight your battle here! This is your land. You conquered it.

JUAN. Columbus discovered it; and I still feel his influence, like a black fog, stifling me!

LUIS. (*mollifyingly*) He is dead. Forgive. He suffered too much injustice to be just.

JUAN. How can my pride forgive? For years I held his solitary outposts; I suffered wounds and fevers; I fought the Indians for him while he went sailing for the Garden of Eden, the mines of Solomon, his Bible-crazed chimeras! He knew my honor would not permit my conspiring against him as others did. So he ignored my services and deliberately condemned me to obscurity! Never one mention of my name in his reports to Spain! It is only since his downfall—— (*Breaking off*) But this, too, is an old story. (*Then with sudden exasperation*) Why should I not sail to find Cathay? He failed in that—but I would succeed! I am no visionary chasing rainbows. (*Desperately*) I tell you I loathe this place! I loathe my petty authority! By God, I could sink all Porto Rico under the sea for one glimpse of Cathay!

LUIS. (*alarmed*) Juan!

JUAN. (*after a pause—ironically*) Well, do not fear that I will leave your precious island. The patent will never come—and if it did, there is a flaw—— (*Despondently, with a great weariness*) It is too late. Cathay is too far. I am too weary. I have fought small things so long that I am small. My spirit has rusted in chains for twenty years. Now it tends to accept them—to gain peace. (*With passionate yearning*) If I could only feel again my old fire, my energy of heart and mind——! If I could be once more the man who fought before Granada——! But the fire smolders. It merely warms my will to dream of the past. It no longer catches flame in deeds. (*With a desolate smile of self-pity*) I begin to dread—another failure. I am too old to find Cathay.

(MENENDEZ *appears in rear in time to hear this last. He is dressed in a Bishop's robes. He looks his years, but his expression of rabid fanaticism has changed to one, not less cruel, of the crafty schemer made complacent by a successful career, the oily intriguer of Church politics. He hesitates with a suspicious, inquisitive glance from one to the other—then advances with a forced air of joviality*) What is this I hear? Too old? Tut-tut! This is heresy, Juan. (*The two turn, startled.* JUAN *stares at him resentfully.* MENENDEZ *exchanges a cold bow of condescension with* LUIS, *then comes to* JUAN *with outstretched hands, smiling oilily*) Have you no greeting for me, old friend?

JUAN. (*takes his hands perfunctorily—then sarcastically*) Who would expect you unattended—like any eavesdropping monk?

MENENDEZ. (*unruffled*) My eagerness to see you. I have great news. I often spoke to the King about you. He now holds you in the highest esteem, and as a proof of his favor I bring you—— (*Then with a sly smile*) But, on second thought, I should not say, I bring you. That is reserved for a worthier hand!

JUAN. (*impatiently*) I dislike mysteries.

MENENDEZ. (*provokingly*) I will give you this hint out of respect for the old age you were lamenting! Prepare to welcome youth—and a prize you have sought for all your life in the Indies—a gift more welcome to you than wine was to Luis before he repented! (*With this parting gibe, he turns away*) Pardon me if I leave you. I must make preparations—for this event. (*He bows mockingly and goes off right*)

JUAN. (*angrily*) Schemer! (*He paces up and down*)

LUIS. (*after pondering a moment—suddenly*) I have it! It must be your patent to explore! He has obtained it from the

King—because he wishes to get rid of you here! You stand in his way—your policy of clemency. He wants to be dictator to introduce torture and slavery! Yet he is afraid to fight you openly, so what craftier scheme than to send you away contented, grateful for a gift, bribed without knowing it?

JUAN. (*resentfully*) Then I will fool the fox! There is no compulsion in such a patent. (*Then confused*) But—it would be my highest hope come true—too late! Too late! I am too old. (*With an attempt at a railing tone*) God's blood, I need to find Cathay—if your Fountain of Youth is there!

LUIS. I hear a crowd coming. I must go. It adds to their spleen to find us together. (*He presses* JUAN'*s hand*) Whatever comes, be firm, old friend. (*He goes out left. The murmur of the crowd increases.* JUAN *sinks on the bench before the fountain, oblivious to it, lost in gloomy thought.* BEATRIZ DE CORDOVA *appears, attended by her duenna and a crowd of richly dressed nobles. She is a beautiful young girl of eighteen or so, the personification of youthful vitality, charm and grace. The nobles point out* JUAN *to her. She dismisses them, motioning for them to be quiet—then comes in and approaches* JUAN, *keeping the fountain between them. She holds a sealed document in her hand. Finally she calls in a trembling, eager voice*)

BEATRIZ. Don Juan! (JUAN *whirls on his bench and stares through the fountain at her. He utters a stunned exclamation as if he saw a ghost. His eyes are held fascinated by her beauty. Then suddenly she laughs—a gay, liquid, clear note—and coming quickly around confronts him*) It is I, Don Juan.

JUAN. (*stares at her still fascinated—then, reminded, springs to his feet and bows low with his old mocking gallantry*) Pardon! I am bewitched! I thought you were the spirit of the fountain. (*Then more mockingly*) Beautiful lady, you do me unmerited honor!

BEATRIZ (*hurt and confused by his tone*) You don't know me? Why, I'm Beatriz. (*As he bows but shows no recognition*) Has Bishop Menendez not told you——?

JUAN. (*suspiciously*) Nothing of you, my lady.

BEATRIZ. I am Beatriz de Cordova——

JUAN. (*guessing—amazed, stares at her—a pause, slowly*) Maria's child!—you!

BEATRIZ. (*letting it all pour forth regardless*) She died a year ago—and—I am your ward now. It was her last wish. My father was dead. There was no near relative whom she would trust. I asked the King to send me here to you. He bade me wait until the Bishop could escort me. He made me the bearer of this gift for you—your dearest wish, he said. (*She gives him the document*)

JUAN. (*unrolls it—a pause as he stares at it dully, then bitterly*) The patent—to find Cathay!

BEATRIZ. Yes! And you can find it where the others failed, I know! You were my dear mother's ideal of Spanish chivalry, of a true knight of the Cross! That was her prophecy, that you would be the first to reach Cathay!

JUAN. She spoke of the man she knew. (*Staring at her fascinatedly—eagerly*) She sends me you—and you are youth! Is it in mockery?

BEATRIZ. (*suddenly*) Oh, Don Juan, I recall something she said I must remember when we should meet. "Bring him tenderness," she said. "That will repay the debt I owe him for saving me for you." She said these words were secrets to tell you alone. What did she mean, Don Juan?

JUAN. (*deeply moved*) Tenderness? Do you bring me that, Beatriz? (*Then as if recalling himself*) No, do not—for it means weakness. Bring me the past instead. Give me back—the man your mother knew.

BEATRIZ. (*who has been scrutinizing him without paying attention to his words*) You are older than I dreamed, Don Juan.

JUAN. (*wounded—with harsh violence*) No tenderness there! Youth! A cuirass of shining steel! A glittering sword! Laughter above the battle! (*Then seeing her look of frightened astonishment at his wild words, he controls himself and adds with a melancholy bitterness*) It was so long ago, Beatriz—that night in Granada—a dimly-remembered dream—— (*Then with a sudden return of his mockingly gallant manner*) Forgive me. I have become a savage lost to manners. (*He kneels and kisses her hand with all his old-time gallantry*) Welcome, dear ward, to Porto Rico! (*She looks down at his bowed head, blushing with pleasure and naïve embarrassment, as*

The Curtain Falls)

SCENE FOUR

SCENE. *Three months later*—MENENDEZ' *official study in the palace—a large, high-ceilinged, bare room with a heavy table at center. The color scheme is dark and gloomy, the atmosphere that of a rigid, narrow ecclesiasticism. In one corner is an altar with high candles burning before it. Heavy hangings shut out the light from the lofty, arched windows. An enormous crucifix hangs on the wall in rear. The room is like an exaggerated monk's cell, but it possesses a somber power over the imagination by the force of its concentration. There is a main entrance at rear, center, and a smaller side door at left, hidden by curtains.*

It is early evening. MENENDEZ *is seated at the table. He is frowningly impatient, listening and waiting for someone. There is the sound of approaching footsteps.* MENENDEZ *turns eagerly in his chair.* QUESADA *enters through the hangings on the left. His face is ominous and set. He wears a sword and pistols over his robe which is tucked up over high riding boots and spurs. He is covered with dust, and has evidently been riding hard. He bows respectfully to* MENENDEZ.

MENENDEZ. I had begun to think you would never come. (*Then with anxiety*) What news?

QUESADA. The meeting is being held. They have gathered in the fort outside the town.

MENENDEZ. Good! It is moving according to my plan, then.

QUESADA. They all agree that Don Juan must resign his patent.

MENENDEZ. Unless he sails to find Cathay at once?

QUESADA. Yes. They are all mad for the gold (*with a sneer*) over there, the report of which I have had rumored about, as you directed.

MENENDEZ. Good. Then we shall be rid of Juan and all the discontented spirits on the island at one stroke!

QUESADA. (*excitedly*) But they also demand that first the Indian, Nano, must be burned at the stake. They believe he has bewitched the Governor. They know of Don Juan's secret interviews with him.

MENENDEZ. (*angrily*) Who told them?

QUESADA. (*after a moment's hesitation—defiantly*) I did.

MENENDEZ. (*angrily*) Fool!

QUESADA. (*alarmed—humbly*) But the dog still refuses baptism.

MENENDEZ. (*sternly*) Is this a time to consider one Indian? Idiot! You know as well as I that my intention has been to attack Juan on one issue, and only one—his failure to sail for Cathay now that he has the King's patent. What have all the Nanos, hung or unhung, to do with that?

QUESADA. Much! If Don Juan were not bewitched by Nano's spells, he would have sailed long since.

MENENDEZ. And you told the rabble that? God pardon you! Was it any part of my orders that you should play upon the mob's lust for blood? I have worked for a peaceable revolt that would awaken Juan to his weakness and shame him into leaving. You have dared to evoke a madness which might easily sweep away all recognized authority. Quick! What was the rabble's mood when you left? (QUESADA *avoids his eyes.* MENENDEZ *pounds the table*) Answer me!

QUESADA. (*evasively*) They had been drinking——

MENENDEZ. (*furiously, a note of alarm creeping in*) Ah!

QUESADA. (*now thoroughly cowed*) They were clamoring to march on the palace. Don Oviedo was trying to restrain them——

MENENDEZ. (*fiercely—with bitter scorn*) You cursed blunderer! No, I am the dolt for having trusted you!

QUESADA. (*kneeling—cowed*) Forgive me, Your Grace!

MENENDEZ. Your action was treachery to me! And I shall punish you! When this expedition sails for that golden fable, Cathay, you shall go with it. Then blunder all you like! (*He rises and strides to the window at rear*)

QUESADA. (*humbly*) I humbly accept my penance.

MENENDEZ. (*bitterly*) Behold the first fruits of your excessive piety! (*He points*) The southern horizon is aflame!

QUESADA. (*rising*) They must have set fire to the Indian villages.

MENENDEZ. Blood and fire! Your merry dance begins well! (*He lets the curtains fall back*) Only Juan can control them now—if he would only promise them to sail at once—but no, he is too proud. He will fight armed rebellion to the last—and we will all go down in the same ruin!

QUESADA. (*scornfully*) He is not the man he was—since Nano bewitched him.

MENENDEZ. (*disgustedly*) Bah! You fool! (*Then intently*) Yet there is truth in what you say. He has grown weak—between Luis' influence and the girl's meddling—— (*Abruptly*)

Come! There is still a chance. Summon Don Juan to me at once! (*This last in a shout of impatience*)

JUAN. (*from outside, rear, mockingly*) There is no need for messengers. (*He enters. In the three months he has aged greatly. His hair and beard have grown perceptibly white. Beneath the bitter, mocking mask there is an expression of deep, hidden conflict and suffering on his face as if he were at war with himself*)

MENENDEZ. (*startled, afraid of what* JUAN *may have overheard*) You heard——?

JUAN. (*scornfully*) Only what you shouted. Am I a monk to listen at keyholes? (*This with a glance at* QUESADA) But I know your intrigues. This meeting of yapping curs—you see, I have heard the rumor—you would have me sail at their bidding, and thus you would be free to rule this island in God's Holy Name! Is it not so?

MENENDEZ. (*controlling his anger*) You have lost your senses. You will not realize that things have reached a crisis! The government has slipped through your fingers while you played at being a loving father——

JUAN. (*stung—fiercely*) It's a lie! (*Controlling himself*) I tell you again, Diego, I will sail at my pleasure, not yours.

MENENDEZ. (*persuasively*) You have kept repeating that—and meanwhile your apathy has ruined us. Your soldiers and sailors are in open mutiny. The mob has risen. (*Urgently*) Juan, do you want rebellion to overwhelm us? You promised them Cathay——

JUAN. (*proudly*) It was you who promised them in my name, you mean, to make certain you would be rid of me!

MENENDEZ. (*tauntingly—noting* JUAN'S *reactions craftily*) I promised because I thought you were still Juan Ponce de Leon. But you are not. You have become merely a slave to a girl's sentimental whims! You are too feeble to govern here and too weak for Cathay. (JUAN'S *hand goes to his sword.* MENENDEZ *continues cuttingly*) Then for the sake of Spain, resign your office and surrender your patent for discovery to someone with the youth and courage to dare!

JUAN. (*infuriated, half drawing his sword*) Take care, Diego! Your cloth cannot condone such insults!

MENENDEZ. (*in a softened, oily tone*) Forgive me, Juan. I insult you for your own sake! Push on to your greatest victory! Do not wait here in a stupor for inglorious defeat!

JUAN. (*shaken*) I shall sail—but first I must know—know for a certainty, beyond all doubt—exactly where—— (*He stops abruptly*)

MENENDEZ. (*inquisitively*) What?

JUAN. (*suspiciously*) Nothing.

QUESADA. (*who has been listening with feverish interest—points to* JUAN *accusingly*) He has gone to Nano every day. Look at his eyes! He is bewitched! (JUAN *starts guiltily but tries to ignore him contemptuously*)

MENENDEZ. Be still, Quesada! (*He looks at* JUAN) These interviews *are* mysterious, Juan.

JUAN. (*quickly—half turning away and averting his eyes —with forced carelessness*) I need accurate information for my voyage that only Nano can give me. That is why I have delayed.

MENENDEZ. (*looking at him sharply*) So? I had thought it might be affection for Beatriz that held you.

JUAN. (*vehemently*) No!

MENENDEZ. (*keenly*) Why are you so vehement? It would be natural enough. You have lived alone. To find a daughter in your declining years——

JUAN. (*pale with rage and agony*) Daughter? How could she look upon me——?

MENENDEZ. (*soothingly but with a taunting intent*) She used to regard you as her hero, her great commander. She must wonder now at this old man's weakness in you.

JUAN. (*frenziedly*) Do you dare taunt me in her name? I *will* sail, I say! I will sail the very first day after I discover —— (*Then distractedly, shaken*) Enough, Diego! I shall do what I wish and when it pleases me! (*He rushes out rear as if furies were hounding him.* MENENDEZ *looks after him, a sneering smile of satisfaction gradually coming over his face as if something were proven to him*)

MENENDEZ. (*half to himself, half to* QUESADA) I should have guessed it before. Yet, who would have thought—— He is bewitched, certainly.

QUESADA. (*eagerly*) Yes!

MENENDEZ. (*dryly*) But you are blaming the wrong witch. The guilty one is sinless. (QUESADA *puzzles over this paradox with open eyes.* MENENDEZ *ponders for a moment, then he turns to* QUESADA) Bring the Lady Beatriz.

QUESADA. Yes, Your Grace. (*He bows and hurries out, left.* MENENDEZ *sits thoughtfully, evidently planning out his campaign. A moment later* BEATRIZ *enters. She bows respectfully*)

BEATRIZ. (*reservedly*) You wish to see me, Your Grace?

MENENDEZ. (*nods and motions her to a chair. He scrutinizes her face carefully for a moment, then begins in a playful, ironical *tone*) Beauty did not leave a stone on stone of ancient Troy. Are you another Helen, Beatriz?

BEATRIZ. (*confused*) I—don't understand.

MENENDEZ. (*coldly and brusquely*) Not understand that rebellion is seething in Porto Rico?—a rebellion that will deal destruction to us all!

BEATRIZ. (*bewildered*) Rebellion? (*Then spiritedly*) Who would dare rebel against Don Juan?

MENENDEZ. (*belittlingly*) Juan is powerless. His own soldiers have taken the lead against him. He is facing ruin! Do you understand? I wish I had words of fire to brand it on your brain! For I tell you on my conscience, as God's minister, you are the one responsible!

BEATRIZ. (*stunned*) I? I? You are jesting! (*Then with haughty resentment*) I harm Don Juan, who is my second father!

MENENDEZ. (*seeming to grow more icy under her anger*) Who has done most in influencing him to softness and lax discipline——

BEATRIZ. (*indignantly*) You mean because I have pitied the suffering of the Indians——?

MENENDEZ. (*dryly*) Let us judge your pity by its results. These heathen no longer fear. They defy our Holy Faith. They sneer at baptism. These Indians shirk their labor. And because Don Juan spends his time with you, he has forgotten not only his duty to govern but his oath to seek Cathay. The soldiers and sailors have waited too long in idleness. Now they revere him no longer as a daring general who will lead them to glory but despise him for a dissembler, delaying because he has lost the courage for action! And so they have conspired. Those are the facts. Will you deny your influence is deep at the root of them? (*Beatriz is too overwhelmed by the ruthlessness of his attack to reply. He pushes his advantage*) And can you deny that a great change has come over Don Juan since your arrival? You cannot have helped but notice this!

BEATRIZ. He has seemed—to become despondent at times.

MENENDEZ. (*vehemently*) Spiritless! Infirm! His thoughts wander like a senile old man's! I believe his mind is failing him!

BEATRIZ. (*horrified*) No! No!

MENENDEZ. You must face the truth! (*Sternly*) When you take a life's ambition from a man like Juan, the man withers away. You have made him forget Cathay. Why? Why have you not urged him to go—for his own sake? When you brought out the patent, you dreamed of him as he dreams of himself—a conqueror and hero!

BEATRIZ. (*hesitatingly*) Father Luis told me we must keep him here—or else his good work would be undone——

MENENDEZ. This uprising will undo it in an hour! (*Then soothingly*) Father Luis is a good man—but blind. You are a girl—and inexperienced—— Come. (*He pauses, watching her keenly, then takes her hand, and leading her to the window, pulls back the curtain*) Look!

BEATRIZ. (*with a shudder of horror*) Ah!

MENENDEZ. Now do you believe in the rebellion—in Juan's danger?

BEATRIZ. (*horrified*) Fire!

MENENDEZ. And murder! In the Indian villages. See what your pity for them has done! And it will not stop there. That is only the first spark of revolution. They'll march here! (*Im-*

pressively) Beatriz, you can save Don Juan. He loves you—as his daughter. Urge him to sail at once! Rouse the hero in him! Give him back his sanity! He is my old friend. I implore you for his sake, Beatriz!

BEATRIZ. (*bewilderedly*) Yes—yes—but give me time to think—to pray for guidance—— (*She kneels before the altar*)

MENENDEZ. (*impatiently*) There is no time! (*There is a noise of hurrying steps and* OVIEDO *enters. He is booted, spurred, covered with dust, his face betraying anxiety and alarm*)

OVIEDO. (*without stopping to see who is there, bursts forth*) Diego! I tried to check them, but they have gone mad! They are marching on the town! Juan will be lost!

MENENDEZ. (*to* BEATRIZ *who has turned around in terror*) You hear!

OVIEDO. The time has come to abandon that sick fool! We must openly lead this rebellion!

BEATRIZ. (*springs to her feet and faces him—her eyes flashing*) Coward! (*He falls back, his hand on his sword, glaring at her*)

MENENDEZ. (*urgently*) Go, Beatriz! (*She passes* OVIEDO *with a scathing glance, and goes out rear.* MENENDEZ *turns to* OVIEDO *with an ironical but worried smile*)

MENENDEZ. If she will but speak to Juan as she did to you, we may still win, my friend!

(*The Curtain Falls*)

SCENE FIVE

SCENE. NANO's *dungeon—a circular cavern, hollowed out by Nature and cut out by man in the solid rock under the Government house. The enclosed space is narrow but lofty, cylindrical in form. A cut-in flight of steps leads from the floor in rear to a trap-door above. The high wall glistens with moisture. A small bench is at right. A lantern stands on one of the lower steps. In the middle of the floor stands a soldier, thick-set, brutal-looking, his sleeves rolled up over his muscular arms. He is blowing with a bellows on a charcoal brazier, glowing red-hot, in which are thrust several irons. On the wall in the rear, his toes barely touching the floor,* NANO *hangs with his arms outstretched over his head, the wrists bound by chains to iron sockets in the rock. His head hangs on one side as if he were in a state of semi-consciousness. His body is thin and wasted.*

The trap-door is opened and a circular patch of gray light falls on the stairs. This is obscured as someone descends. It is Juan. He shuts the trap-door behind him and comes down. He stops when he is opposite NANO's *head, and, leaning over, stares at the savage's face. The latter opens his eyes. His head stiffens proudly erect on his shoulders. He and* JUAN *stare into each other's eyes.* JUAN *drops his guiltily, turns away and descends to the floor, where the soldier is standing at attention.*

JUAN. (*harshly*) Has he spoken?

SOLDIER. Not one word, sir.

JUAN. Then you have not obeyed——

SOLDIER. (*indicates the irons in the fire*) I have tried every trick I know—but he's made of iron.

JUAN. (*looks up at* NANO *with intense hatred*) Dog! (*Then he turns to the soldier*) Go and keep guard above.

SOLDIER. Yes, sir. (*He bends down to pick up the brazier*)

JUAN. (*harshly*) No.

SOLDIER. (*with a glance at him—understandingly*) Yes, sir. (*He goes up the stairs, opens the trap-door and disappears, letting it fall shut behind him.* JUAN *sinks on the stone bench at right and stares up at* NANO, *who looks back at him with unflinching defiance. A pause*)

JUAN. (*his eyes now fixed dully on the floor—half-aloud to himself*) Diego did not lie. The storm is gathering. (*With bitter hopelessness*) What matter? I could pray that it might be a deluge annihilating mankind—but for Beatriz. (*He groans, then raises his eyes again to* NANO) Why do you look at me? I can never read your eyes. They see in another world. What are you? Flesh, but not our flesh. Earth. I come after—or before—but lost, blind in a world where my eyes deflect on surfaces. What values give you your loan of life? Answer! I must know the terms in which to make appeal! (*The savage is silent, motionless. A pause. Then* JUAN, *as if suddenly reminded, jumps to his feet in a frenzy of impatience*) Answer me, dog! I must find the will to act—or be dishonored!

NANO. (*solemnly—in a faint voice*) The Gods are angry.

JUAN. (*with wild joy*) You speak! At last! Nano, why have you kept dumb while I implored——?

NANO. The Gods have stopped your ears.

JUAN. (*going on obsessed, regardless*) Juan Ponce de Leon—to torture a helpless captive! Why did you bring me to such shame? Why would you not answer my question?

NANO. (*with contempt*) My tongue grew weary. For a moon I answered every day.

JUAN. (*fiercely*) But you lied! Tell me the truth now! Where is the fountain?

NANO. (*indifferently, shutting his eyes*) Only the Gods know.

JUAN. The same lie! You told me at first that men of your former tribe knew! You must know! This is your revenge—for the death of your wives and children! Must I swear to you again they were killed in spite of my strict orders? Come! Forget them! I will give you your choice of all your women on the island—your freedom—I will petition the King to honor you—give you back your lands—anything if you will answer me! (NANO *remains silent.* JUAN *utters a furious cry and, rushing to the brazier, takes a red-hot coal with the tongs and holds it before the Indian's eyes*) Dog! I will burn that scorn from your eyes! (*The Indian stares at the hot iron immovably.* JUAN *lets it fall to the floor with a desperate groan of misery*) Pardon! Forgiveness in Christ's name! It is you who torture me! Nano, I burn to hell! I love! (*He suddenly stops, chilled to despair by the implacable isolation in the savage's face. He throws himself down on the bench in an apathy. Finally he slowly draws his sword and speaks in a dead voice*) Either you speak or you die. I swear it.

NANO. (*with aloof contempt*) What is death?

JUAN. (*dully*) I will die, too. Perhaps in the grave there

is oblivion and peace. (*After a pause*) You are a fool, Nano. If you would help me I could make you pilot of the fleet to guide us to your land. The fountain once found, you would be free. No harm should come to your people. Do you never long for your old home?

NANO. (*who has been listening with quickened interest*) Home? To the land of flowers. My home of many warriors. (*After a pause*) You will let me guide the great winged canoes—to my home?

JUAN. (*eagerly*) Yes. (*In great suspense*) Will you help me? Tell me! (*He has sprung to his feet*)

NANO. Only the Gods—— (*He checks himself abruptly*)

JUAN. (*frenziedly*) Ah! (*He raises his sword as if to run the savage through*)

NANO. (*looking into Juan's eyes without noticing the threat*) The tongues of the white devils are false. How can I trust your word?

JUAN. I take my sacred oath! (*He raises his hand*)

NANO. Your God is a God of lies.

JUAN. (*wildly*) By your God then—since mine has forsaken me!

NANO. (*lifts his head and murmurs some supplication, as if begging forgiveness—then looks at* JUAN *with savage triumph*) I will guide you—but remember the way is long!

JUAN. (*triumphantly*) At last! What does it matter how long or difficult! (*Raising his arms*) Ah, God's blood, I already feel new life, the will to live! I can conquer now! (*A pounding of a sword-butt on the trap-door. Then it is flung open*)

SOLDIER. Pardon, Excellency——

BEATRIZ' VOICE. (*calls down*) Don Juan! Don Juan!

JUAN. (*exultantly*) Her voice! A happy omen! (*He hurries up the stairs*)

NANO. (*again lifting his eyes to heaven—with religious fervor*) Great Spirit, forgive my lie. His blood shall atone!

(*The Curtain Falls*)

SCENE SIX

SCENE. *Same as Scene Three—Courtyard of the Governor's House—a stifling twilight. The sky is darkening with clouds.*

BEATRIZ' *voice—from the left—calls down as at the end of preceding scene.*

BEATRIZ. Don Juan! Don Juan! (*His voice is heard, "Beatriz." She enters, pale and agitated, runs to rear and looks for signs of the insurrection—then hurries back just in time to meet* JUAN, *who enters, left. He is in a tense state of hectic excitement, his face ghastly pale, his obsessed eyes burning feverishly, his drawn sword still in his hand. She starts back from him, frightened by his appearance*)

JUAN. (*in a strained, high-pitched tone*) Was it the fountain called—or you, Beatriz? You, for you are the fountain! (*He takes her hand impetuously and kisses it*)

BEATRIZ. (*flurriedly*) I came to warn you——

JUAN. (*with a sharp glance*) Warn? Then you have seen Diego? Bah! (*He makes a gesture of contempt with his sword as if brushing all revolutions aside*) When the hour comes, I shall be strong. The will breathes in me again. Forget all else, Beatriz. Give me your thoughts! Have you been happy here with me?

BEATRIZ. (*not knowing what to say or do*) Yes—yes. (*Trying to return to her mission*) But——

JUAN. You came as a benediction—that cursed me. (*Abruptly*) Have you not noticed how much older I have grown?

BEATRIZ. (*convinced he is out of his head—resolved to humor him—frightened but pityingly*) You can become young again.

JUAN. (*exultantly*) I will! (*Then mysteriously*) This is a strange world with many wonders still undiscovered.

BEATRIZ. (*seeing a chance to bring in her point—quickly*) Then discover them. The search will make you young.

JUAN. (*deeply and superstitiously impressed*) From your own lips! It is another blessed augury! (*Eagerly*) But pretend I am young. What then?

BEATRIZ. Why then you would be happy.

JUAN. (*intensely*) You promise——? Have you never loved?

BEATRIZ. (*bewildered*) Loved?

JUAN. Since you speak of happiness.

BEATRIZ. I loved my mother—my father—I love you, Don Juan.

JUAN. (*avidly*) Ah, say that again! Those words are blood to my heart!

BEATRIZ. (*earnestly*) I love you as I loved my father——

JUAN. (*brusquely—wounded to the quick*) Has love never stolen into your dreams? You are no nun. Come, tell me the image of the one you dream of as a lover.

BEATRIZ. (*resolved to pass this off jestingly*) It is a great secret. You insist? Well then, it is your double—— (JUAN *utters a cry of joy, bending toward her. She adds hastily*) You as my mother described you in the wars before Granada.

JUAN. (*bitterly*) When I had youth. But I loved only glory then. Did she not tell you that?

BEATRIZ. Why then—that is why she said, bring him tenderness.

JUAN. (*somberly*) You have fulfilled her wish—or was it her revenge? (*Then abruptly*) And what if I should myself become that double?—the knight of Granada with your gift of tenderness—what then?

BEATRIZ. (*frightened by his strangeness*) Ah, now, you are jesting, Don Juan. (*She forces a laugh*)

JUAN. (*passionately*) No, Beatriz! (*She instinctively shrinks away from him. He calms himself*) No more now. I fear your laughter. First let the consummation—— Then you will not laugh. You—— (*Trying to read her mystified eyes—miserably uncertain*) What will you do?

BEATRIZ. (*controlling her timidity—softly persuasive*) You are ill, Don Juan. Will you listen to my cure for you?

JUAN. Yes.

BEATRIZ (*with energy*) Sail and find Cathay!

JUAN. (*with a start, tormentedly*) You, too, condemn me! But I swear to you I have longed to go! I have hated my own cowardice! I have played the traitor to every dream, every great hope—— But, Beatriz, when I go, I will leave my life behind with you. So—until I knew—I was afraid of losing what I have—— (*Then with a quick change to something approaching triumphant decision*) But that is past! My will has risen from the dead. It is decreed by your own lips. I shall sail at once!

BEATRIZ. Oh, I am glad!

JUAN. (*sadly*) Glad I am leaving you?

BEATRIZ. No, I shall be sad and lonely. It is for your own welfare——

JUAN. But promise me one boon——

BEATRIZ. (*eagerly*) Anything!

JUAN. Promise you will not marry until I return—or you hear I am dead?

BEATRIZ. (*confused*) I have never even thought of marrying.

JUAN. (*in deadly earnest in spite of his pitiful pretense at a joking tone*) Until I present my double to you——?

BEATRIZ. (*relieved and laughing easily*) Why, I might change my mind then, Don Juan.

JUAN. Will you seal that pledge with a kiss? (*He forces a smile to conceal his longing*)

BEATRIZ. (*uncertainly—forcing a laugh*) Yes, Don Juan. (*She lifts her face to him. He starts to kiss her on the lips but something in her face stops him and he ends by kissing her reverentially on the forehead—forcing a smile*)

JUAN. There—upon your forehead—for remembrance. The other—for tenderness—is still a promise of my dream. (*There is a sound of hurrying steps and* JUAN *moves away from* BEATRIZ *guiltily.* LUIS *enters from the rear. His face is agitated, full of alarm and anxiety*)

BEATRIZ. (*greeting him eagerly, glad of the interruption*) Father Luis.

LUIS. Juan! I bring you terrible news. (*He sees* JUAN'S *drawn sword*) Ah, you know! It is time you drew your sword.

JUAN. (*scornfully*) You mean the scum rises? When I tell them the fleet sails tomorrow——

LUIS. Will you give them Nano to burn at the stake? That is their first demand. (BEATRIZ *gives a horrified cry*)

JUAN. (*stunned—unbelievingly*) Surrender Nano? No, it is impossible. You have heard rumors——

LUIS. Quesada has roused their cruelty to frenzy. (*He points to where a red glow is mounting up in the sky*) See! They are burning the Indian quarter. May God have mercy!

JUAN. (*in a rage*) Kill Nano? The curs! I shall order a company of my guard——

LUIS. (*looking at him pityingly*) Your guard is leading the mob! (*Reproachfully*) Juan, Juan, why have you lived in a dream! I warned you time after time. If you had been governor in anything but name——

JUAN. (*sinking on the bench—stupidly*) Call the guard. I must order them to disperse.

BEATRIZ. (*pityingly*) His mind is sick——

LUIS. (*rather peremptorily*) Will you leave us, Beatriz?

BEATRIZ. (*obediently*) Yes, Father. (*Then excitedly*) I must see Bishop Menendez—— (*She hurries out, right*)

LUIS. (*comes and slaps* JUAN *on the back—sternly*) Juan! Awake, in God's name!

JUAN. (*startled to action, springs to his feet*) I shall protect his life with my own!

LUIS. In order to torture him yourself?

JUAN. (*vehemently but guiltily*) A lie! (*Suspicious—resentfully*) Have you seen him? I gave orders——

LUIS. It is weeks since I was permitted to see him; and you have avoided meeting me. Why?

JUAN. (*harshly*) I have no patience with your converting. I need Nano as he is.

LUIS. Because you prefer his heathen myths——

JUAN. (*controlling an outburst of rage*) Myths? Why myths? Cathay is there. (*He points*)

LUIS. I was not speaking of Cathay. You are sailing tomorrow? Does this mean you have finally wrung from this poor Indian's agonies a faith in magic fountains——?

JUAN. (*losing control of himself—raging*) Fool! You are like those dullards who, when Columbus said the earth was round, brayed at him for blaspheming! Listen to me! I do not believe Nano, I believe in Nature. Nature is part of God. She can perform miracles. Since this land was discovered have we not found wonders undreamed of before? The points in Nano's story hold true to the facts we know. His home is a beautiful mainland—"A land of flowers," in his own words. Is not Cathay also known as the "Flowery Land"? There are great walled cities with roofs of gold inland to the West. Is not that Marco Polo's land beyond all doubt? And the fountain is in Cathay. All the evidence from around the world proves that! And I shall find it!

LUIS. (*pityingly*) But this evidence is merely fable, legend, the dreams of poets!

JUAN. (*furiously*) Have praying and fasting made you an imbecile? What evidence had Columbus? And you—you believe Christ lived and died. Well, have you talked with men who saw Him in the manger, or on the cross?

LUIS. Juan, this is blasphemy!

JUAN. (*with bitter despair*) Then let it be! I have prayed to Him in vain.

LUIS. Juan!

JUAN. (*with all the power of his will in the words*) Let me be damned forever if Nature will only grant me youth upon this earth again!

LUIS. (*horrified*) Juan! You defy your God!

JUAN. There is no God but Love—no heaven but youth!

LUIS. *(looks at his tortured face intently—suddenly realizes—in a tone of great pity)* So that is it—I have been blind. I thought your love saw in her—a child, a daughter!

JUAN. *(intensely)* A child—yes—for a time—but one morning standing by the fountain she was a woman. More than a woman! She was the Spirit of Youth, Hope, Ambition, Power to dream and dare! She was all that I had lost. She was Love and the Beauty of Love! So I loved her, loved her with all the intensity of Youth's first love—when youth was dead! Oh, it was monstrous folly, I admit. I called myself a senile fool! I suffered with the damned. I lived in hell without the recompense of being dead! And I loved her more—and more! *(His head sinks down on his hands. A great sob racks his whole body)*

LUIS. *(overcome by compassion, his voice trembling)* Old friend—God in His Mercy have pity on you! *(He is interrupted by the hurried entrance of* BEATRIZ *from the right)*

BEATRIZ *(indignantly)* Bishop Menendez says he can do nothing—that you must give Nano up! *(The angry tumult of a mob marching is heard from the distance. Frightenedly)* Listen! Oh, Don Juan, you will save him, will you not?

JUAN. *(starting up—in a voice in which rage and apprehension are blended)* I must! *(He listens to the rising murmur of the mob. As he does so his whole body stiffens into defiant determination. He becomes in an instant the commander again)* Cowardly rabble! *(He springs to the entrance on the left and shouts to the soldier on guard)* Bring Nano! *(He comes back to where* BEATRIZ *and* LUIS *are standing and looks around the courtyard as if measuring his position)* I shall face them here. Take Beatriz away, Luis.

BEATRIZ. I wish to stay with you!

MENENDEZ. (*enters from the right*) Juan! (*Seeing his drawn sword—apprehensively*) What? You will defy them? Then you are lost! Yield to them, I advise you. Give Nano to justice. (*While he is speaking* NANO *is half carried in by the soldiers. He is limp and exhausted*)

JUAN. (*with wild scorn*) Ah, High Priest! Deliver him up, eh?

MENENDEZ. Juan! You are impious! (*Angrily*) It is sacrilege—to compare this Indian dog—you mock our Blessed Savior! You are cursed—I wash my hands—His will be done! (*He turns and strides back into the house, right*)

LUIS. (*at a nearer roar from the mob*) Juan! Escape! There is still time——

JUAN. Run from jackals! Is my honor dead?

LUIS. (*as a smashing battering sounds from outside*) They are at the outer gate! Come, Beatriz, in God's name! (*She struggles but he succeeds in getting her as far as the entrance, right. A last crashing smash is heard as the outer gate gives way. A moment later the advance guard of the mob pour in—all of the lower rabble, these. Some wave torches above their heads. All are armed with pikes, knives, and various crude weapons that they have picked up or stolen*)

JUAN. (*in a roar of command*) Back! (*They hesitate for a moment. Then they see* NANO *and with yells of fury rush for him around the fountain.* JUAN *springs to meet them. With quick thrusts and cuts of his sword he kills or wounds four of the foremost, who drop to the ground. The rest fall back frightened and awed for the moment. In this lull the remainder of the mob pour in from the rear, crowding and jostling each other. They are a nondescript crowd, ranging from nobles, richly dressed, soldiers, sailors, to the riff-raff of the criminal element in bright-colored rags. There are a number of monks among them, Franciscans who urge them on, a few Dominicans who plead for restraint*)

THE MOB. Don Juan! It's the Governor—push back there! —To the flames with the Indian dog! Seize him! Stand aside, Don Juan! Heretic! He's bewitched! The dog refused baptism! Torture!

JUAN. (*sternly*) I will kill the man who touches this Indian! (*He walks up and down before them, his sword ready to thrust, looking from eye to eye—scathingly*) Scoundrels! Where is your valor now? Prick up your courage! (*Mockingly*) Come! Who wishes to die?

A NOBLE. We demand justice! (*Yells of approval from the crowd. They push in closer.* JUAN *levels his sword at the breast of the nearest who springs back with a frightened cry. The mob sways and surges, close packed and indecisive, cowed by* JUAN's *eyes*)

QUESADA. (*suddenly pushing his way to the front of the crowd—pointing at* NANO, *frantically*) Give him up! You are bewitched! (*The mob are again aroused. There are cries of "To the stake! Torture!" etc.*)

JUAN. No! (*Yells of rage. The mob surges forward.* JUAN *raises his sword*) I will kill the first one who—— (*They recoil again, all but* QUESADA. *With his free hand* JUAN *sweeps him to one side contemptuously—then fiercely threatening the crowd*) Will you rebel against the Governor of your King? Then you are traitors to Spain! And, by God's blood, I will hang one of you on every tree! (*The crowd gives way by inches, sullenly, their yells reduced for the moment to a rebellious muttering: "The King will remove you! Hang the Indians! Hang them! Hang Nano!" etc.)*

A SOLDIER. We mean no harm to you, Don Juan. Keep your word to us. Order the fleet to sail. (*A yell of acclamation from the soldiers and sailors*)

QUESADA. And give over that dog! The Inquisition shall know you protect infidels!

JUAN. I am Spain's soldier, not the Inquisition's! Soldiers and sailors! I tell you it is in Spain's service this Indian's life is spared. The fleet sails tomorrow—and we need Nano to pilot our voyage! (*A tumult from the bewildered crowd. Shouts of various nature: "The fleet sails! Tomorrow! Hurrah! He jokes! He mocks us! Spare him? No luck with a heathen on board! What does he mean? Guide us? No! The curse of the Church!" But the mob is puzzled, blundering, and* JUAN *continues with a sort of condescension as if he were speaking to children*) Silence! Since you are so stupid, I must explain. This Nano was born on the mainland—Cathay!—our goal, do you understand?—and I have put off sailing while I questioned him. We must have his knowledge. He must be our pilot. (*With a fierce glance at* NANO *as if to let his threat strike home*) And if he fails in his promise to me, I will gladly give him to you for punishment.

QUESADA. (*furiously*) You say this to save him!

JUAN. Soldiers, sailors, I appeal to you! Can this mad monk lead you to conquest? You must decide between us. (*The crowd are all turning his way, becoming greedily enthusiastic.* JUAN *sees the psychological moment to play a trump card*) But to convince you finally, listen to Nano. Speak, Nano!

Tell them what you told me—of the golden cities. Speak! (*Then under cover of the crowd's shouts of "Down with the dog! Torture! Hear! Let him speak! Don Juan says let him!" etc., he adds in a fierce whisper to the Indian*) If you wish ever to see your home again!

NANO. (*mechanically, in a clear monotonous voice, with expressionless face*) A big land—far mighty cities—gold——

JUAN. You hear? The cities of gold! (*The crowd murmurs excitedly*)

NANO. There is much gold. The houses have gold on them.

A SOLDIER. Cipango! We'll storm their cities for them!

A SAILOR. Loot, my bullies!

JUAN. Glory and gold for all of you! And now go! (*The crowd are jubilant. Shouts of "Up anchor! Ahoy Cathay! At last! We sail! Sack! Riches! Gold!" etc.* JUAN *shouts above the tumult*) Go! Disperse! Tomorrow we sail! (*A voice cries, "Long live Don Juan!" The whole mob takes it up.* JUAN *begins to give way under the strain—wearily*) Go. Go.

THE MOB. (*led by a sailor, takes up a sort of chanty song in mighty chorus, dancing wildly, waving their torches, crowding out, rear*)

The Cities of Gold
In far Cathay—
Their great Khan is old,
And his wealth untold
In prize for our bold
Who sail away.
Aye!
His gold for our bold who sail away!!

BEATRIZ. (*as the last of the mob disappear—rushing up to* JUAN *with great admiration*) You have saved him! What they have said of you is true indeed—lion by nature as well as name!

JUAN. (*bitterly*) Lion? No! Tricky politician! If I had been the Juan of long ago, I would not have plead or bargained with such curs. I would have—— (*He raises his sword threateningly—then lets his arm sink limply. The sword slips from his fingers and falls to the ground*)

BEATRIZ. (*kneels quickly and presents its hilt to him*) I give you back your sword—to bring good fortune. Now you must find the golden cities!

JUAN. (*taking it—longingly*) I care only for the one, Beatriz—the golden city of Youth, where you are queen. (*She looks into his face smilingly, mystified as—*

The Curtain Falls)

SCENE SEVEN

SCENE. *Four months later—a strip of beach on the Florida coast—a bright, moonlight night. The forest runs diagonally from right, front, to left, rear—a wall of black shadow. The sand gleams a pallid white in the moonlight. The rhythmic ebb and flow of waves is heard—their voice on a windless night of calm.*

As the curtain rises, an INDIAN *is discovered, standing in the moonlight, just out of the shadow of the forest. He is old, but still erect and warrior-like, a chief by his demeanor. His body, naked save for a piece of deerskin at his waist, is elaborately painted, as is his face. A knot of feathers is in his hair. A tomahawk and flint knife are at his waist. He is motionless and silent as a statue, one hand clasping his unslung bow as if it were a staff, but he peers intently at some object in the ocean before him. Finally, he gives an ejaculation of surprise and makes a motion of summons to the forest behind him. The* MEDICINE MAN *glides out of the darkness to his side. This latter is incredibly old and shrunken, daubed with many insignia in paint, wearing many ornaments of bone and shell. They confer together in low tones with much pantomime. A man is evidently swimming toward them from some strange object out at sea. Other* INDIANS *steal from the forest, form a group in the shadow behind the two, point out to sea, gesticulate. At a sharp command from the* CHIEF, *they unsling their bows, fit arrows to strings, crouch in an ambush in the shadow. The* CHIEF *does likewise and stands waiting, prepared for what may come.* NANO *walks up the beach from front, left. His naked body glistens with drops of water. He sees the* CHIEF *and stops, raising his right hand above his head. The* CHIEF *makes a sign. The other* INDIANS *dart from their ambush and surround* NANO.

CHIEF. Bind him.

NANO. (*calmly*) Is a brother an enemy? (*They all start with surprise at hearing their own language.* NANO *goes on*) This is the land of my fathers. I am Nano, a son of Boanu, who was a chief. (*They all stare at him. The* CHIEF *makes a sign to the* MEDICINE MAN, *who comes forward and examines* NANO'S *face intently*)

MEDICINE MAN. His words are truth. He is Nano—or an evil spirit in his body. (*He shakes a charm at him*) Are you from the Land of the Dead?

NANO. I am of the living. They did not chain me. They think I fear the sea. I come to warn you. I swam from the great canoes. They are the warships of the Spaniards.

CHIEF. (*mystified*) What are Spaniards? Their winged canoes are like the boats of Gods.

NANO. These are no Gods. They are men who die from wounds. Their faces are white, but they are evil. They wear shirts that arrows cannot pierce. They have strange sticks that spit fire and kill. Their devils make them strong. But they are not true warriors. They are thieves and rapers of women.

CHIEF. Have they no God?

NANO. (*with scorn*) Their God is a thing of earth! It is this! (*He touches a gold ornament that the* CHIEF *wears*)

MEDICINE MAN. (*mystified*) Gold? Gold is sacred to the Sun. It can be no God itself.

NANO. (*contemptuously*) They see only things, not the spirit behind things. Their hearts are muddy as a pool in which deer have trampled. Listen. Their Medicine Men tell of a God who came to them long ago in the form of a man. He taught them to scorn things. He taught them to look for the spirit behind things. In revenge, they killed him. They tortured him as a sacrifice to their Gold Devil. They crossed two big sticks. They drove little sticks through his hands and feet and pinned him on the others—thus. (*He illustrates. A murmur of horror and indignation goes up among them*)

MEDICINE MAN. To torture a God! How did they dare?

NANO. Their devils protected them. And now each place they go, they carry that figure of a dying God. They do this to strike fear. They command you to submit when you see how even a God who fought their evil was tortured. (*Proudly*) But I would not.

MEDICINE MAN. (*suspiciously*) If you defied them, how are you alive?

NANO. I am craftier than they. They have an old chief who is cursed with madness. Him I told of the Spring of Life. I said I would find it for him.

MEDICINE MAN. Only the Gods can reveal it. Why have you told this lie?

NANO. (*fiercely*) Revenge! I have made a plan. Is there a spring near?

CHIEF. (*mystified*) Yes. In the forest.

NANO. (*with satisfaction*) Good! Listen. This mad chief is the mightiest among them. Without him they would turn cowards. Tomorrow night I will lead him to the spring. You must lie hidden. We will kill him there. Is this clear?

CHIEF. Yes.

NANO. I will swim back now. I escaped to tell you of my plan and warn you. They would lay waste your land as they did mine. They killed my wives and children. They burned. They tortured. They chained warriors neck to neck. They beat them with a whip to dig in the fields like squaws. This old chief led them. My heart is fire. Until he dies, it will know no peace.

CHIEF. I begin to feel your hatred.

NANO. Then remember to hide by the spring.

CHIEF. We will not forget.

NANO. It is well. (*He turns and strides down to the sea. They stand watching him in silence*)

MEDICINE MAN. (*uneasily, thoughtful*) Only devils could build great canoes that fly with wings. My brothers, they are evil spirits. Nano has made war with them. They have beaten him. Can we trust his plan?

CHIEF. What is your counsel?

MEDICINE MAN. I have heard the voice of the Great Spirit speaking in the night. Let us first try to propitiate their devils.

CHIEF. I do not know how to war with devils. That is your duty. Let us summon the council. (*He makes a sign at which his followers disappear silently into the wood. He and the* MEDICINE MAN *follow as—*

The Curtain Falls)

SCENE EIGHT

SCENE. *The same. High noon of the following day—glaring sunlight on the beach, an atmosphere of oppressive heat and languor. The earth seems dead, preserved in some colorless, molten fluid. The forest is a matted green wall. The sound of the sea has the quality of immense exhaustion.*

On the beach, a sort of makeshift altar is being erected—two round boulders supporting a flat slab of rock. On top of the slab is placed a shallow bowl made of bark. A group of INDIANS, *under the direction of the* MEDICINE MAN, *are hurriedly putting on the finishing touches to this shrine. They keep casting awed apprehensive glances seaward. The* MEDICINE MAN *is binding two branches of a tree together in the form of a cross. All the* INDIANS *are feathered and painted as for an unusual solemn occasion.*

THE INDIANS. (*their eyes on the sea as they work—frightenedly*) The small canoes leave the great winged ones. They are coming! The sun gleams on their shirts that arrows cannot pierce. Their fire-sticks glitter in the sun. Their faces are turned. Their faces are pale! They are watching us!

MEDICINE MAN. (*finishing his work*) Keep your hearts brave! (*Giving the cross to two* INDIANS) Here. This is their totem pole. Stand it there. (*They dig a hole in the sand before the altar and set the cross there; but they make the mistake of setting it head down. The* MEDICINE MAN *grunts with satisfaction)* They will think we adore the same devil. They will leave us in peace.

INDIAN. *(his eyes on the sea)* The last canoe has left the great ships. *(He gives a cry of fear echoed by the others)* Aie! Fire and smoke! *(They cower. The hollow boom of a cannon fired in salute reverberates over the sea. They all shrink with terror, bowing their heads)*

INDIAN. *(awe-struck)* The Thunder fights with them!

INDIAN. They are white Gods!

MEDICINE MAN. *(frightened himself, but rallying his followers sternly)* You have the hearts of squaws. Quick! Where is the gold? *(An* INDIAN *comes to him with an earthenware vessel. He empties it out on the bowl on the top of the altar. It is full of gold nuggets of different sizes. They form a heap glowing in the sun)*

INDIANS. They come! They come!

MEDICINE MAN. *(sternly)* Pretend to worship their gold devil but pray to our Great Father, the Sun. He can defeat all devils. Pray to him! *(An* INDIAN *starts to beat rhythmically on the small drum. The* MEDICINE MAN *lifts his shrill voice in the first strains of the chant. Immediately the others all join in as if hypnotized)* Great Father, Mighty One, Ruler of Earth. Maker of Days. Ripener of the Corn. Creator of Life. Look down upon us out of your Sky-Tent. Let our song rise to you. Let it enter your heart. Mighty One, hear us. Hide not your face in clouds. Bless us at the dawn. And at the day's end. *(They form a circle and dance about the altar, their eyes raised to the sun overhead. Their chant hides the noise of the* SPANIARDS *landing. Then the* SPANIARDS *appear from the left, front. First comes* JUAN, *his face wild and haggard, his eyes obsessed. He is accompanied by* LUIS. *Following him are a squad of* SOLDIERS, *guarding* NANO, *who is in chains. Then come four* FRANCISCAN MONKS, *led by* QUESADA, *who wears a sword and pistol over his robe. The others carry crosses. Following them is a group of* NOBLES, *richly dressed. Then come ranks of* SOLDIERS. *They all stare at this Indian ceremony with contemptuous scorn*)

JUAN. (*irritably*) Make them cease their accursed noise, Luis. Let Nano speak to them.

LUIS. (*advancing toward the* INDIANS—*in a loud but friendly voice, raising his right hand*) Peace, brothers. (*The* INDIANS *stop, petrified, staring with awe at the white men. The* MEDICINE MAN *lifts his right hand and advances a step toward* LUIS. QUESADA *notices the cross, utters a furious exclamation, strides forward to verify his suspicion. When he sees that it is indeed upside down his face grows livid with fury*)

QUESADA. The cross head down! The black mass! (*He pulls out his pistol*) Blaspheming dog! (*He fires. The* MEDICINE MAN *falls. The other* INDIANS *who have shrunk back toward the woods in terror at his first move, now turn tail in panic and flee*)

LUIS. (*in horror*) Stop, Quesada! (QUESADA *pulls up the cross and is setting it back upright when the* MEDICINE MAN, *by a last dying effort, draws his knife, and writhing to his feet, plunges it into* QUESADA'S *back. They both fall together, the* INDIAN *dead.* QUESADA *shudders and is still. A yell of rage goes up from the* SPANIARDS. *They rush forward toward the woods as if to pursue the* INDIANS *but* JUAN *shouts a command*)

JUAN. Halt! Fools! (*They stop prudently but sullenly.* JUAN *turns to* LUIS, *who is kneeling beside* QUESADA) Is he dead?

LUIS. Yes. (*Crossing himself*) May his soul rest in peace. (*All echo this, crossing themselves*)

JUAN. An eye for an eye, a tooth for a tooth. (*Mockingly*) And now it is his eye, his tooth. (*Then with a shudder*) Take him away. This is a bloody baptism for Cathay. (*Turning to* NANO *as the* SOLDIERS *carry the bodies aside*) Is this the land, Nano?

NANO. (*his eyes smoldering with hate*) Yes.

JUAN. You said it was a wonder land—a land of flowers. I see no flowers.

NANO. (*in a sinister tone*) In the forest—flowers grow by a spring——

JUAN. (*harshly—with an apprehensive glance about*) Silence!

A NOBLE. (*from the group that has been stirring impatiently*) Your Excellency. The banners of Castile and Aragon wait on your pleasure.

JUAN. (*making a confused gesture as if wiping cobwebs from his brain*) Yes—yes—I must take possession. Bring the banners. (*He kneels on one knee. They all do likewise*) In the name of Jesus Christ, Our Lord, and of his most gracious Majesty, the sovereign of Castile and Aragon, I do hereby annex to his dominions this land and all its environs. And I call the land Florida. (*He bends and kisses the sand. The banners are planted in the ground, where they hang motionless from their poles.* JUAN, *having made this effort, seems to fall into a stupor*)

A NOBLE. (*in a mocking whisper*) A pretty name!

A NOBLE. He has grown imbecile. Will he go spring-hunting here, too? My faith, with all the water he has drunk in the past four months, he must be flooded. (*They all snicker at this*)

A NOBLE. (*impatiently*) Will he never get off his knees and let us rise?

LUIS. (*sensing what is going on behind their backs—to* JUAN—*who seems to be praying with bowed head—plucking his sleeve*) Juan! Come!

JUAN. (*vaguely*) I was praying—to what God, who knows? (*He rises to his feet weakly. At this, they all rise*)

A NOBLE. (*pointing excitedly*) Look! In that bowl on the stones. Is it not gold? (*They all rush forward to the altar. The* NOBLE *picks up a piece of it—his voice hoarse with greedy triumph*) Gold! (*They all grab at the bowl, upsetting its contents on the sand. They bend down and clutch for it crying*) Gold! This must be a rich land! There must be more! The Golden Cities are near! Cathay at last! (*The* SOLDIERS *forget discipline, break ranks, form a disorderly, pushing crowd about their leaders. Even the* MONKS *edge forward inquisitively*)

LUIS. (*urgently*) Juan! Look! This is disgraceful!

JUAN. (*coming to himself with a start—in a furious tone of command*) Get back to your ranks! A brave example you set, nobles of Spain! (*His personality is compelling. They all slink to their former order again, muttering rebelliously.* JUAN *seems suddenly seized with a wild exultation*) Cathay! We have found Cathay! This is the land—the Flowery Land! Our dreams lie hidden here! Sing the Te Deum! Sing! (*There is an oppressive silence for a moment, in which the heat, the sun glaring on the beach, the green of the forest, all nature seems to lay upon these men a mysterious spell, a sudden exhausted recognition of their own defeat. Then the* FRANCISCAN MONKS *raise their voices mechanically and spiritlessly in the Te Deum. Other listless voices gradually join theirs as—*

The Curtain Falls)

SCENE NINE

SCENE. *About midnight—in the forest. Gigantic tree-trunks, entwined with vines in flower, are in the foreground. Festoons of Spanish moss hang clear to the ground from the branches. Through the network one sees a circular clearing, grass-grown, flooded with moonlight. There is the soft murmur of a spring which bubbles from the ground in the center of this open space.* INDIANS *are crouched in ambush among the trees, motionless, their eyes fixed on the clearing.*

The stillness is broken by the whistled call of a bird. The INDIANS *stir alertly. One of them whistles in answer to the call. An* INDIAN *creeps swiftly in from the left. The* CHIEF *comes from his place of ambush to meet him.*

CHIEF. He comes?

INDIAN. He has entered the forest.

CHIEF. I will give Nano the signal when we are ready. Go. Hide. (*The* INDIAN *takes a place with the others. The* CHIEF *fits an arrow to his bow and crouches in the shadow. There is a pause of silence—then the noise of someone pushing his way through the woods at the rear of the clearing.* NANO *appears there, followed by* JUAN)

JUAN. Why do you stop?

NANO. This is the place.

JUAN. (*looking around him disappointedly*) This?

NANO. There is the spring.

JUAN. (*stepping forward to look at it—with growing anger*) It looks a common spring like any other. Beware, dog! In these past months you have shown me many springs——

NANO. (*quickly*) The voyage was long. There were many islands. You forced me to lead you to a spring on each. But I told you the Spring of Life was here.

JUAN. I feared your revenge might lie. (*Relapsed into a mood of somber preoccupation—bitterly*) I drank of every one. I closed my eyes. I felt the stirring of rebirth. Fool! Always the mirror in the spring showed me the same loathsome blighted face—— (*He groans—then with a harsh laugh*) A sacred grove, the legend says! Some of those springs bubbled from sandy water! Beautiful maidens? There were none. At one place I found an old hag filling her bowl, who drank and mumbled at me. (*Then in a harsh tone of command*) Nano! I command you to tell me if you have lied. (*Distractedly*) I must have certainty, be it of faith or despair!

NANO. This is the spring.

JUAN. (*looking around him*) But where are the trees with golden fruit, the maidens, the fountain——? (*Bewildered, staring—grasping at hope*) And yet—this spot has singular beauty. I feel enchantment. But why do I shudder? (*A low whistled signal comes from the* CHIEF *hidden on the edge of the clearing.* JUAN *starts*) Sssh! What was that?

NANO. A bird. (*Insistently*) It is a magic spring. Drink!

JUAN. (*bending over the spring*) A mirror of moonlight. The dead eyes of a corpse stare back in mine. (*He kneels by the spring as if fascinated*) I dare not drink. To whom can I pray? Beatriz! Oh, to hear your voice once more, to see your face! And yet I see you everywhere. Your spirit inspires all things wherever there is beauty. I hear you call in the song of the waves, the wind is your breath, the trees reach out with your arms, the dawn and sunset promise with your lips! You are everywhere and nowhere—part of all life but mine! (*He breaks off, turning distrustful, harried eyes on the impatient* NANO—*bitterly*) I am a spectacle for laughter, eh? A grotesque old fool!

NANO. (*in a fierce tone of command*) Drink!

JUAN. (*hectically—goading himself to action*) The test. Spirit of Eternal Youth, I pray to you! Beatriz! (*He bends down and drinks. As he does so* NANO *darts away from him to the woods in front*)

NANO. (*hurriedly*) Kill when he stands again! (*The* INDIANS *can be seen raising their bows, taking aim*)

JUAN. (*having drunk, remains kneeling by the spring—in a trembling tone of hesitating joy*) New life thrills in me! Is it youth? Do I dream? Then let me never wake till the end of time! (*Then harshly*) Coward! How often have you looked death in the face. Are you afraid of life? Open! Open and see! (*He opens his eyes and stares down into the spring. A terrible groan tears from his breast*) O God! (*His grief is turned immediately into a frenzy of rage*) Treacherous dog. You betrayed me. (*He leaps to his feet, drawing his sword. There is a twanging of many bows, the whiz of a flight of arrows.* JUAN *falls, clutches at the grass, is still. The* INDIANS *pour out into the clearing but keep a cautious distance from* JUAN)

NANO. (*with more courage than they, he bends down over the body*) He wore no shining shirt. He is dead. (*He does *a wild dance of savage triumph beside the body—then stops as suddenly)* Quick. To their camp. The great Spirit has made them helpless. Be brave and kill! *(He runs swiftly into the woods, followed by the whole band, brandishing their weapons. There is a pause. Then the fierce yells of the savages as they fall upon the sleeping camp, the howls of terror of the* SPANIARDS, *the screams of the dying, a few futile musket-shots)*

(The Curtain Falls)

SCENE TEN

SCENE. *The same clearing in the woods some hours later. There is no intervening fringe of trees in this scene, the open space is in full view. The Spring is at center. The wall of forest forms a semicircular background. As the curtain rises, there is a pitch-blackness and silence except for the murmur of the Spring. Then the sound of someone struggling to rise from the ground, falling back again with a groan of pain.* JUAN'S *voice comes out of the darkness.*

JUAN. (*as if he had just regained consciousness—then with a groan of rage and pain as memory returns*) Fool! Why did I look? I might have died in my dream. (*A pause—weakly*) Sleep seems humming in my ears. Or is it—death!—death, the Merciful One! (*He stirs and his voice suddenly grows strident*) No, No! Why have I lived! To die alone like a beast in the wilderness? (*With a bitter mocking despair*) O Son of God, is this Thy justice? Does not the Savior of Man know magnanimity? True, I prayed for a miracle which was not Thine. Let me be damned then, but (*passionately*) let me believe in Thy Kingdom! Show me Thy miracle—a sign—a word—a second's vision of what I am that I should have lived and died! A test, Lord God of Hosts! (*He laughs with a scornful bravado*) Nothing! (*But even as he speaks a strange unearthly light *begins to flood down upon a spot on the edge of the clearing on the right. Startled in spite of himself)* This light—the moon has waned—— *(Beneath the growing light a form takes shape —a tall woman's figure, like a piece of ancient sculpture, shrouded in long draperies of a blue that is almost black. The face is a pale mask with features indistinguishable save for the eyes that stare straight ahead with a stony penetration that sees through and beyond things. Her arms are rigid at her sides, the palms of the hands turned outward.* JUAN *stares at her, defiance striving with his awe)* What are you? *(Forcing a sneer)* An angel in answer to my prayer? *(He cannot control a shudder—tries to calm himself. He stares at the figure—after a pause, boldly)* Or are you Death? Why then I have often laughed in your eyes! *(Tauntingly)* Off with your mask, coward! *(Mockingly but uneasy)* Delightful Lady, you are enigmatic. One must embrace you with bold arms, tear off your masquerade. That was my pastime once—to play at love as gaming. Were I the Juan of long ago—but you see I am old now and wounded. *(He pauses. The figure is frozen. He asks a bit falteringly)* Are you—death? Then wait—— *(In passionate invocation)* O Beatriz! Let me hear your voice again in mercy of farewell! *(As if in answer to this the voice of* BEATRIZ *sings from the darkness)*

VOICE. Love is a flower
Forever blooming
Life is a fountain
Forever leaping
Upward to catch the golden sunlight

Upward to reach the azure heaven
Failing, falling,
Ever returning,
To kiss the earth that the flower may live.

JUAN. (*raptly*) Youth! (*As the song is sung, the same mystical light floods down slowly about the Spring, which is transformed into a gigantic fountain, whose waters, arched with rainbows, seem to join earth and sky, forming a shimmering veil, which hides the background of forest.* JUAN *and the* FIGURE *are left at the edge of this, on the outside. The form of* BEATRIZ *appears within as if rising from the spring. She dances in ecstasy—the personified spirit of the fountain.* JUAN *cries with a voice trembling with joy*) The Fountain! Let me drink! (*He tries to drag himself to it but cannot—in anguish*) Must I die——? (*Making a furious gesture of defiance at the* FIGURE *and struggling to rise*) No! I defy you! (*Exhausted, he sinks back crying beseechingly*) Beatriz! (*But she seems not to see or hear him.* JUAN *half sobs in despair*) She will not see! She will not hear! Fountain, cruel as the heart of youth, what mercy have you for the old and wounded? (*He sinks down overcome by weakness.* BEATRIZ *vanishes from the fountain. In her place appears the form of a Chinese poet. He is a venerable old man with the mild face of a dreamer and scholar. He carries a block and writes upon it with a brush, absorbed in contemplation.* JUAN *looking up and seeing him —startled*) What are you? (*Groping at some clue in his memory*) I know—that night in Granada—the Moor's tale—— (*Excitedly*) Of the poet from the East who told his father the Fountain lie! Are you not that poisoner of life? (*The* POET *raises his hand as if in summons. The form of the Moorish minstrel of Scene One appears at his side*) The Moor! (*Raging*) Infidel dog! Your lie has cursed me! (*The form of* NANO *appears at the other side of the Chinese poet.* JUAN *struggles to reach his sword in a fury*) Murderer! (*Then his eyes are caught by a fourth figure which materializes beside the Moor. It is* LUIS *as he was in Scene One. With a cry of joy*) Luis—old friend—— (*Then as* LUIS *seems neither to see nor hear him, he sinks back helplessly*) No—another mocking phantom! (*He watches the Chinese poet, who seems to be reading what he has written to all of them*) See! The dead lie to the living. It passes on—from East to West—round the round world—from old worlds to new—cheating the old and wounded —Ha! (*He laughs harshly and wildly. The Chinese poet takes the Indian by one hand, the Moor by the other. These latter stretch out their hands to* LUIS, *who takes them, thus completing the circle.* BEATRIZ' *voice can be heard singing*)

VOICE. Life is a field
Forever growing
Beauty a fountain
Forever flowing
Upward beyond the source of sunshine
Upward beyond the azure heaven,
Born of God but
Ever returning
To merge with earth that the field may live.

(*As she sings, the four forms disappear as if they were dissolved in the fountain*)

JUAN. (*lost in the ecstasy of her song*) Sing on, Youth! (*With a start as the song stops—stupidly*) The ghosts are gone. What is the answer to their riddle? I am no poet. I have striven for what the hand can grasp. What is left when Death makes the hand powerless? (*Addresses the* FIGURE *pitifully, trying to mock*) O Mighty Relaxer of hands, have you no vision for the graspers of earth? (*The* FIGURE *raises a summoning hand. One by one, within the fountain, solemn figures materialize. First the Chinese poet, now robed as a Buddhist priest; then the Moorish minstrel, dressed as a priest of Islam; and then the* MEDICINE MAN *as he was in Scene Eight, decked out in all the paint and regalia of his office; lastly,* LUIS, *the Dominican monk of the present. Each one carries the symbol of his religion before him. They appear clearly for a moment, then fade from sight, seeming to dissolve in the fountain.* JUAN *has stared at them with straining eyes—in a bewildered voice*) All faiths—they vanish—are one and equal—within—— (*Awe and reverence creeping into his voice*) What are you, Fountain? That from which all life springs and to which it must return—God! Are all dreams of you but the one dream? (*Bowing his head miserably*) I do not know. Come back, Youth. Tell me this secret! (*For a moment the voice of* BEATRIZ *is heard from the darkness*)

Death is a mist
Veiling sunrise.

(JUAN *seems to fall into a rapt spell. The form of an old Indian woman appears from the left. She falters forward, a wooden bowl under her arm, as if she were going to fill it at the fountain*)

JUAN. (*recognizing her aghast*) Damned hag! I remember you waited beside a spring to mock me! Begone! (*But the old woman stretches out her hands to him with a mysterious beseeching.* JUAN *shudders—then after a struggle with himself, gets to his feet painfully*) So be it. Sit here by me. I am old, too—and, poor woman, you cannot fill your bowl there. Come. (*He grasps her hands. In a flash her mask of age disappears. She is* BEATRIZ. JUAN *gazes at her in an ecstasy—faltering, his mind groping*) Beatriz! Age—Youth—— They are the same rhythm of eternal life! (*Without his noticing it,* BEATRIZ *recedes from him and vanishes in the Fountain. He raises his face to the sky—with halting joy*) Light comes! Light creeps into my soul! (*Then he sees the* FIGURE *walk slowly from its place and vanish in the Fountain*) Death is no more! (*The* FIGURE *materializes again within the Fountain but this time there is no mask, the face is that of* BEATRIZ, *her form grown tall, majestic, vibrant with power. Her arms are raised above her head. Her whole body soars upward. A radiant, dancing fire, proceeding from the source of the Fountain, floods over and envelopes her until her figure is like the heart of its flame.* JUAN *stares at this vision for a moment, then sinks on his knees—exultantly*) I see! Fountain Everlasting, time without end! Soaring flame of the spirit transfiguring Death! All is within! All things dissolve, flow on eternally! O aspiring fire of life, sweep the dark soul of man! Let us burn in thy unity! (BEATRIZ' *voice rises triumphantly*)

VOICE. God is a flower
Forever blooming
God is a fountain
Forever flowing.

(*The song ceases. The light fades. There is darkness.* JUAN'S *voice is heard sobbing with happiness*)

JUAN. O God, Fountain of Eternity, Thou art the All in One, the One in All—the Eternal Becoming which is Beauty! (*He falls unconscious. A pause. Then the faint misty light of the dawn floats over the clearing.* JUAN *is seen lying where he had fallen. There is the noise of someone approaching from the woods in the rear,* LUIS *and a brother* DOMINICAN *enter from the forest*)

LUIS. (*seeing* JUAN) God be praised! (*He rushes forward and kneels by* JUAN'S *body.* JUAN *stirs and groans*) He moves! Juan! It's Luis! Our friends were murdered. A boat from the fleet is waiting——

JUAN. (*in a dreaming ecstasy*) God—Thou art all——

DOMINICAN. He prays.

LUIS. Delirium. Let us carry him. We'll sail for the nearest settlement——

JUAN. (*as they raise him*) Light! I see and know!

LUIS. It is the dawn, Juan.

JUAN. (*exultantly*) The dawn! (*They carry him out as*

The Curtain Falls)

SCENE ELEVEN

SCENE. *Some months later. The courtyard of a Dominican monastery in Cuba. A crude little home-made fountain is in center. This is the only adornment of the quadrangle of bald, sunbaked earth, enclosed on the left and in the rear by a high white wall, on the right by the monastery building itself. The entrance to this is an arched doorway surmounted by a crucifix of carved wood. Two niches on either side of this door shelter primitive wooden figures of the Holy Family and Saint Dominic. In the wall, center, is another arched door with a cross above it. Beyond the wall nature can be seen and felt—vivid, colorful, burgeoning with the manifold, compelling life of the tropics. Palm trees lean over the wall casting their graceful shadows within. Vines in flower have climbed to the top and are starting to creep down inside.*

A sunset sky of infinite depth glows with mysterious splendor.

As the curtain rises, JUAN *and the* FATHER SUPERIOR *are discovered.* JUAN *is asleep, reclining on a sort of improvised invalid's chair, his cloak wrapped around him, facing the fountain. He is pale and emaciated but his wasted countenance has gained an entirely new quality, the calm of a deep spiritual serenity. The* FATHER SUPERIOR *is a portly monk with a simple round face, gray hair and beard. His large eyes have the opaque calm of a ruminating cow's. The door in the rear is opened and* LUIS *enters. He closes the door carefully and tiptoes forward.*

LUIS. (*in a whisper*) He is sleeping?

FATHER SUPERIOR. As you see, Father.

LUIS. (*looking down at* JUAN) How calm his face is—as if he saw a vision of peace.

FATHER SUPERIOR. It is a blessed miracle he has lived so long.

LUIS. He has been waiting. (*Sadly*) And now, I am afraid his desire is fulfilled—but not as he dreamed. Rather the cup of gall and wormwood——

FATHER SUPERIOR. (*mystified*) You mean the caravel brings him bad tidings?

LUIS. Yes; and I must wake him to prepare his mind.

FATHER SUPERIOR. I will leave you with him. It is near vesper time. (*He turns and goes into the monastery*)

LUIS. (*touching* JUAN *on the arm—gently*) Juan, awake. (JUAN *opens his eyes*) The caravel has anchored.

JUAN. From Porto Rico?

LUIS. Yes.

JUAN. (*with an air of certainty—with exultant joy*) Then Beatriz is here!

LUIS. (*disturbed—evasively*) There has been a frightful insurrection of the Indians. Diego was killed. (*Hastily*) But I will not trouble you with that. (*Then slowly*) Beatriz comes to nurse you—(*With warning emphasis*)—her second father, those were her words.

JUAN. (*smiling*) You need not emphasize. I know her heart. (*Then earnestly*) But I must tell her my truth. (*Then with a sort of pleading for assurance*) It is for that I have waited, to tell her of the love I bore her—now—as farewell—when she cannot misunderstand. (*Proudly*) My love was no common thing. It was the one time Beauty touched my life. I wish to live in her memory as what she was to me. (*Sinking back—with a flickering smile, weakly*) Come, old friend, are you grown so ascetic you deny my right to lay this Golden City—the only one I ever conquered—at the feet of Beauty?

LUIS. (*kindly persuasive*) Silence is better, Juan. You should renounce——

JUAN. (*gently*) All is renounced. But do you begrudge a traveler if he begs a flower from this earth, a last token of the world's grace, to lend farewell the solace of regret?

LUIS. (*more and more troubled*) Juan—I—I speak because—you have suffered—and now—I would not have you suffer more, dear friend. (*Then blurting out most brusquely*) The caravel brings you a surprise. Your nephew, Juan, has arrived from Spain and comes from Porto Rico to greet you.

JUAN. (*vaguely*) My nephew? (*The sound of voices comes from inside the monastery*) Beatriz! (*The* FATHER SUPERIOR *appears in the doorway ushering in* BEATRIZ *and* JUAN'S *nephew. They are followed by the Duenna and the* NEPHEW'S *Servant, who carries his master's cloak and a lute. During the following scene these two remain standing respectfully by the doorway for a time, then go back into the monastery, the Servant leaving the cloak and lute on the ground beside the doorway. The* FATHER SUPERIOR *retires immediately.* LUIS, *after a clasp of* JUAN'S *hand, also withdraws, exchanging greetings as he passes the* NEPHEW *and* BEATRIZ. BEATRIZ *glows with fulfillment, is very apparently deeply in love. The* NEPHEW *is a slender, graceful young cavalier. He is dressed richly*)

BEATRIZ. (*halting a moment with a shocked exclamation as*

she sees JUAN's *wasted face—then rushing forward and flinging herself on her knees beside his chair. Hastily*) Don Juan! Oh, this is happiness—to find you still—recovered from your wounds! Oh, I'll say prayers of thanksgiving! (*Impulsively she kisses him*)

JUAN. (*thrilled—choked—unable to say but one word*) Beatriz! Beatriz!

NEPHEW. (*kneels and kisses* JUAN's *hand. Startled,* JUAN's *eyes search his face keenly, apprehensive of what he, too, plainly sees there*) I greet you, sir. God grant you may soon be strong again.

JUAN. (*weakly*) Soon—I shall be strong—against all wounds. (*After a pause*) And so your name is Juan, too?

NEPHEW. In your honor. Though I can add no honor to it, I hope to bear it worthily.

JUAN. (*hostility creeping into his tone*) You come out here adventuring?

NEPHEW. I come to serve Spain!

JUAN. (*harshly*) A heart as steeled as your sword. Have you that?

BEATRIZ. (*eagerly—somewhat hurt by* JUAN's *reception*) Oh, he is brave! When the mob tried to storm the palace it was Juan who led the defenders.

JUAN. (*more and more agitated—trying to hide his growing resentment under effusive amiability*) Bravely done! But you have doubtless heard great tales of mountains of jewels—Golden Cities of Cathay—you hope to grow rich.

NEPHEW. (*proudly*) I do not care for riches; and as for Golden Cities, I only wish to plant Spain's banner on their citadels!

JUAN. (*inspired by respect in spite of himself*) Brave dreams! Echoes blown down the wind of years.

BEATRIZ. (*looking at the* NEPHEW *with great pride as* JUAN *searches her face*) He is as you were in my mother's tales. (*She and the* NEPHEW *are held by each other's eyes*)

JUAN. (*after a conquering struggle with his bitterness—fatalistically*) So—thus old heart—in silence. (*Then rousing himself—intensely*) But with joy! with joy! (*They look at him in puzzled alarm. He smiles gently at* BEATRIZ) Then you have found him at last—my double?

BEATRIZ. (*blushing, confusedly*) I—I do not know, Don Juan.

JUAN. Then I know. (*Musing a bit sadly*) You have stolen my last gesture. An old man had a tale to tell you—oh, so brave a tale!—but now he sees that if youth cannot, age must keep its secrets! A sad old ghost to haunt your memory, that would be a poor wedding gift. (*They again look from him to each other, mystified and apprehensive.* JUAN *suddenly looks up at them—with a startling directness*) You love each other! (*He hurries on with feverish gayety*) Forgive—I'm a rough soldier—and there is need for haste. Quick. Do you not ask my blessing?

BEATRIZ. (*falling on her knees beside him—happily*) Oh, yes, good Don Juan! (*The* NEPHEW *kneels beside her*)

JUAN. (*he raises his hands over their heads*) Youth of this earth—love—hail—and farewell! May you be blessed forever! (*He touches their heads with his hands—then sinks back, closing his eyes. They rise and stand looking down at him uncertainly*)

NEPHEW. (*after a pause—in a whisper*) He wishes to sleep.

BEATRIZ. *(as they walk apart, in a whisper, the tears in her eyes)* Oh, Juan, I'm afraid—and yet—I am not sad.

NEPHEW. *(takes her in his arms passionately)* My life! My soul! *(He kisses her)*

BEATRIZ. My love!

NEPHEW. Life is beautiful! The earth sings for us! Let us sing, too! *(He strides over to where the lute is and picks it up)*

BEATRIZ. *(happily)* Yes—— *(Then reminded)* Ssshh! *(She points at* JUAN*)*

NEPHEW. *(urgingly)* He is asleep. We can go out beyond the walls. *(He puts his arms around her and leads her out through the door in rear)*

JUAN. *(opening his eyes and looking after them, a tender smile on his lips)* Yes! Go where Beauty is! Sing! *(From outside the voices of* BEATRIZ *and his* NEPHEW *are heard mingling in their version of the fountain song)*

Love is a flower
Forever blooming
Beauty a fountain
Forever flowing
Upward into the source of sunshine,
Upward into the azure heaven;
One with God but
Ever returning
To kiss the earth that the flower may live.

*(*JUAN *listens in an ecstasy, bows his head, weeps. Then he sinks back with closed eyes exhaustedly.* LUIS *enters from the monastery)*

LUIS. (*hurries forward in alarm*) Juan! (*He hears the song and is indignant*) Have they lost all feeling? I will soon stop—— (*He starts for the door in rear*)

JUAN. (*in a ringing voice*) No! I am that song! One must accept, absorb, give back, become oneself a symbol! Juan Ponce de Leon is past! He is resolved into the thousand moods of beauty that make up happiness—color of the sunset, of tomorrow's dawn, breath of the great Trade wind—sunlight on grass, an insect's song, the rustle of leaves, an ant's ambitions. (*In an ecstasy*) Oh, Luis, I begin to know eternal youth! I have found my Fountain! O Fountain of Eternity, take back this drop, my soul! (*He dies.* LUIS *bows his head and weeps*)

FATHER SUPERIOR. (*enters from the right*) Vespers. (*Then in a voice of awe as he stares at* JUAN) Is he—dead?

LUIS. (*aroused—exaltedly*) No! He lives in God! Let us pray. (LUIS *sinks on his knees beside* JUAN'S *body, the* FATHER SUPERIOR *beside him. He lifts his eyes and clasped hands to heaven and prays fervently. The voices of* BEATRIZ *and the* NEPHEW *in the fountain song seem to rise to an exultant pitch. Then the chant of the monks swells out, deep and vibrant. For a moment the two strains blend into harmony, fill the air in an all-comprehending hymn of the mystery of life as*

The Curtain Falls)

THE MOON OF THE CARIBBEES

A Play in One Act

CHARACTERS

YANK DRISCOLL OLSON DAVIS COCKY SMITTY PAUL	*seamen of the British tramp steamer,* Glencairn

LAMPS, *the lamp-trimmer*

CHIPS, *the carpenter*

OLD TOM, *the donkeyman*

BIG FRANK DICK MAX PADDY	*firemen on the* Glencairn

BELLA SUSIE VIOLET PEARL	*West Indian negresses*

THE FIRST MATE

Two other seamen—SCOTTY and IVAN—and several other members of the stokehole-engine-room crew.

NOTE.—With the exception of "In the Zone," the action of all the plays following takes place in years preceding the outbreak of the World War.

THE MOON OF THE CARIBBEES

SCENE. *A forward section of the main deck of the British tramp steamer* Glencairn, *at anchor off an island in the West Indies. The full moon, half-way up the sky, throws a clear light on the deck. The sea is calm and the ship motionless.*

On the left two of the derrick booms of the foremast jut out at an angle of forty-five degrees, black against the sky. In the rear the dark outline of the port bulwark is sharply defined against a distant strip of coral beach, white in the moonlight, fringed with coco-palms whose tops rise clear of the horizon. On the right is the forecastle with an open doorway in the center leading to the seamen's and firemen's compartments. On either side of the doorway are two closed doors opening on the quarters of the bo'sun, the ship's carpenter, the messroom steward, and the donkeyman—what might be called the petty officers of the ship. Near each bulwark there is also a short stairway, like a section of fire escape, leading up to the forecastle head (the top of the forecastle)—the edge of which can be seen on the right.

In the center of the deck, and occupying most of the space, is the large, raised square of the number one hatch, covered with canvas, battened down for the night.

A melancholy negro chant, faint and far-off, drifts, crooning, over the water.

Most of the seamen and firemen are reclining or sitting on the hatch. PAUL *is leaning against the port bulwark, the upper part of his stocky figure outlined against the sky.* SMITTY *and*

COCKY *are sitting on the edge of the forecastle head with their legs dangling over. Nearly all are smoking pipes or cigarettes. The majority are dressed in patched suits of dungaree. Quite a few are in their bare feet and some of them, especially the firemen, have nothing on but a pair of pants and an under-shirt. A good many wear caps.*

There is the low murmur of different conversations going on in the separate groups as the curtain rises. This is followed by a sudden silence in which the singing from the land can be plainly heard.

DRISCOLL. (*a powerfully built Irishman who is sitting on the edge of the hatch, front—irritably*) Will ye listen to them naygurs? I wonder now, do they call that keenin' a song?

SMITTY. (*a young Englishman with a blond mustache. He is sitting on the forecastle head looking out over the water with his chin supported on his hands*) It doesn't make a chap feel very cheerful, does it? (*He sighs*)

COCKY. (*a wizened runt of a man with a straggling gray mustache—slapping* SMITTY *on the back*) Cheero, ole dear! Down't be ser dawhn in the marf, Duke. She loves yer.

SMITTY. (*gloomily*) Shut up, Cocky! (*He turns away from* COCKY *and falls to dreaming again, staring toward the spot on shore where the singing seems to come from*)

BIG FRANK. (*a huge fireman sprawled out on the right of the hatch—waving a hand toward the land*) They bury some-body—py chimminy Christmas, I tink so from way it sound.

YANK. (*a rather good-looking rough who is sitting beside* DRISCOLL) What d'yuh mean, bury? They don't plant 'em down here, Dutchy. They eat 'em to save fun'ral expenses. I guess this guy went down the wrong way an' they got indigestion.

COCKY. Indigestion! Ho yus, not 'arf! Down't yer know as them blokes 'as two stomacks like a bleedin' camel?

DAVIS. (*a short, dark man seated on the right of hatch*) An' you seen the two, I s'pect, ain't you?

COCKY. (*scornfully*) Down't be showin' yer igerance be tryin' to make a mock o' me what has seen more o' the world than yeself ever will.

MAX. (*a Swedish fireman—from the rear of hatch*) Spin dat yarn, Cocky.

COCKY. It's Gawd's troof, what I tole yer. I 'eard it from a bloke what was captured pris'ner by 'em in the Solomon Islands. Shipped wiv 'im one voyage. 'Twas a rare treat to 'ear 'im tell what 'appened to 'im among 'em. (*Musingly*) 'E was a funny bird, 'e was—'ailed from Mile End, 'e did.

DRISCOLL. (*with a snort*) Another lyin' cockney, the loike av yourself!

LAMPS. (*a fat Swede who is sitting on a camp stool in front of his door talking with* CHIPS) Where you meet up with him, Cocky?

CHIPS. (*a lanky Scotchman—derisively*) In New Guinea, I'll lay my oath!

COCKY. (*defiantly*) Yus! It *was* in New Guinea, time I was shipwrecked there. (*There is a perfect storm of groans and laughter at this speech*)

YANK. (*getting up*) Yuh know what we said yuh'd get if yuh sprung any of that lyin' New Guinea dope on us again, don't yuh? Close that trap if yuh don't want a duckin' over the side.

COCKY. Ow, I was on'y tryin' to edicate yer a bit. (*He sinks into dignified silence*)

YANK. (*nodding toward the shore*) Don't yuh know this is the West Indies, yuh crazy mut? There ain't no cannibals here. They're only common niggers.

DRISCOLL. (*irritably*) Whativir they are, the divil take their cryin'. It's enough to give a man the jigs listenin' to 'em.

YANK. (*with a grin*) What's the matter, Drisc? Yuh're as sore as a boil about somethin'.

DRISCOLL. I'm dyin' wid impatience to have a dhrink; an' that blarsted bumboat naygur woman took her oath she'd bring back rum enough for the lot av us whin she came back on board tonight.

BIG FRANK. (*overhearing this—in a loud eager voice*) You say the bumboat voman vill bring booze?

DRISCOLL. (*sarcastically*) That's right—tell the Old Man about ut, an' the Mate, too. (*All of the crew have edged nearer to* DRISCOLL *and are listening to the conversation with an air of suppressed excitement.* DRISCOLL *lowers his voice impressively and addresses them all*) She said she cud snake ut on board in the bottoms av thim baskets av fruit they're goin' to bring wid 'em to sell to us for'ard.

THE DONKEYMAN. (*an old gray-headed man with a kindly, wrinkled face. He is sitting on a camp stool in front of his door, right front*) She'll be bringin' some black women with her this time—or times has changed since I put in here last.

DRISCOLL. She said she wud—two or three—more, maybe, I dunno. (*This announcement is received with great enthusiasm by all hands*)

COCKY. What a bloody lark!

OLSON. Py yingo, we have one hell of a time!

DRISCOLL. (*warningly*) Remimber ye must be quiet about ut, ye scuts—wid the dhrink, I mane—ivin if the bo'sun is ashore. The Old Man ordered her to bring no booze on board or he wudn't buy a thing off av her for the ship.

PADDY. (*a squat, ugly Liverpool Irishman*) To the divil wid him!

BIG FRANK. (*turning on him*) Shud up, you tamn fool, Paddy! You vant make trouble? (*To* DRISCOLL) You und me, ve keep dem quiet, Drisc.

DRISCOLL. Right ye are, Dutchy. I'll split the skull av the first wan av ye starts to foight. (*Three bells are heard striking*)

DAVIS. Three bells. When's she comin', Drisc?

DRISCOLL. She'll be here any minute now, surely. (*To* PAUL, *who has returned to his position by the bulwark after hearing* DRISCOLL'*s news*) D'you see 'em comin', Paul?

PAUL. I don't see anyting like bumboat. (*They all set themselves to wait, lighting pipes, cigarettes, and making themselves comfortable. There is a silence broken only by the mournful singing of the negroes on shore*)

SMITTY. (*slowly—with a trace of melancholy*) I wish they'd stop that song. It makes you think of—well—things you ought to forget. Rummy go, what?

COCKY. (*slapping him on the back*) Cheero, ole love! We'll be 'avin our rum in arf a mo', Duke. (*He comes down to the deck, leaving* SMITTY *alone on the forecastle head*)

BIG FRANK. Sing someting, Drisc. Den ve don't hear dot yelling.

DAVIS. Give us a chanty, Drisc.

PADDY. Wan all av us knows.

MAX. We all sing in on chorus.

OLSON. "Rio Grande," Drisc.

BIG FRANK. No, ve don't know dot. Sing "Viskey Johnny."

CHIPS. "Flyin' Cloud."

COCKY. Now! Guv us "Maid o' Amsterdam."

LAMPS. "Santa Anna" iss a good one.

DRISCOLL. Shut your mouths, all av you. (*Scornfully*) A chanty is ut ye want? I'll bet me whole pay day there's not wan in the crowd 'ceptin' Yank here, an' Ollie, an' meself, an' Lamps an' Cocky, maybe, wud be sailors enough to know the main from the mizzen on a windjammer. Ye've heard the names of chanties but divil a note av the tune or a loine av the words do ye know. There's hardly a rale deep-water sailor lift on the seas, more's the pity.

YANK. Give us "Blow The Man Down." We all know some of that. (*A chorus of assenting voices*) Yes!—Righto!—Let 'er drive! Start 'er, Drisc! (*etc.*)

DRISCOLL. Come in then, all av ye. (*He sings*) As I was a-roamin' down Paradise Street——

ALL. Wa-a-ay, blow the man down!

DRISCOLL. As I was a-roamin' down Paradise Street——

ALL. Give us some time to blow the man down!

CHORUS

Blow the man down, boys, oh, blow the man down!
Wa-a-ay, blow the man down!
As I was a-roamin' down Paradise Street—
Give us some time to blow the man down!

DRISCOLL. A pretty young maiden I chanced for to meet.

ALL. Wa-a-ay, blow the man down!

DRISCOLL. A pretty young maiden I chanced for to meet.

ALL. Give us some time to blow the man down!

CHORUS

Blow the man down, boys, oh, blow the man down!
Wa-a-ay, blow the man down!
A pretty young maiden I chanced for to meet.
Give us some time to blow the man down!

PAUL. (*just as* DRISCOLL *is clearing his throat preparatory to starting the next verse*) Hay, Drisc! Here she come, I tink. Some bumboat comin' dis way. (*They all rush to the side and look toward the land*)

YANK. There's five or six of them in it—and they paddle like skirts.

DRISCOLL. (*wildly elated*) Hurroo, ye scuts! 'Tis thim right enough. (*He does a few jig steps on the deck*)

OLSON. (*after a pause during which all are watching the approaching boat*) Py yingo, I see six in boat, yes, sir.

DAVIS. I kin make out the baskets. See 'em there amidships.

BIG FRANK. Vot kind booze dey bring—viskey?

DRISCOLL. Rum, foine West Indy rum wid a kick in ut loike a mule's hoind leg.

LAMPS. Maybe she don't bring any; maybe skipper scare her.

DRISCOLL. Don't be throwin' cold water, Lamps. I'll skin her black hoide off av her if she goes back on her worrd.

YANK. Here they come. Listen to 'em gigglin'. (*Calling*) Oh, you kiddo! (*The sound of women's voices can be heard talking and laughing*)

DRISCOLL. (*calling*) Is ut you, Mrs. Old Black Joe?

A WOMAN'S VOICE. 'Ullo, Mike! (*There is loud feminine laughter at this retort*)

DRISCOLL. Shake a leg an' come abord thin.

THE WOMAN'S VOICE. We're a-comin'.

DRISCOLL. Come on, Yank. You an' me'd best be goin' to give 'em a hand wid their truck. 'Twill put 'em in good spirits.

COCKY. (*as they start off left*) Ho, you ain't 'arf a fox, Drisc. Down't drink it all afore we sees it.

DRISCOLL. (*over his shoulder*) You'll be havin' yours, me sonny bye, don't fret. (*He and* YANK *go off left*)

COCKY. (*licking his lips*) Gawd blimey, I can do wiv a wet.

DAVIS. Me, too!

CHIPS. I'll bet there ain't none of us'll let any go to waste.

BIG FRANK. I could trink a whole barrel mineself, py chimminy Christmas!

COCKY. I 'opes all the gels ain't as bloomin ugly as 'er. Looked like a bloody organ-grinder's monkey, she did. Gawd, I couldn't put up wiv the likes of 'er!

PADDY. Ye'll be lucky if any of thim looks at ye, ye squint-eyed runt.

COCKY. (*angrily*) Ho, yus? You ain't no bleedin' beauty prize yeself, me man. A 'airy ape, I calls yer.

PADDY. (*walking toward him—truculently*) Whot's thot? Say ut again if ye dare.

COCKY. (*his hand on his sheath-knife—snarling*) 'Airy ape! That's wot I says! (PADDY *tries to reach him but the others keep them apart*)

BIG FRANK. (*pushing* PADDY *back*) Vot's the matter mit you, Paddy. Don't you hear vat Driscoll say—no fighting?

PADDY. (*grumblingly*) I don't take no back-talk from that deck-scrubbin' shrimp.

COCKY. Blarsted coal-puncher! (DRISCOLL *appears wearing a broad grin of satisfaction. The fight is immediately forgotten by the crowd, who gather around him with exclamations of eager curiosity.* How is it, Drisc? Any luck? Vot she bring, Drisc? Where's the gels? *etc.*)

DRISCOLL. (*with an apprehensive glance back at the bridge*) Not so loud, for the love av hivin! (*The clamor dies down*) Yis, she has ut wid her. She'll be here in a minute wid a pint bottle or two for each wan av ye—three shillin's a bottle. So don't be impashunt.

COCKY. (*indignantly*) Three bob! The bloody cow!

SMITTY. (*with an ironic smile*) Grand larceny, by God! (*They all turn and look up at him surprised to hear him speak*)

OLSON. Py yingo, we don't pay so much.

BIG FRANK. Tamn black tief!

PADDY. We'll take ut away from her and give her nothin'.

THE CROWD. (*growling*) Dirty thief! Dot's right! Give her nothin'! Not a bloomin' 'apenny! (*etc.*)

DRISCOLL. (*grinning*) Ye can take ut or lave ut, me sonny byes. (*He casts a glance in the direction of the bridge and then reaches inside his shirt and pulls out a pint bottle*) 'Tis foine rum, the rale stuff. (*He drinks*) I slipped this wan out av wan of the baskets whin they wasn't lookin'. (*He hands the bottle to* OLSON *who is nearest him*) Here ye are, Ollie. Take a small sup an' pass ut to the nixt. 'Tisn't much but 'twill serve to take the black taste out av your mouths if ye go aisy wid ut. An' there's buckets more av ut comin'. (*The *bottle passes from hand to hand, each man taking a sip and smacking his lips with a deep "Aa-ah" of satisfaction*)

DAVIS. Where's she now, Drisc?

DRISCOLL. Up havin' a worrd wid the skipper, makin' arrangements about the money, I s'pose.

DAVIS. An' where's the other gels?

DRISCOLL. Wid her. There's foive av thim she took aboard—two swate little slips av things, near as white as you an' me are, for that gray-whiskered auld fool, an' the mates—an' the engineers too, maybe. The rist of thim'll be comin' for'ard whin she comes.

COCKY. 'E ain't 'arf a funny ole bird, the skipper. Gawd blimey! 'Member when we sailed from 'ome 'ow 'e stands on the bridge lookin' like a bloody ole sky pilot? An' 'is missus dawhn on the bloomin' dock 'owlin' fit to kill 'erself? An' 'is kids 'owlin' an' wavin' their 'andkerchiefs? (*With great moral indignation*) An' 'ere 'e is makin' up to a bleedin' nigger! There's a captain for yer! Gawd blimey! Bloody crab, I calls 'im!

DRISCOLL. Shut up, ye insect! Sure, it's not you should be talkin', an' you wid a woman an' childer weepin' for ye in iviry divil's port in the wide worrld, if we can believe your own tale av ut.

COCKY. (*still indignant*) I ain't no bloomin' captain. I ain't. I ain't got no missus—reg'lar married, I means. I ain't——

BIG FRANK. (*putting a huge paw over* COCKY'S *mouth*) You aint' going talk so much, you hear? (COCKY *wriggles away from him*) Say, Drisc, how ve pay dis voman for booze? Ve ain't got no cash.

DRISCOLL. It's aisy enough. Each girl'll have a slip av

paper wid her an' whin you buy anythin' you write ut down and the price beside ut and sign your name. If ye can't write have some one who can do ut for ye. An' rimimber this: Whin ye buy a bottle av dhrink or (*with a wink*) somethin' else forbid, ye must write down tobaccy or fruit or somethin' the loike av that. Whin she laves the skipper'll pay what's owin' on the paper an' take ut out av your pay. Is ut clear to ye now?

ALL. Yes—Clear as day—Aw right, Drisc—Righto—Sure (*etc.*)

DRISCOLL. An' don't forgit what I said about bein' quiet wid the dhrink, or the Mate'll be down on our necks an' spile the fun. (*A chorus of assent*)

DAVIS. (*looking aft*) Ain't this them comin'? (*They all look in that direction. The silly laughter of a woman is heard*)

DRISCOLL. Look at Yank, wud ye, wid his arrm around the middle av wan av thim. That lad's not wastin' any toime. (*The four women enter from the left, giggling and whispering to each other. The first three carry baskets on their heads. The youngest and best-looking comes last.* YANK *has his arm about her waist and is carrying her basket in his other hand. All four are distinct negro types. They wear light-colored, loose-fitting clothes and have bright bandana handkerchiefs on their heads. They put down their baskets on the hatch and sit down beside them. The men crowd around, grinning*)

BELLA. (*she is the oldest, stoutest, and homeliest of the four—grinning back at them*) 'Ullo, boys.

THE OTHER GIRLS. 'Ullo, boys.

THE MEN. Hello, yourself—Evenin'—Hello—How are you? (*etc.*)

BELLA. (*genially*) Hope you had a nice voyage. My name's Bella, this here's Susie, yander's Violet, and her there (*pointing to the girl with* YANK) is Pearl. Now we all knows each other.

PADDY. (*roughly*) Never mind the girls. Where's the dhrink?

BELLA. (*tartly*) You're a hawg, ain't you? Don't talk so loud or you don't git any—you nor no man. Think I wants the ole captain to put me off the ship, do you?

YANK. Yes, nix on hollerin', you! D'yuh wanta queer all of us?

BELLA. (*casting a quick glance over her shoulder*) Here! Some of you big strapping boys sit back of us on the hatch there so's them officers can't see what we're doin'. (DRISCOLL *and several of the others sit and stand in back of the girls on the hatch.* BELLA *turns to* DRISCOLL) Did you tell 'em they gotter sign for what they gits—and *how* to sign?

DRISCOLL. I did—what's your name again—oh, yis—Bella, darlin'.

BELLA. Then it's all right; but you boys has gotter go inside the fo'castle when you gits your bottle. No drinkin' out here on deck. I ain't takin' no chances. (*An impatient murmur of assent goes up from the crowd*) Ain't that right, Mike?

DRISCOLL. Right as rain, darlin'. (BIG FRANK *leans over and says something to him in a low voice.* DRISCOLL *laughs and slaps his thigh*) Listen, Bella, I've somethin' to ask ye for my little friend here who's bashful. Ut has to do wid the ladies so I'd best be whisperin' ut to ye meself to kape them from blushin'. (*He leans over and asks her a question*)

BELLA. (*firmly*) Four shillin's.

DRISCOLL. (*laughing*) D'you hear that, all av ye? Four shillin's ut is.

PADDY. (*angrily*) To hell wid this talkin'. I want a dhrink.

BELLA. Is everything all right, Mike?

DRISCOLL. (*after a look back at the bridge*) Sure. Let her droive!

BELLA. All right, girls. (*The girls reach down in their baskets in under the fruit which is on top and each pulls out a pint bottle. Four of the men crowd up and take the bottles*) Fetch a light, Lamps, that's a good boy. (LAMPS *goes to his room and returns with a candle. This is passed from one girl to another as the men sign the sheets of paper for their bottles*) Don't you boys forget to mark down cigarettes or tobacco or fruit, remember! Three shillin's is the price. Take it into the fo'castle. For Gawd's sake, don't stand out here drinkin' in the moonlight. (*The four go into the forecastle. Four more take their places.* PADDY *plants himself in front of* PEARL *who is sitting by* YANK *with his arm still around her*)

PADDY. (*gruffly*) Gimme thot! (*She holds out a bottle which he snatches from her hand. He turns to go away*)

YANK. (*sharply*) Here, you! Where d'yuh get that stuff? You ain't signed for that yet.

PADDY. (*sullenly*) I can't write me name.

YANK. Then I'll write it for yuh. (*He takes the paper from* PEARL *and writes*) There ain't goin' to be no welchin' on little Bright Eyes here—not when I'm around, see? Ain't I right, kiddo?

PEARL. (*with a grin*) Yes, suh.

BELLA. (*seeing all four are served*) Take it into the

fo'castle, boys. (PADDY *defiantly raises his bottle and gulps down a drink in the full moonlight.* BELLA *sees him*) Look at 'im! Look at the dirty swine! (PADDY *slouches into the forecastle*) Wants to git me in trouble. That settles it! We all got to git inside, boys, where we won't git caught. Come on, girls. (*The girls pick up their baskets and follow* BELLA. YANK *and* PEARL *are the last to reach the doorway. She lingers behind him, her eyes fixed on* SMITTY, *who is still sitting on the forecastle head, his chin on his hands, staring off into vacancy*)

PEARL. (*waving a hand to attract his attention*) Come ahn in, pretty boy. Ah likes you.

SMITTY. (*coldly*) Yes; I want to buy a bottle, please. (*He goes down the steps and follows her into the forecastle. No one remains on deck but* THE DONKEYMAN, *who sits smoking his pipe in front of his door. There is the subdued babble of voices from the crowd inside but the mournful cadence of the song from the shore can again be faintly heard.* SMITTY *reappears and closes the door to the forecastle after him. He shudders and shakes his shoulders as if flinging off something which disgusted him. Then he lifts the bottle which is in his hand to his lips and gulps down a long drink.* THE DONKEYMAN *watches him impassively.* SMITTY *sits down on the hatch facing him. Now that the closed door has shut off nearly all the noise, the singing from shore comes clearly over the moonlit water*)

SMITTY. (*listening to it for a moment*) Damn that song of theirs. (*He takes another big drink*) What do you say, Donk?

THE DONKEYMAN. (*quietly*) Seems nice an' sleepy-like.

SMITTY. (*with a hard laugh*) Sleepy! If I listened to it long—sober—I'd never go to sleep.

THE DONKEYMAN. 'Tain't sich bad music, is it? Sounds

kinder pretty to me—low an' mournful—same as listenin' to the organ outside o' church of a Sunday.

SMITTY. (*with a touch of impatience*) I didn't mean it was bad music. It isn't. It's the beastly memories the damn thing brings up—for some reason. (*He takes another pull at the bottle*)

THE DONKEYMAN. Ever hear it before?

SMITTY. No; never in my life. It's just a something about the rotten thing which makes me think—of—well, oh, the devil! (*He forces a laugh*)

THE DONKEYMAN. (*spitting placidly*) Queer things, mem'ries. I ain't ever been bothered much by 'em.

SMITTY. (*looking at him fixedly for a moment—with quiet scorn*) No, you wouldn't be.

THE DONKEYMAN. Not that I ain't had my share o' things goin' wrong; but I puts 'em out o' me mind, like, an' fergets 'em.

SMITTY. But suppose you couldn't put them out of your mind? Suppose they haunted you when you were awake and when you were asleep—what then?

THE DONKEYMAN. (*quietly*) I'd git drunk, same's you're doin'.

SMITTY. (*with a harsh laugh*) Good advice. (*He takes another drink. He is beginning to show the effects of the liquor. His face is flushed and he talks rather wildly*) We're poor little lambs who have lost our way, eh, Donk? Damned from here to eternity, what? God have mercy on such as we! True, isn't it, Donk?

THE DONKEYMAN. Maybe; I dunno. (*After a slight pause*) What ever set you goin' to sea? You ain't made for it.

SMITTY. (*laughing wildly*) My old friend in the bottle here, Donk.

THE DONKEYMAN. I done my share o' drinkin' in my time. (*Regretfully*) Them was good times, those days. Can't hold up under drink no more. Doctor told me I'd got to stop or die. (*He spits contentedly*) So I stops.

SMITTY. (*with a foolish smile*) Then I'll drink one for you. Here's your health, old top! (*He drinks*)

THE DONKEYMAN. (*after a pause*) S'pose there's a gel mixed up in it some place, ain't there?

SMITTY. (*stiffly*) What makes you think so?

THE DONKEYMAN. Always is when a man lets music bother 'im. (*After a few puffs at his pipe*) An' she said she threw you over 'cause you was drunk; an' you said you was drunk 'cause she threw you over. (*He spits leisurely*) Queer thing, love, ain't it?

SMITTY. (*rising to his feet with drunken dignity*) I'll trouble you not to pry into my affairs, Donkeyman.

THE DONKEYMAN. (*unmoved*) That's everybody's affair, what I said. I been through it many's the time. (*Genially*) I always hit 'em a whack on the ear an' went out and got drunker'n ever. When I come home again they always had somethin' special nice cooked fur me to eat. (*Puffing at his pipe*) That's the on'y way to fix 'em when they gits on their high horse. I don't s'pose you ever tried that?

SMITTY. (*pompously*) Gentlemen don't hit women.

THE DONKEYMAN. (*placidly*) No; that's why they has mem'ries when they hears music. (SMITTY *does not deign to reply to this but sinks into a scornful silence.* DAVIS *and the girl* VIOLET *come out of the forecastle and close the door behind them. He is staggering a bit and she is laughing shrilly*).

DAVIS. (*turning to the left*) This way, Rose, or Pansy, or Jessamine, or black Tulip, or Violet, or whatever the hell flower your name is. No one'll see us back here. (*They go off left*)

THE DONKEYMAN. There's love at first sight for you—an' plenty more o' the same in the fo'c's'tle. No mem'ries jined with that.

SMITTY. (*really repelled*) Shut up, Donk. You're disgusting. (*He takes a long drink*)

THE DONKEYMAN. (*philosophically*) All depends on how you was brung up, I s'pose. (PEARL *comes out of the forecastle. There is a roar of voices from inside. She shuts the door behind her, sees* SMITTY *on the hatch, and comes over and sits beside him and puts her arm over his shoulder*)

THE DONKEYMAN. (*chuckling*) There's love for you, Duke.

PEARL. (*patting* SMITTY's *face with her hand*) 'Ullo, pretty boy. (SMITTY *pushes her hand away coldly*) What you doin' out here all alone by yourself?

SMITTY. (*with a twisted grin*) Thinking and—(*he indicates the bottle in his hand*)—drinking to stop thinking. (*He drinks and laughs maudlinly. The bottle is three-quarters empty*)

PEARL. You oughtn't drink so much, pretty boy. Don't you know that? You have big, big headache come mawnin'.

SMITTY. (*dryly*) Indeed?

PEARL. That's true. Ah knows what Ah say. (*Cooingly*) Why you run 'way from me, pretty boy? Ah likes you. Ah don' like them other fellahs. They act too rough. You ain't rough. You're a genelman. Ah knows. Ah can tell a genelman fahs Ah can see 'im.

SMITTY. Thank you for the compliment; but you're wrong, you see. I'm merely—a ranker. (*He adds bitterly*) And a rotter.

PEARL. (*patting his arm*) No, you ain't. Ah knows better. You're a genelman. (*Insinuatingly*) Ah wouldn't have nothin' to do with them other men, but (*she smiles at him enticingly*) you is diff'rent. (*He pushes her away from him disgustedly. She pouts*) Don' you like me, pretty boy?

SMITTY. (*a bit ashamed*) I beg your pardon. I didn't mean to be rude, you know, really. (*His politeness is drunkenly exaggerated*) I'm a bit off color.

PEARL. (*brightening up*) Den you do like me—little ways?

SMITTY. (*carelessly*) Yes, yes, why shouldn't I? (*He suddenly laughs wildly and puts his arm around her waist and presses her to him*) Why not? (*He pulls his arm back quickly with a shudder of disgust, and takes a drink.* PEARL *looks at him curiously, puzzled by his strange actions. The door from the forecastle is kicked open and* YANK *comes out. The uproar of shouting, laughing and singing voices has increased in violence.* YANK *staggers over toward* SMITTY *and* PEARL)

YANK. (*blinking at them*) What the hell—oh, it's you, Smitty the Duke. I was goin' to turn one loose on the jaw of any guy'd cop my dame, but seein' it's you—— (*Sentimentally*) Pals is pals and any pal of mine c'n have anythin' I got, see? (*Holding out his hand*) Shake, Duke. (SMITTY *takes his hand and he pumps it up and down*) You'n me's frens. Ain't I right?

SMITTY. Right it is, Yank. But you're wrong about this girl. She isn't with me. She was just going back to the fo'c's'tle to you. (PEARL *looks at him with hatred gathering in her eyes*)

YANK. Tha' right?

SMITTY. On my word!

YANK. (*grabbing her arm*) Come on then, you, Pearl! Le's have a drink with the bunch. (*He pulls her to the entrance where she shakes off his hand long enough to turn on* SMITTY *furiously*)

PEARL. You swine! You can go to hell! (*She goes into the forecastle, slamming the door*)

THE DONKEYMAN. (*spitting calmly*) There's love for you. They're all the same—white, brown, yeller 'n' black. A whack on the ear's the only thing'll learn 'em. (SMITTY *makes no reply but laughs harshly and takes another drink; then sits staring before him, the almost empty bottle tightly clutched in one hand. There is an increase in volume of the muffled clamor from the forecastle and a moment later the door is thrown open and the whole mob, led by Driscoll, pours out on deck. All of them are very drunk and several of them carry bottles in their hands.* BELLA *is the only one of the women who is absolutely sober. She tries in vain to keep the men quiet.* PEARL *drinks from* YANK'S *bottle every moment or so, laughing shrilly, and leaning against* YANK, *whose arm is about her waist.* PAUL *comes out last carrying an accordion. He staggers over and stands on top of the hatch, his instrument under his arm*)

DRISCOLL. Play us a dance, ye square-head swab!—a rale, God-forsaken son av a turkey trot wid guts to ut.

YANK. Straight from the old Barbary Coast in Frisco!

PAUL. I don't know. I try. (*He commences tuning up*)

YANK. Ataboy! Let 'er rip! (DAVIS *and* VIOLET *come back and join the crowd.* THE DONKEYMAN *looks on them all with a detached, indulgent air.* SMITTY *stares before him and does not seem to know there is anyone on deck but himself*)

BIG FRANK. Dance? I don't dance. I trink! (*He suits the action to the word and roars with meaningless laughter*)

DRISCOLL. Git out av the way thin, ye big hulk, an' give us some room. (BIG FRANK *sits down on the hatch, right. All of the others who are not going to dance either follow his example or lean against the port bulwark*)

BELLA. (*on the verge of tears at her inability to keep them in the forecastle or make them be quiet now they are out*) For Gawd's sake, boys, don't shout so loud! Want to git me in trouble?

DRISCOLL. (*grabbing her*) Dance wid me, me cannibal quane. (*Someone drops a bottle on deck and it smashes*)

BELLA. (*hysterically*) There they goes! There they goes! Captain'll hear that! Oh, my Lawd!

DRISCOLL. Be damned to him! Here's the music! Off ye go! (PAUL *starts playing "You Great Big Beautiful Doll" with a note left out every now and then. The four couples commence dancing—a jerk-shouldered version of the old Turkey Trot as it was done in the sailor-town dives, made more grotesque by the fact that all the couples are drunk and keep lurching into each other every moment. Two of the men start dancing together, intentionally bumping into the others.* YANK *and* PEARL *come around in front of* SMITTY *and, as they pass him,* PEARL *slaps him across the side of the face with all her might, and laughs viciously. He jumps to his feet with his fists clenched but sees who hit him and sits down again smiling bitterly.* YANK *laughs boisterously*)

YANK. Wow! Some wallop! One on you, Duke.

DRISCOLL. (*hurling his cap at* PAUL) Faster, ye toad! (PAUL *makes frantic efforts to speed up and the music suffers in the process*)

BELLA. (*puffing*) Let me go. I'm wore out with you steppin' on my toes, you clumsy Mick. (*She struggles but* DRISCOLL *holds her tight*)

DRISCOLL. God blarst you for havin' such big feet, thin. Aisy, aisy, Mrs. Old Black Joe! 'Tis dancin'll take the blubber off ye. (*He whirls her around the deck by main force.* COCKY, *with* SUSIE, *is dancing near the hatch, right, when* PADDY, *who is sitting on the edge with* BIG FRANK, *sticks his foot out and the wavering couple stumble over it and fall flat on the deck. A roar of laughter goes up.* COCKY *rises to his feet, his face livid with rage, and springs at* PADDY, *who promptly knocks him down.* DRISCOLL *hits* PADDY *and* BIG FRANK *hits* DRISCOLL. *In a flash a wholesale fight has broken out and the deck is a surging crowd of drink-maddened men hitting out at each other indiscriminately, although the general idea seems to be a battle between seamen and firemen. The women shriek and take refuge on top of the hatch, where they huddle in a frightened group. Finally there is the flash of a knife held high in the moonlight and a loud yell of pain*)

DAVIS. (*somewhere in the crowd*) Here's the Mate comin'! Let's git out o' this! (*There is a general rush for the forecastle. In a moment there is no one left on deck but the little group of women on the hatch;* SMITTY, *still dazedly rubbing his cheek;* THE DONKEYMAN *quietly smoking on his stool; and* YANK *and* DRISCOLL, *their faces battered up considerably, their undershirts in shreds, bending over the still form of* PADDY, *which lies stretched out on the deck between them. In the silence the mournful chant from the shore creeps slowly out to the ship*)

DRISCOLL. (*quickly—in a low voice*) Who knoifed him?

YANK. (*stupidly*) I didn't see it. How do I know? Cocky, I'll bet. (*The* FIRST MATE *enters from the left. He is a tall, strongly-built man dressed in a plain blue uniform*)

THE MATE. (*angrily*) What's all this noise about? (*He sees the man lying on the deck*) Hello! What's this? (*He bends down on one knee beside* PADDY)

DRISCOLL. (*stammering*) All av us—was in a bit av a harmless foight, sir—an'—I dunno—— (*The* MATE *rolls* PADDY *over and sees a knife wound on his shoulder*)

THE MATE. Knifed, by God. (*He takes an electric flash from his pocket and examines the cut*) Lucky it's only a flesh wound. He must have hit his head on deck when he fell. That's what knocked him out. This is only a scratch. Take him aft and I'll bandage him up.

DRISCOLL. Yis, sor. (*They take* PADDY *by the shoulders and feet and carry him off left. The* MATE *looks up and sees the women on the hatch for the first time*)

THE MATE. (*surprised*) Hello! (*He walks over to them*) Go to the cabin and get your money and clear off. If I had my way, you'd never—— (*His foot hits a bottle. He stoops down and picks it up and smells of it*) Rum, by God! So that's the trouble! I thought their breaths smelled damn queer. (*To the women, harshly*) You needn't go to the skipper for any money. You won't get any. That'll teach you to smuggle rum on a ship and start a riot.

BELLA. But, Mister——

THE MATE. (*sternly*) You know the agreement—rum—no money.

BELLA. (*indignantly*) Honest to Gawd, Mister, I never brung no——

THE MATE (*fiercely*) You're a liar! And none of your lip or I'll make a complaint ashore tomorrow and have you locked up.

BELLA. (*subdued*) Please, Mister——

THE MATE. Clear out of this, now! Not another word out of you! Tumble over the side damn quick! The others are waiting for you. Hop, now! (*They walk quickly—almost run—off to the left.* THE MATE *follows them, nodding to* THE DONKEYMAN, *and ignoring the oblivious* SMITTY. *There is absolute silence on the ship for a few moments. The melancholy song of the negroes drifts crooning over the water.* SMITTY *listens to it intently for a time; then sighs heavily, a sigh that is half a sob*)

SMITTY. God! (*He drinks the last drop in the bottle and throws it behind him on the hatch*)

THE DONKEYMAN. (*spitting tranquilly*) More mem'ries? (SMITTY *does not answer him. The ship's bell tolls four bells.* THE DONKEYMAN *knocks out his pipe*) I think I'll turn in. (*He opens the door to his cabin, but turns to look at* SMITTY*—kindly*) You can't hear it in the fo'c's'tle—the music, I mean—an' there'll likely be more drink in there, too. Good-night. (*He goes in and shuts the door*)

SMITTY. Good-night, Donk. (*He gets wearily to his feet*

and walks with bowed shoulders, staggering a bit, to the forecastle entrance and goes in. There is silence for a second or so, broken only by the haunted, saddened voice of that brooding music, faint and far-off, like the mood of the moonlight made audible)

(*The Curtain Falls*)

BOUND EAST FOR CARDIFF

A Play in One Act

CHARACTERS

YANK
DRISCOLL
COCKY
DAVIS
SCOTTY
OLSON
PAUL
SMITTY
IVAN
THE CAPTAIN
THE SECOND MATE

BOUND EAST FOR CARDIFF

SCENE. *The seamen's forecastle of the British tramp steamer* Glencairn *on a foggy night midway on the voyage between New York and Cardiff. An irregular-shaped compartment, the sides of which almost meet at the far end to form a triangle. Sleeping bunks about six feet long, ranged three deep with a space of three feet separating the upper from the lower, are built against the sides. On the right above the bunks three or four port-holes can be seen. In front of the bunks, rough wooden benches. Over the bunks on the left, a lamp in a bracket. In the left foreground, a doorway. On the floor near it, a pail with a tin dipper. Oilskins are hanging from a hook near the doorway.*

The far side of the forecastle is so narrow that it contains only one series of bunks.

In under the bunks a glimpse can be had of sea-chests, suit-cases, sea-boots, etc., jammed in indiscriminately.

At regular intervals of a minute or so the blast of the steamer's whistle can be heard above all the other sounds.

Five men are sitting on the benches talking. They are dressed in dirty patched suits of dungaree, flannel shirts, and all are in their stocking feet. Four of the men are pulling on pipes and the air is heavy with rancid tobacco smoke. Sitting on the top bunk in the left foreground, a Norwegian, PAUL, *is softly playing some folk-song on a battered accordion. He stops from time to time to listen to the conversation.*

In the lower bunk in the rear a dark-haired, hard-featured man is lying apparently asleep. One of his arms is stretched limply over the side of the bunk. His face is very pale, and drops of clammy perspiration glisten on his forehead.

It is nearing the end of the dog-watch—about ten minutes to eight in the evening.

COCKY. (*a weazened runt of a man. He is telling a story. The others are listening with amused, incredulous faces, interrupting him at the end of each sentence with loud derisive guffaws*) Makin' love to me, she was! It's Gawd's truth! A bloomin' nigger! Greased all over with cocoanut oil, she was. Gawd blimey, I couldn't stand 'er. Bloody old cow, I says; and with that I fetched 'er a biff on the ear wot knocked 'er silly, an'—— (*He is interrupted by a roar of laughter from the others*)

DAVIS. (*a middle-aged man with black hair and mustache*) You're a liar, Cocky.

SCOTTY. (*a dark young fellow*) Ho-ho! Ye werr neverr in New Guinea in yourr life, I'm thinkin'.

OLSON. (*a Swede with a drooping blond mustache—with ponderous sarcasm*) Yust tink of it! You say she wass a cannibal, Cocky?

DRISCOLL. (*a brawny Irishman with the battered features of a prize-fighter*) How cud ye doubt ut, Ollie? A quane av the naygurs she musta been surely. Who else wud think herself aqual to fallin' in love wid a beauthiful, divil-may-care rake av a man the loike av Cocky? (*A burst of laughter from the crowd*)

COCKY. (*indignantly*) Gawd strike me dead if it ain't true, every bleedin' word of it. 'Appened ten year ago come Christmas.

SCOTTY. 'Twas a Christmas dinner she had her eyes on.

DAVIS. He'd a been a tough old bird.

DRISCOLL. 'Tis lucky for both av ye ye escaped; for the quane av the cannibal isles wad a died av the bellyache the day afther Christmas, divil a doubt av ut. (*The laughter at this is long and loud*)

COCKY. (*sullenly*) Blarsted fat-'eads! (*The sick man in the lower bunk in the rear groans and moves restlessly. There is a hushed silence. All the men turn and stare at him*)

DRISCOLL. Ssshh! (*In a hushed whisper*) We'd best not be talkin' so loud and him tryin' to have a bit av a sleep. (*He tiptoes softly to the side of the bunk*) Yank! You'd be wantin' a drink av wather, maybe? (YANK *does not reply.* DRISCOLL *bends over and looks at him*) It's asleep he is, sure enough. His breath is chokin' in his throat loike wather gurglin' in a poipe. (*He comes back quietly and sits down. All are silent, avoiding each other's eyes*)

COCKY. (*after a pause*) Pore devil! It's over the side for 'im, Gawd 'elp 'im.

DRISCOLL. Stop your croakin'! He's not dead yet and, praise God, he'll have many a long day yet before him.

SCOTTY. (*shaking his head doubtfully*) He's bod, mon, he's verry bod.

DAVIS. Lucky he's alive. Many a man's light woulda gone out after a fall like that.

OLSON. You saw him fall?

DAVIS. Right next to him. He and me was goin' down in number two hold to do some chippin'. He puts his leg over careless-like and misses the ladder and plumps straight down to the bottom. I was scared to look over for a minute, and then I heard him groan and I scuttled down after him. He was hurt bad inside, for the blood was drippin' from the side of his mouth. He was groanin' hard, but he never let a word out of him.

COCKY. An' you blokes remember when we 'auled 'im in 'ere? Oh, 'ell, 'e says, oh, 'ell—like that, and nothink else.

OLSON. Did the captain know where he iss hurted?

COCKY. That silly ol' josser! Wot the 'ell would 'e know abaht anythink?

SCOTTY. (*scornfully*) He fiddles in his mouth wi' a bit of glass.

DRISCOLL. (*angrily*) The divil's own life ut is to be out on the lonely sea wid nothin' betune you and a grave in the ocean but a spindle-shanked, gray-whiskered auld fool the loike av him. 'Twas enough to make a saint shwear to see him wid his gold watch in his hand, tryin' to look as wise as an owl on a tree, and all the toime he not knowin' whether 'twas cholery or the barber's itch was the matther with Yank.

SCOTTY. (*sardonically*) He gave him a dose of salts, na doot?

DRISCOLL. Divil a thing he gave him at all, but looked in the book he had wid him, and shook his head, and walked out widout sayin' a word, the second mate afther him no wiser than himself, God's curse on the two av thim!

COCKY. (*after a pause*) Yank was a good shipmate, pore beggar. Lend me four bob in Noo Yark, 'e did.

DRISCOLL. (*warmly*) A good shipmate he was and is, none betther. Ye said no more than the truth, Cocky. Five years and more ut is since first I shipped wid him, and we've stuck together iver since through good luck and bad. Fights we've had, God help us, but 'twas only when we'd a bit av drink taken, and we always shook hands the nixt mornin'. Whativer was his was mine, and many's the toime I'd a been on the beach or worse, but for him. And now—— (*His voice trembles as he fights to control his emotion*) Divil take me if I'm not startin' to blubber loike an auld woman, and he not dead at all, but goin' to live many a long year yet, maybe.

DAVIS. The sleep'll do him good. He seems better now.

OLSON. If he wude eat something——

DRISCOLL. Wud ye have him be eatin' in his condishun? Sure it's hard enough on the rest av us wid nothin' the matther wid our insides to be stomachin' the skoff on this rusty lime-juicer.

SCOTTY. (*indignantly*) It's a starvation ship.

DAVIS. Plenty o' work and no food—and the owners ridin' around in carriages!

OLSON. Hash, hash! Stew, stew! Marmalade, py damn! (*He spits disgustedly*)

COCKY. Bloody swill! Fit only for swine is wot I say.

DRISCOLL. And the dish-wather they disguise wid the name av tea! And the putty they call bread! My belly feels loike I'd swalleyed a dozen rivets at the thought av ut! And sea-biscuit that'd break the teeth av a lion if he had the misfortune to take a bite at one! (*Unconsciously they have all raised their voices, forgetting the sick man in their sailor's delight at finding something to grumble about*).

PAUL. (*swings his feet over the side of his bunk, stops play-*

ing his accordion, and says slowly) And rot-ten po-tay-toes! *(He starts in playing again. The sick man gives a groan of pain)*

DRISCOLL. *(holding up his hand)* Shut your mouths, all av you. 'Tis a hell av a thing for us to be complainin' about our guts, and a sick man maybe dyin' listenin' to us. *(Gets up and shakes his fist at the Norwegian)* God stiffen you, ye square-head scut! Put down that organ av yours or I'll break your ugly face for you. Is that banshee schreechin' fit music for a sick man? *(The Norwegian puts his accordion in the bunk and lies back and closes his eyes.* DRISCOLL *goes over and stands beside* YANK. *The steamer's whistle sounds particularly loud in the silence)*

DAVIS. Damn this fog! *(Reaches in under a bunk and yanks out a pair of sea-boots, which he pulls on)* My lookout next, too. Must be nearly eight bells, boys. *(With the exception of* OLSON, *all the men sitting up put on oilskins, sou'westers, sea-boots, etc., in preparation for the watch on deck.* OLSON *crawls into a lower bunk on the right)*

SCOTTY. My wheel.

OLSON. *(disgustedly)* Nothin' but yust dirty weather all dis voyage. I yust can't sleep when weestle blow. *(He turns his back to the light and is soon fast asleep and snoring)*

SCOTTY. If this fog keeps up, I'm tellin' ye, we'll no be in Cardiff for a week or more.

DRISCOLL. 'Twas just such a night as this the auld Dover wint down. Just about this toime ut was, too, and we all sittin' round in the fo'castle, Yank beside me, whin all av a suddint we heard a great slitherin' crash, and the ship heeled over till we was all in a heap on wan side. What came afther I disremimber exactly, except 'twas a hard shift to get the boats over the side before the auld teakittle sank. Yank was in the same boat wid me, and sivin morthal days we drifted wid scarcely a drop of wather or a bite to chew on. 'Twas Yank here that held me down whin I wanted to jump into the ocean, roarin' mad wid the thirst. Picked up we were on the same day wid only Yank in his senses, and him steerin' the boat.

COCKY. (*protestingly*) Blimey but you're a cheerful blighter, Driscoll! Talkin' abaht shipwrecks in this 'ere blushin' fog. (YANK *groans and stirs uneasily, opening his eyes.* DRISCOLL *hurries to his side*)

DRISCOLL. Are ye feelin' any betther, Yank?

YANK. (*in a weak voice*) No.

DRISCOLL. Sure, you must be. You look as sthrong as an ox. (*Appealing to the others*) Am I tellin' him a lie?

DAVIS. The sleep's done you good.

COCKY. You'll be 'avin your pint of beer in Cardiff this day week.

SCOTTY. And fish and chips, mon!

YANK. (*peevishly*) What're yuh all lyin' fur? D'yuh think I'm scared to—— (*He hesitates as if frightened by the word he is about to say*)

DRISCOLL. Don't be thinkin' such things! (*The ship's bell is heard heavily tolling eight times. From the forecastle head above the voice of the lookout rises in a long wail:* Aaall's welll. *The men look uncertainly at* YANK *as if undecided whether to say good-by or not*)

YANK. (*in an agony of fear*) Don't leave me, Drisc! I'm dyin', I tell yuh. I won't stay here alone with everyone snorin'. I'll go out on deck. (*He makes a feeble attempt to rise, but sinks back with a sharp groan. His breath comes in wheezy *gasps*) Don't leave me, Drisc! (*His face grows white and his head falls back with a jerk*)

DRISCOLL. Don't be worryin', Yank. I'll not move a step out av here—and let that divil av a bosun curse his black head off. You speak a word to the bosun, Cocky. Tell him that Yank is bad took and I'll be stayin' wid him a while yet.

COCKY. Right-o. (COCKY, DAVIS, *and* SCOTTY *go out quietly*)

COCKY. (*from the alleyway*) Gawd blimey, the fog's thick as soup.

DRISCOLL. Are ye satisfied now, Yank? (*Receiving no answer, he bends over the still form*) He's fainted, God help him! (*He gets a tin dipper from the bucket and bathes* YANK'S *forehead with the water.* YANK *shudders and opens his eyes*)

YANK. (*slowly*) I thought I was goin' then. Wha' did yuh wanta wake me up fur?

DRISCOLL. (*with a forced gayety*) It is wishful for heaven ye are?

YANK. (*gloomily*) Hell, I guess.

DRISCOLL. (*crossing himself involuntarily*) For the love av the saints don't be talkin' loike that! You'd give a man the creeps. It's chippin' rust on deck you'll be in a day or two wid the best av us. (YANK *does not answer, but closes his eyes wearily. The seaman who has been on lookout,* SMITTY, *a young Englishman, comes in and takes off his dripping oilskins. While he is doing this the man whose turn at the wheel has been relieved enters. He is a dark burly fellow with a round stupid face. The Englishman steps softly over to* DRISCOLL. *The other crawls into a lower bunk*)

SMITTY. (*whispering*) How's Yank?

DRISCOLL. Betther. Ask him yourself. He's awake.

YANK. I'm all right, Smitty.

SMITTY. Glad to hear it, Yank. (*He crawls to an upper bunk and is soon asleep*)

IVAN. (*the stupid-faced seaman, who comes in after* SMITTY, *twists his head in the direction of the sick man*) You feel gude, Jank?

YANK. (*wearily*) Yes, Ivan.

IVAN. Dot's gude. (*He rolls over on his side and falls asleep immediately*)

YANK. (*after a pause broken only by snores—with a bitter laugh*) Good-by and good luck to the lot of you!

DRISCOLL. Is ut painin' you again?

YANK. It hurts like hell—here. (*He points to the lower part of his chest on the left side*) I guess my old pump's busted. Ooohh! (*A spasm of pain contracts his pale features. He presses his hand to his side and writhes on the thin mattress of his bunk. The perspiration stands out in beads on his forehead*)

DRISCOLL. (*terrified*) Yank! Yank! What is ut? (*Jumping to his feet*) I'll run for the captain. (*He starts for the doorway*)

YANK. (*sitting up in his bunk, frantic with fear*) Don't leave me, Drisc! For God's sake don't leave me alone! (*He leans over the side of his bunk and spits.* DRISCOLL *comes back to him*) Blood! Ugh!

DRISCOLL. Blood again! I'd best be gettin' the captain.

YANK. No, no, don't leave me! If yuh do I'll git up and follow you. I ain't no coward, but I'm scared to stay here with all of them asleep and snorin'. (DRISCOLL, *not knowing what to do, sits down on the bench beside him. He grows calmer and sinks back on the mattress)* The captain can't do me no good, yuh know it yourself. The pain ain't so bad now, but I thought it had me then. It was like a buzz-saw cuttin' into me.

DRISCOLL. *(fiercely)* God blarst ut!

(The CAPTAIN *and the* SECOND MATE *of the steamer enter the forecastle. The* CAPTAIN *is an old man with gray mustache and whiskers. The* MATE *is clean-shaven and middle-aged. Both are dressed in simple blue uniforms)*

THE CAPTAIN. *(taking out his watch and feeling* YANK'S *pulse)* And how is the sick man?

YANK. *(feebly)* All right, sir.

THE CAPTAIN. And the pain in the chest?

YANK. It still hurts, sir, worse than ever.

THE CAPTAIN. *(taking a thermometer from his pocket and putting it into* YANK'S *mouth)* Here. Be sure and keep this in under your tongue, not over it.

THE MATE. *(after a pause)* Isn't this your watch on deck, Driscoll?

DRISCOLL. Yes, sorr, but Yank was fearin' to be alone, and——

THE CAPTAIN. That's all right, Driscoll.

DRISCOLL. Thank ye, sorr.

THE CAPTAIN. *(stares at his watch for a moment or so; then takes the thermometer from* YANK'S *mouth and goes to the lamp to read it. His expression grows very grave. He beckons the* MATE *and* DRISCOLL *to the corner near the doorway.* YANK *watches them furtively. The* CAPTAIN *speaks in a low voice to the* MATE*)* Way up, both of them. *(To* DRISCOLL*)* He has been spitting blood again?

DRISCOLL. Not much for the hour just past, sorr, but before that——

THE CAPTAIN. A great deal?

DRISCOLL. Yes, sorr.

THE CAPTAIN. He hasn't eaten anything?

DRISCOLL. No, sorr.

THE CAPTAIN. Did he drink that medicine I sent him?

DRISCOLL. Yes, sorr, but it didn't stay down.

THE CAPTAIN. (*shaking his head*) I'm afraid—he's very weak. I can't do anything else for him. It's too serious for me. If this had only happened a week later we'd be in Cardiff in time to——

DRISCOLL. Plaze help him some way, sorr!

THE CAPTAIN. (*impatiently*) But, my good man, I'm not a doctor. (*More kindly as he sees* DRISCOLL'S *grief*) You and he have been shipmates a long time?

DRISCOLL. Five years and more, sorr.

THE CAPTAIN. I see. Well, don't let him move. Keep him quiet and we'll hope for the best. I'll read the matter up and send him some medicine, something to ease the pain, anyway. (*Goes over to* YANK) Keep up your courage! You'll be better tomorrow. (*He breaks down lamely before* YANK'S *steady gaze*) We'll pull you through all right—and—hm—well—coming, Robinson? Dammit! (*He goes out hurriedly, followed by the* MATE)

DRISCOLL. (*trying to conceal his anxiety*) Didn't I tell you you wasn't half as sick as you thought you was? The Captain'll have you out on deck cursin' and swearin' loike a trooper before the week is out.

YANK. Don't lie, Drisc. I heard what he said, and if I didn't

I c'd tell by the way I feel. I know what's goin' to happen. I'm goin' to—— (*He hesitates for a second—then resolutely*) I'm goin' to die, that's what, and the sooner the better!

DRISCOLL. (*wildly*) No, and be damned to you, you're not. I'll not let you.

YANK. It ain't no use, Drisc. I ain't got a chance, but I ain't scared. Gimme a drink of water, will yuh, Drisc? My throat's burnin' up. (DRISCOLL *brings the dipper full of water and supports his head while he drinks in great gulps*)

DRISCOLL. (*seeking vainly for some word of comfort*) Are ye feelin' more aisy-loike now?

YANK. Yes—now—when I know it's all up. (*A pause*) You mustn't take it so hard, Drisc. I was just thinkin' it ain't as bad as people think—dyin'. I ain't never took much stock in the truck them sky-pilots preach. I ain't never had religion; but I know whatever it is what comes after it can't be no worser'n this. I don't like to leave you, Drisc, but—that's all.

DRISCOLL. (*with a groan*) Lad, lad, don't be talkin'.

YANK. This sailor life ain't much to cry about leavin'—just one ship after another, hard work, small pay, and bum grub; and when we git into port, just a drunk endin' up in a fight, and all your money gone, and then ship away again. Never meetin' no nice people; never gittin' outa sailor-town, hardly, in any port; travelin' all over the world and never seein' none of it; without no one to care whether you're alive or dead. (*With a bitter smile*) There ain't much in all that that'd make yuh sorry to lose it, Drisc.

DRISCOLL. (*gloomily*) It's a hell av a life, the sea.

YANK. (*musingly*) It must be great to stay on dry land all your life and have a farm with a house of your own with cows and pigs and chickens, 'way in the middle of the land where yuh'd never smell the sea or see a ship. It must be great to have a wife, and kids to play with at night after supper when your work was done. It must be great to have a home of your own, Drisc.

DRISCOLL. (*with a great sigh*) It must, surely; but what's the use av thinkin' av ut? Such things are not for the loikes av us.

YANK. Sea-farin' is all right when you're young and don't care, but we ain't chickens no more, and somehow, I dunno, this last year has seemed rotten, and I've had a hunch I'd quit—with you, of course—and we'd save our coin, and go to Canada or Argentine or some place and git a farm, just a small one, just enough to live on. I never told yuh this, 'cause I thought you'd laugh at me.

DRISCOLL. (*enthusiastically*) Laugh at you, is ut? When I'm havin' the same thoughts myself, toime afther toime. It's a grand idea and we'll be doin' ut sure if you'll stop your crazy notions—about—about bein' so sick.

YANK. (*sadly*) Too late. We shouldn'ta made this trip, and then—— How'd all the fog git in here?

DRISCOLL. Fog?

YANK. Everything looks misty. Must be my eyes gittin' weak, I guess. What was we talkin' of a minute ago? Oh, yes, a farm. It's too late. (*His mind wandering*) Argentine, did I say? D'yuh remember the times we've had in Buenos Aires? The moving pictures in Barracas? Some class to them, d'yuh remember?

DRISCOLL. (*with satisfaction*) I do that; and so does the

piany player. He'll not be forgettin' the black eye I gave him in a hurry.

YANK. Remember the time we was there on the beach and had to go to Tommy Moore's boarding house to git shipped? And he sold us rotten oilskins and sea-boots full of holes, and shipped us on a skysail-yarder round the Horn, and took two months' pay for it. And the days we used to sit on the park benches along the Paseo Colon with the vigilantes lookin' hard at us? And the songs at the Sailor's Opera where the guy played ragtime—d'yuh remember them?

DRISCOLL. I do, surely.

YANK. And La Plata—phew, the stink of the hides! I always liked Argentine—all except that booze, caña. How drunk we used to git on that, remember?

DRISCOLL. Cud I forget ut? My head pains me at the menshun av that divil's brew.

YANK. Remember the night I went crazy with the heat in Singapore? And the time you was pinched by the cops in Port Said? And the time we was both locked up in Sydney for fightin'?

DRISCOLL. I do so.

YANK. And that fight on the dock at Cape Town—— (*His voice betrays great inward perturbation*)

DRISCOLL. (*hastily*) Don't be thinkin' av that now. 'Tis past and gone.

YANK. D'yuh think He'll hold it up against me?

DRISCOLL. (*mystified*) Who's that?

YANK. God. They say He sees everything. He must know it was done in fair fight, in self-defense, don't yuh think?

DRISCOLL. Av course. Ye stabbed him, and be damned to

him, for the skulkin' swine he was, afther him tryin' to stick you in the back, and you not suspectin'. Let your conscience be aisy. I wisht I had nothin' blacker than that on my sowl. I'd not be afraid av the angel Gabriel himself.

YANK. (*with a shudder*) I c'd see him a minute ago with the blood spurtin' out of his neck. Ugh!

DRISCOLL. The fever, ut is, that makes you see such things. Give no heed to ut.

YANK. (*uncertainly*) You don't think He'll hold it up agin me—God, I mean.

DRISCOLL. If there's justice in hiven, no! (YANK *seems comforted by this assurance*)

YANK. (*after a pause*) We won't reach Cardiff for a week at least. I'll be buried at sea.

DRISCOLL. (*putting his hands over his ears*) Ssshh! I won't listen to you.

YANK. (*as if he had not heard him*) It's as good a place as any other, I s'pose—only I always wanted to be buried on dry land. But what the hell'll I care—then? (*Fretfully*) Why should it be a rotten night like this with that damned whistle blowin' and people snorin' all round? I wish the stars was out, and the moon, too; I c'd lie out on deck and look at them, and it'd make it easier to go—somehow.

DRISCOLL. For the love av God don't be talkin' loike that!

YANK. Whatever pay's comin' to me yuh can divvy up with the rest of the boys; and you take my watch. It ain't worth much, but it's all I've got.

DRISCOLL. But have you no relations at all to call your own?

YANK. No, not as I know of. One thing I forgot: You know Fanny the barmaid at the Red Stork in Cardiff?

DRISCOLL. Sure, and who doesn't?

YANK. She's been good to me. She tried to lend me half a crown when I was broke there last trip. Buy her the biggest box of candy yuh c'n find in Cardiff. (*Breaking down—in a choking voice*) It's hard to ship on this voyage I'm goin' on—alone! (DRISCOLL *reaches out and grasps his hand. There is a pause, during which both fight to control themselves*) My throat's like a furnace. (*He gasps for air*) Gimme a drink of water, will yuh, Drisc? (DRISCOLL *gets him a dipper of water*) I wish this was a pint of beer. Oooohh! (*He chokes, his face convulsed with agony, his hands tearing at his shirt-front. The dipper falls from his nerveless fingers*)

DRISCOLL. For the love av God, what is ut, Yank?

YANK. (*speaking with tremendous difficulty*) S'long, Drisc! (*He stares straight in front of him with eyes starting from their sockets*) Who's that?

DRISCOLL. Who? What?

YANK. (*faintly*) A pretty lady dressed in black. (*His face twitches and his body writhes in a final spasm, then straightens out rigidly*)

DRISCOLL. (*pale with horror*) Yank! Yank! Say a word to me for the love av hiven! (*He shrinks away from the bunk, making the sign of the cross. Then comes back and puts a trembling hand on* YANK'S *chest and bends closely over the body*)

COCKY. (*from the alleyway*) Oh, Driscoll! Can you leave Yank for arf a mo' and give me a 'and?

DRISCOLL. (*with a great sob*) Yank! (*He sinks down on his knees beside the bunk, his head on his hands. His lips move in some half-remembered prayer*)

COCKY. (*enters, his oilskins and sou'wester glistening with drops of water*) The fog's lifted. (COCKY *sees* DRISCOLL *and stands staring at him with open mouth.* DRISCOLL *makes the sign of the cross again*)

COCKY. (*mockingly*) Sayin' 'is prayers! (*He catches sight of the still figure in the bunk and an expression of awed understanding comes over his face. He takes off his dripping sou'-wester and stands, scratching his head*)

COCKY. (*in a hushed whisper*) Gawd blimey!

(*The Curtain Falls*)

THE LONG VOYAGE HOME

A Play in One Act

CHARACTERS

FAT JOE, *proprietor of a dive*

NICK, *a crimp*

MAG, *a barmaid*

OLSON
DRISCOLL
COCKY
IVAN } *seamen of the British tramp steamer* Glencairn

KATE

FREDA

TWO ROUGHS

THE LONG VOYAGE HOME

SCENE. *The bar of a low dive on the London water-front—a squalid, dingy room dimly lighted by kerosene lamps placed in brackets on the walls. On the left, the bar. In front of it, a door leading to a side room. On the right, tables with chairs around them. In the rear, a door leading to the street.*

A slovenly barmaid with a stupid face sodden with drink is mopping off the bar. Her arm moves back and forth mechanically and her eyes are half shut as if she were dozing on her feet. At the far end of the bar stands FAT JOE, *the proprietor, a gross bulk of a man with an enormous stomach. His face is red and bloated, his little piggish eyes being almost concealed by rolls of fat. The thick fingers of his big hands are loaded with cheap rings, and a gold watch-chain of cable-like proportions stretches across his checked waistcoat.*

At one of the tables, front, a round-shouldered young fellow is sitting, smoking a cigarette. His face is pasty, his mouth weak, his eyes shifting and cruel. He is dressed in a shabby suit, which must have once been cheaply flashy, and wears a muffler and a cap.

It is about nine o'clock in the evening.

JOE. (*yawning*) Blimey if bizness ain't 'arf slow tonight. I donnow wot's 'appened. The place is like a bleedin' tomb. Where's all the sailormen, I'd like to know? (*Raising his voice*)

Ho, you Nick! (NICK *turns around listlessly*) Wot's the name o' that wessel put in at the dock below jest arter noon?

NICK (*laconically*) *Glencairn*—from Bewnezerry. (Buenos Aires.)

JOE. Ain't the crew been paid orf yet?

NICK. Paid orf this arternoon, they tole me. I 'opped on board of 'er an' seen 'em. 'Anded 'em some o' yer cards, I did. They promised faithful they'd 'appen in tonight—them as whose time was done.

JOE. Any two-year men to be paid orf?

NICK. Four—three Britishers an' a square-'ead.

JOE. (*indignantly*) An' yer popped orf an' left 'em? An' me a-payin' yer to 'elp an' bring 'em in 'ere!

NICK. (*grumblingly*) Much you pays me! An' I ain't slingin' me 'ook abaht the 'ole bleedin' town fur now man. See?

JOE. I ain't speakin' on'y fur meself. Down't I always give yer yer share, fair an' square, as man to man?

NICK. (*with a sneer*) Yus—b'cause you 'as to.

JOE. 'As to? Listen to 'im! There's many'd be 'appy to 'ave your berth, me man!

NICK. Yus? Wot wiv the peelers li'ble to put me away in the bloody jail fur crimpin', an' all?

JOE. (*indignantly*) We down't do no crimpin'.

NICK. (*sarcastically*) Ho, now! Not arf!

JOE. (*a bit embarrassed*) Well, on'y a bit now an' agen when there ain't no reg'lar trade. (*To hide his confusion he turns to the barmaid angrily. She is still mopping off the bar, her chin on her breast, half-asleep*) 'Ere, me gel, we've 'ad enough o' that. You been a-moppin', an' a-moppin', an' a-moppin' the blarsted bar fur a 'ole 'our. 'Op it aht o' this! You'd fair guv a bloke the shakes a-watchin' yer.

MAG. (*beginning to sniffle*) Ow, you do frighten me when you 'oller at me, Joe. I ain't a bad gel, I ain't. Gawd knows I tries to do me best fur you. (*She bursts into a tempest of sobs*)

JOE. (*roughly*) Stop yer grizzlin'! An' 'op it aht of 'ere!

NICK. (*chuckling*) She's drunk, Joe. Been 'ittin' the gin, eh, Mag?

MAG. (*ceases crying at once and turns on him furiously*) You little crab, you! Orter wear a muzzle, you ort! A-openin' of your ugly mouth to a 'onest woman what ain't never done you no 'arm. (*Commencing to sob again*) H'abusin' me like a dawg cos I'm sick an' orf me oats, an' all.

JOE. Orf yer go, me gel! Go hupstairs and 'ave a sleep. I'll wake yer if I wants yer. An' wake the two gels when yer goes hup. It's 'arpas' nine an' time as some one was a-comin' in, tell 'em. D'yer 'ear me?

MAG. (*stumbling around the bar to the door on left—sobbing*) Yus, yus, I 'ears you. Gawd knows wot's goin' to 'appen to me, I'm that sick. Much you cares if I dies, down't you? (*She goes out*)

JOE. (*still brooding over* NICK's *lack of diligence—after a pause*) Four two-year men paid orf wiv their bloody pockets full o' sovereigns—an' yer lorst 'em. (*He shakes his head sorrowfully*)

NICK. (*impatiently*) Stow it! They promised faithful they'd come, I tells yer. They'll be walkin' in in 'arf a mo'. There's lots o' time yet. (*In a low voice*) 'Ave yer got the drops? We might wanter use 'em.

JOE. (*taking a small bottle from behind the bar*) Yus; 'ere it is.

NICK. (*with satisfaction*) Righto! (*His shifty eyes peer about the room searchingly. Then he beckons to* JOE, *who comes over to the table and sits down*) Reason I arst yer about the drops was 'cause I seen the capt'n of the Amindra this arternoon.

JOE. The Amindra? Wot ship is that?

NICK. Bloody windjammer—skys'l-yarder—full-rigged—painted white—been layin' at the dock above 'ere fur a month. You knows 'er.

JOE. Ho, yus. I knows now.

NICK. The capt'n says as 'e wants a man special bad—ter-night. They sails at daybreak ter-morrer.

JOE. There's plenty o' 'ands lyin' abaht waitin' fur ships, I should fink.

NICK. Not fur this ship, ole buck. The capt'n an' mate are bloody slave-drivers, an' they're bound down round the 'Orn. They 'arf starved the 'ands on the larst trip 'ere, an' no one'll dare ship on 'er. (*After a pause*) I promised the capt'n faithful I'd get 'im one, and ter-night.

JOE. (*doubtfully*) An' 'ow are yer goin' to git 'im?

NICK. (*with a wink*) I was thinkin' as one of 'em from the *Glencairn*'d do—them as was paid orf an' is comin' 'ere.

JOE. (*with a grin*) It'd be a good 'aul, that's the troof. (*Frowning*) If they comes 'ere.

NICK. They'll come, an' they'll all be rotten drunk, wait an' see. (*There is the noise of loud, boisterous singing from the street*) Sounds like 'em, now. (*He opens the street door and looks out*) Gawd blimey if it ain't the four of 'em! (*Turning *to* JOE *in triumph)* Naw, what d'yer say? They're lookin' for the place. I'll go aht an' tell 'em. *(He goes out.* JOE *gets into position behind the bar, assuming his most oily smile. A moment later the door is opened, admitting* DRISCOLL, COCKY, IVAN *and* OLSON. DRISCOLL *is a tall, powerful Irishman;* COCKY, *a wizened runt of a man with a straggling gray mustache;* IVAN, *a hulking oaf of a peasant;* OLSON, *a stocky, middle-aged Swede with round, childish blue eyes. The first three are all very drunk, especially* IVAN, *who is managing his legs with difficulty.* OLSON *is perfectly sober. All are dressed in their ill-fitting shore clothes and look very uncomfortable.* DRISCOLL *has unbuttoned his stiff collar and its ends stick out sideways. He has lost his tie.* NICK *slinks into the room after them and sits down at a table in rear. The seamen come to the table, front)*

JOE. *(with affected heartiness)* Ship ahoy, mates! 'Appy to see yer 'ome safe an' sound.

DRISCOLL. *(turns round, swaying a bit, and peers at him across the bar)* So ut's you, is ut? *(He looks about the place with an air of recognition)* 'An the same damn rat's-hole, sure enough. I remimber foive or six years back 'twas here I was sthripped av me last shillin' whin I was aslape. *(With sudden fury)* God stiffen ye, come none av your dog's thricks on me this trip or I'll—— *(He shakes his fist at* JOE*)*

JOE. *(hastily interrupting)* Yer must be mistaiken. This is a 'onest place, this is.

COCKY. *(derisively)* Ho, yus! An' you're a bleedin' angel, I s'pose?

IVAN. *(vaguely taking off his derby hat and putting it on again—plaintively)* I don' li-ike dis place.

DRISCOLL. *(going over to the bar—as genial as he was furious a moment before*) Well, no matther, 'tis all past an' gone an' forgot. I'm not the man to be holdin' harrd feelin's on me first night ashore, an' me dhrunk as a lord. (*He holds out his hand, which* JOE *takes very gingerly*) We'll all be havin' a dhrink, I'm thinkin'. Whiskey for the three av us—*Irish* whiskey!

COCKY. (*mockingly*) An' a glarse o' ginger beer fur our blarsted love-child 'ere. (*He jerks his thumb at* OLSON)

OLSON. (*with a good-natured grin*) I bane a good boy dis night, for one time.

DRISCOLL. (*bellowing, and pointing to* NICK *as* JOE *brings the drinks to the table*) An' see what that crimpin' son av a crimp'll be wantin'—an' have your own pleasure. (*He pulls a sovereign out of his pocket and slams it on the bar*)

NICK. Guv me a pint o' beer, Joe. (JOE *draws the beer and takes it down to the far end of the bar.* NICK *comes over to get it and* JOE *gives him a significant wink and nods toward the door on the left.* NICK *signals back that he understands*)

COCKY. (*drink in hand—impatiently*) I'm that bloody dry! (*Lifting his glass to* DRISCOLL) Cheero, ole dear, cheero!

DRISCOLL. (*pocketing his change without looking at it*) A toast for ye: Hell roast that divil av a bo'sun! (*He drinks*)

COCKY. Righto! Gawd strike 'im blind! (*He drains his glass*)

IVAN. (*half-asleep*) Dot's gude. (*He tosses down his drink in one gulp.* OLSON *sips his ginger ale.* NICK *takes a swallow of his beer and then comes round the bar and goes out the door on left*)

COCKY. (*producing a sovereign*) Ho there, you Fatty! Guv us another!

JOE. The saime, mates?

COCKY. Yus.

DRISCOLL. No, ye scut! I'll be havin' a pint av beer. I'm dhry as a loime kiln.

IVAN. (*suddenly getting to his feet in a befuddled manner and nearly upsetting the table*) I don' li-ike dis place! I wan' see girls—plenty girls. (*Pathetically*) I don' li-ike dis place. I wan't dance with girl.

DRISCOLL. (*pushing him back on his chair with a thud*) Shut up, ye Rooshan baboon! A foine Romeo you'd make in your condishun. (IVAN *blubbers some incoherent protest—then suddenly falls asleep*)

JOE. (*bringing the drinks—looks at* OLSON) An' you, matey?

OLSON. (*shaking his head*) Noting dis time, thank you.

COCKY. (*mockingly*) A-saivin' of 'is money, 'e is! Goin' back to 'ome an' mother. Goin' to buy a bloomin' farm an' punch the blarsted dirt, that's wot 'e is! (*Spitting disgustedly*) There's a funny bird of a sailorman for yer, Gawd blimey!

OLSON. (*wearing the same good-natured grin*) Yust what I like, Cocky. I wus on farm long time when I wus kid.

DRISCOLL. Lave him alone, ye bloody insect! 'Tis a foine sight to see a man wid some sense in his head instead av a damn fool the loike av us. I only wisht I'd a mother alive to call me own. I'd not be dhrunk in this divil's hole this minute, maybe.

COCKY. (*commencing to weep dolorously*) Ow, down't talk, Drisc! I can't bear to 'ear you. I ain't never 'ad no mother, I ain't——

DRISCOLL. Shut up, ye ape, an' don't be makin' that squealin'. If ye cud see your ugly face, wid the big red nose av ye all screwed up in a knot, ye'd never shed a tear the rist av your loife. (*Roaring into song*) We ar're the byes av We-e-exford who fought wid hearrt an' hand! (*Speaking*) To hell wid Ulster! (*He drinks and the others follow his example*) An' I'll strip to any man in the city av London won't dhrink to that toast. (*He glares truculently at* JOE, *who immediately downs his beer.* NICK *enters again from the door on the left and comes up to* JOE *and whispers in his ear. The latter nods with satisfaction*)

DRISCOLL. (*glowering at them*) What divil's thrick are ye up to now, the two av ye? (*He flourishes a brawny fist*) Play fair wid us or ye deal wid me!

JOE. (*hastily*) No trick, shipmate! May Gawd kill me if that ain't troof!

NICK. (*indicating* IVAN, *who is snoring*) On'y your mate there was arskin' fur gels an' I thorght as 'ow yer'd like 'em to come dawhn and 'ave a wet wiv yer.

JOE. (*with a smirking wink*) Pretty, 'olesome gels they be, ain't they, Nick?

NICK. Yus.

COCKY. Aar! I knows the gels you 'as, not 'arf! They'd fair blind yer, they're that 'omely. None of yer bloomin' gels fur me, ole Fatty. Me an' Drisc knows a place, down't we, Drisc?

DRISCOLL. Divil a lie, we do. An' we'll be afther goin' there in a minute. There's music there an' a bit av a dance to liven a man.

JOE. Nick, 'ere, can play yer a tune, can't yer, Nick?

NICK. Yus.

JOE. An' yer can 'ave a dance in the side room 'ere.

DRISCOLL. Hurroo! Now you're talkin'. (*The two women,* FREDA *and* KATE, *enter from the left.* FREDA *is a little, sallow-faced blonde.* KATE *is stout and dark*)

COCKY. (*in a loud aside to* DRISCOLL) Gawd blimey, look at 'em! Ain't they 'orrible? (*The women come forward to the table, wearing their best set smiles*)

FREDA. (*in a raspy voice*) 'Ullo, mates.

KATE. 'Ad a good voyage?

DRISCOLL. Rotten; but no matther. Welcome, as the sayin' is, an' sit down, an' what'll ye be takin' for your thirst? (*To* KATE) You'll be sittin' by me, darlin'—what's your name?

KATE. (*with a stupid grin*) Kate. (*She stands by his chair*)

DRISCOLL. (*putting his arm around her*) A good Irish name, but you're English by the trim av ye, an' be damned to you. But no matther. Ut's fat ye are, Katy dear, an' I never cud endure skinny wimin. (FREDA *favors him with a viperish glance and sits down by* OLSON) What'll ye have?

OLSON. No, Drisc. Dis one bane on me. (*He takes out a roll of notes from his inside pocket and lays one on the table.* JOE, NICK, *and the women look at the money with greedy eyes.* IVAN *gives a particularly violent snore*)

FREDA. Waike up your fren'. Gawd, 'ow I 'ates to 'ear snorin'.

DRISCOLL. (*springing to action, smashes* IVAN's *derby over his ears*) D'you hear the lady talkin' to ye, ye Rooshan swab? (*The only reply to this is a snore.* DRISCOLL *pulls the battered remains of the derby off* IVAN's *head and smashes it back again*) Arise an' shine, ye dhrunken swine! (*Another snore. The women giggle.* DRISCOLL *throws the beer left in his glass into* IVAN's *face. The Russian comes to in a flash, spluttering. There is a roar of laughter*)

IVAN. (*indignantly*) I tell you—dot's someting I don' li-ike!

COCKY. Down't waste good beer, Drisc.

IVAN. (*grumblingly*) I tell you—dot is not ri-ight.

DRISCOLL. Ut's your own doin', Ivan. Ye was moanin' for girrls an' whin they come you sit gruntin' loike a pig in a sty. Have ye no manners? (IVAN *seems to see the women for the first time and grins foolishly*)

KATE. (*laughing at him*) Cheero, ole chum, 'ows Russha?

IVAN. (*greatly pleased—putting his hand in his pocket*) I buy a drink.

OLSON. No; dis one bane on me. (*To* JOE) Hey, you faller!

JOE. Wot'll it be, Kate?

KATE. Gin.

FREDA. Brandy.

DRISCOLL. An' Irish whiskey for the rist av us—wid the excipshun av our timperance friend, God pity him!

FREDA. (*to* OLSON) You ain't drinkin'?

OLSON. (*half-ashamed*) No.

FREDA. (*with a seductive smile*) I down't blame yer. You got sense, you 'ave. I on'y tike a nip o' brandy now an' agen fur my 'ealth. (JOE *brings the drinks and* OLSON'S *change.* COCKY *gets unsteadily to his feet and raises his glass in the air*)

COCKY. 'Ere's a toff toast for yer: The ladies, Gawd— (*He hesitates—then adds in a grudging tone*)—bless 'em.

KATE. (*with a silly giggle*) Oo-er! That wasn't what you was goin' to say, you bad Cocky, you! (*They all drink*)

DRISCOLL. (*to* NICK) Where's the tune ye was promisin' to give us?

NICK. Come ahn in the side 'ere an' you'll 'ear it.

DRISCOLL. (*getting up*) Come on, all av ye. We'll have a

tune an' a dance if I'm not too dhrunk to dance, God help me. (COCKY *and* IVAN *stagger to their feet.* IVAN *can hardly stand. He is leering at* KATE *and snickering to himself in a maudlin fashion. The three, led by* NICK, *go out the door on the left.* KATE *follows them.* OLSON *and* FREDA *remain seated*)

COCKY. (*calling over his shoulder*) Come on an' dance, Ollie.

OLSON. Yes, I come. (*He starts to get up. From the side room comes the sound of an accordion and a boisterous whoop from* DRISCOLL, *followed by a heavy stamping of feet*)

FREDA. Ow, down't go in there. Stay 'ere an' 'ave a talk wiv me. They're all drunk an' you ain't drinkin'. (*With a smile up into his face*) I'll think yer don't like me if yer goes in there.

OLSON. (*confused*) You wus wrong, Miss Freda. I don't—I mean I do like you.

FREDA. (*smiling—puts her hand over his on the table*) An' I likes you. Yer a genelman. You don't get drunk an' hinsult poor gels wot 'as a 'ard an' uneppy life.

OLSON. (*pleased but still more confused—wriggling his feet*) I bane drunk many time, Miss Freda.

FREDA. Then why ain't yer drinkin' now? (*She exchanges a quick, questioning glance with* JOE, *who nods back at her—then she continues persuasively*) Tell me somethin' abaht yeself.

OLSON. (*with a grin*) There ain't noting to say, Miss Freda. I bane poor devil sailorman, dat's all.

FREDA. Where was you born—Norway? (OLSON *shakes his head*) Denmark?

OLSON. No. You guess once more.

FREDA. Then it must be Sweden.

OLSON. Yes. I wus born in Stockholm.

FREDA. (*pretending great delight*) Ow, ain't that funny! I was born there, too—in Stockholm.

OLSON. (*astonished*) You wus born in Sweden?

FREDA. Yes; you wouldn't think it, but it's Gawd's troof. (*She claps her hands delightedly*)

OLSON. (*beaming all over*) You speak Swedish?

FREDA. (*trying to smile sadly*) Now. Y'see my ole man an' woman come 'ere to England when I was on'y a baby an' they was speakin' English b'fore I was old enough to learn. Sow I never knew Swedish. (*Sadly*) Wisht I 'ad! (*With a smile*) We'd 'ave a bloomin' lark of it if I 'ad, wouldn't we?

OLSON. It sound nice to hear the old talk yust once in a time.

FREDA. Righto! No place like yer 'ome, I says. Are yer goin' up to—to Stockholm b'fore yer ships away agen?

OLSON. Yes. I go home from here to Stockholm. (*Proudly*) As passenger!

FREDA. An' you'll git another ship up there arter you've 'ad a vacation?

OLSON. No. I don't never ship on sea no more. I got all sea I want for my life—too much hard work for little money. Yust work, work, work on ship. I don't want more.

FREDA. Ow, I see. That's why you give up drinkin'.

OLSON. Yes. (*With a grin*) If I drink I yust get drunk and spend all money.

FREDA. But if you ain't gointer be a sailor no more, what'll yer do? You been a sailor all yer life, ain't yer?

OLSON. No. I work on farm till I am eighteen. I like it, too —it's nice—work on farm.

FREDA. But ain't Stockholm a city same's London? Ain't no farms there, is there?

OLSON. We live—my brother and mother live—my father iss dead—on farm yust a little way from Stockholm. I have plenty money, now. I go back with two years' pay and buy more land yet; work on farm. (*Grinning*) No more sea, no more bum grub, no more storms—yust nice work.

FREDA. Ow, ain't that luv'ly! I s'pose you'll be gittin' married, too?

OLSON. (*very much confused*) I don't know. I like to, if I find nice girl, maybe.

FREDA. Ain't yer got some gel back in Stockholm? I bet yer 'as.

OLSON. No. I got nice girl once before I go on sea. But I go on ship, and I don't come back, and she marry other faller. (*He grins sheepishly*)

FREDA. Well, it's nice for yer to be goin' 'ome, anyway.

OLSON. Yes. I tank so. (*There is a crash from the room on left and the music abruptly stops. A moment later* COCKY *and* DRISCOLL *appear, supporting the inert form of* IVAN *between them. He is in the last stage of intoxication, unable to move a muscle.* NICK *follows them and sits down at the table in rear*)

DRISCOLL. (*as they zigzag up to the bar*) Ut's dead he is, I'm thinkin', for he's as limp as a blarsted corpse.

COCKY. (*puffing*) Gawd, 'e ain't 'arf 'eavy!

DRISCOLL. (*slapping* IVAN'S *face with his free hand*) Wake up, ye divil, ye. Ut's no use. Gabriel's trumpet itself cudn't rouse him. (*To* JOE) Give us a dhrink, for I'm perishing wid the thirst. 'Tis harrd worrk, this.

JOE. Whiskey?

DRISCOLL. *Irish* whiskey, ye swab. (*He puts down a coin on *the bar.* JOE *serves* COCKY *and* DRISCOLL. *They drink and then swerve over to* OLSON'*s table*)

OLSON. Sit down and rest for time, Drisc.

DRISCOLL. No, Ollie, we'll be takin' this lad home to his bed. Ut's late for wan so young to be out in the night. An' I'd not trust him in this hole as dhrunk as he is, an' him wid a full pay day on him. (*Shaking his fist at* JOE) Oho, I know your games, me sonny bye!

JOE. (*with an air of grievance*) There ye goes again—hinsultin' a 'onest man!

COCKY. Ho, listen to 'im! Guv 'im a shove in the marf, Drisc.

OLSON. (*anxious to avoid a fight—getting up*) I help you take Ivan to boarding house.

FREDA. (*protestingly*) Ow, you ain't gointer leave me, are yer? An' we 'avin sech a nice talk, an' all.

DRISCOLL. (*with a wink*) Ye hear what the lady says, Ollie. Ye'd best stay here, me timperance lady's man. An' we need no help. 'Tis only a bit av a way and we're two strong men if we are dhrunk. Ut's no hard shift to take the remains home. But ye can open the door for us, Ollie. (OLSON *goes to the door and opens it*) Come on, Cocky, an' don't be fallin' aslape yourself. (*They lurch toward the door. As they go out* DRISCOLL *shouts back over his shoulder*) We'll be comin' back in a short time, surely. So wait here for us, Ollie.

OLSON. All right. I wait here, Drisc. (*He stands in the doorway uncertainly.* JOE *makes violent signs to* FREDA *to bring him back. She goes over and puts her arms around* OLSON'*s shoulder.* JOE *motions to* NICK *to come to the bar. They whisper together excitedly*)

FREDA. (*coaxingly*) You ain't gointer leave me, are yer,

dearie? (*Then irritably*) Fur Gawd's sake, shet that door! I'm fair freezin' to death wiv the fog. (OLSON *comes to himself with a start and shuts the door*)

OLSON. (*humbly*) Excuse me, Miss Freda.

FREDA. (*leading him back to the table—coughing*) Buy me a drink o' brandy, will yer? I'm sow cold.

OLSON. All you want, Miss Freda, all you want. (*To* JOE, *who is still whispering instructions to* NICK) Hey, Yoe! Brandy for Miss Freda. (*He lays a coin on the table*)

JOE. Righto! (*He pours out her drink and brings it to the table*) 'Avin' somethink yeself, shipmate?

OLSON. No. I don' tank so. (*He points to his glass with a grin*) Dis iss only belly-wash, no? (*He laughs*)

JOE. (*hopefully*) 'Ave a man's drink.

OLSON. I would like to—but no. If I drink one I want drink one tousand. (*He laughs again*)

FREDA. (*Responding to a vicious nudge from* JOE'*s elbow*) Ow, tike somethin'. I ain't gointer drink all be meself.

OLSON. Den give me a little yinger beer—small one. (JOE *goes back of the bar, making a sign to* NICK *to go to their table.* NICK *does so and stands so that the sailor cannot see what* JOE *is doing*)

NICK. (*to make talk*) Where's yer mates popped orf ter? (JOE *pours the contents of the little bottle into* OLSON'*s glass of ginger beer*)

OLSON. Dey take Ivan, dat drunk faller, to bed. They come back. (JOE *brings* OLSON'*s drink to the table and sets it before him*)

JOE. (*to* NICK*—angrily*) 'Op it, will yer? There ain't no time to be dawdlin'. See? 'Urry!

NICK. Don't worry, ole bird, I'm orf. (*He hurries out the door.* JOE *returns to his place behind the bar*)

OLSON. (*after a pause—worriedly*) I tank I should go after dem. Cocky iss very drunk, too, and Drisc——

FREDA. Aar! The big Irish is all right! Don't yer 'ear 'im say as 'ow they'd surely come back 'ere, an' fur you to wait fur 'em?

OLSON. Yes; but if dey don't come soon I tank I go see if dey are in boarding house all right.

FREDA. Where is the boardin' 'ouse?

OLSON. Yust little way back from street here.

FREDA. You stayin' there, too?

OLSON. Yes—until steamer sail for Stockholm—in two day.

FREDA. (*she is alternately looking at* JOE *and feverishly trying to keep* OLSON *talking so he will forget about going away after the others*) Yer mother won't be arf glad to see yer agen, will she? (OLSON *smiles*) Does she know yer comin'?

OLSON. No. I tought I would yust give her surprise. I write to her from Bonos Eres but I don't tell her I come home.

FREDA. Must be old, ain't she, yer ole lady?

OLSON. She iss eighty-two. (*He smiles reminiscently*) You know, Miss Freda, I don't see my mother or my brother in—let me tank— (*He counts laboriously on his fingers*) must be more than ten year. I write once in while and she write many time; and my brother he write me, too. My mother say in all letter I should come home right away. My brother he write same ting, too. He want me to help him on farm. I write back always I come soon; and I mean all time to go back home at end of voyage. But I come ashore, I take one drink, I take many drinks, I get drunk, I spend all money, I have to ship away for other voyage. So dis time I say to myself: Don't drink one drink, Ollie, or, sure, you don't get home. And I want go home dis time. I feel homesick for farm and to see my people again. (*He smiles*) Yust like little boy, I feel homesick. Dat's why I don't drink noting tonight but dis—belly-wash! (*He roars with childish laughter, then suddenly becomes serious*) You know, Miss Freda, my mother get very old, and I want see her. She might die and I would never——

FREDA. (*moved a lot in spite of herself*) Ow, don't talk like that! I jest 'ates to 'ear anyone speakin' abaht dyin'. (*The door to the street is opened and* NICK *enters, followed by two rough-looking, shabbily-dressed men, wearing mufflers, with caps pulled down over their eyes. They sit at the table nearest to the door.* JOE *brings them three beers, and there is a whispered consultation, with many glances in the direction of* OLSON)

OLSON. (*starting to get up—worriedly*) I tank I go round to boarding house. I tank someting go wrong with Drisc and Cocky.

FREDA. Ow, down't go. They kin take care of theyselves. They ain't babies. Wait 'arf a mo'. You ain't 'ad yer drink yet.

JOE. (*coming hastily over to the table, indicates the men in the rear with a jerk of his thumb*) One of them blokes wants yer to 'ave a wet wiv 'im.

FREDA. Righto! (*To* OLSON) Let's drink this. (*She raises her glass. He does the same*) 'Ere's a toast fur yer: Success to yer bloomin' farm an' may yer live long an' 'appy on it. Skoal! (*She tosses down her brandy. He swallows half his glass of ginger beer and makes a wry face*)

OLSON. Skoal! (*He puts down his glass*)

FREDA. (*with feigned indignation*) Down't yer like my toast?

OLSON. (*grinning*) Yes. It iss very kind, Miss Freda.

FREDA. Then drink it all like I done.

OLSON. Well—— (*He gulps down the rest*) Dere! (*He laughs*)

FREDA. Done like a sport!

ONE OF THE TOUGHS. (*with a laugh*) Amindra, ahoy!

NICK. (*warningly*) Sssshh!

OLSON. (*turns around in his chair*) Amindra? Iss she in port? I sail on her once long time ago—three mast, full rig, skys'l-yarder? Iss dat ship you mean?

THE ROUGH. (*grinning*) Yus; right you are.

OLSON. (*angrily*) I know dat damn ship—worst ship dat sail to sea. Rotten grub and dey make you work all time—and the Captain and Mate wus Bluenose devils. No sailor who know anyting ever ship on her. Where iss she bound from here?

THE ROUGH. Round Cape 'Orn—sails at daybreak.

OLSON. Py yingo, I pity poor fallers make dat trip round Cape Stiff dis time year. I bet you some of dem never see port once again. (*He passes his hand over his eyes in a dazed way. His voice grows weaker*) Py golly, I feel dizzy. All the room go round and round like I wus drunk. (*He gets weakly to his feet*) Good-night, Miss Freda. I bane feeling sick. Tell Drisc —I go home. (*He takes a step forward and suddenly collapses over a chair, rolls to the floor, and lies there unconscious*)

JOE. (*from behind the bar*) Quick, nawh! (NICK *darts forward with* JOE *following.* FREDA *is already beside the unconscious man and has taken the roll of money from his inside pocket. She strips off a note furtively and shoves it into her bosom, trying to conceal her action, but* JOE *sees her. She hands the roll to* JOE, *who pockets it.* NICK *goes through all the other pockets and lays a handful of change on the table*)

JOE. (*impatiently*) 'Urry, 'urry, can't yer? The other blokes'll be 'ere in 'arf a mo'. (*The two roughs come forward*) 'Ere, you two, tike 'im in under the arms like 'e was drunk. (*They do so*) Tike 'im to the Amindra—yer knows that, don't yer?—two docks above. Nick'll show yer. An' you, Nick, down't yer leave the bleedin' ship till the capt'n guvs yer this bloke's advance—full month's pay—five quid, d'yer 'ear?

NICK. I knows me bizness, ole bird. (*They support* OLSON *to the door*)

THE ROUGH. (*as they are going out*) This silly bloke'll 'ave the s'prise of 'is life when 'e wakes up on board of 'er. (*They laugh. The door closes behind them.* FREDA *moves quickly for the door on the left but* JOE *gets in her way and stops her*)

JOE. (*threateningly*) Guv us what yer took!

FREDA. Took? I guv yer all 'e 'ad.

JOE. Yer a liar! I seen yer a-playin' yer sneakin' tricks, but yer can't fool Joe. I'm too old a 'and. (*Furiously*) Guv it to me, yer bloody cow! (*He grabs her by the arm*)

FREDA. Lemme alone! I ain't got no——

JOE. (*hits her viciously on the side of the jaw. She crumples up on the floor*) That'll learn yer! (*He stoops down and fumbles in her bosom and pulls out the banknote, which he stuffs into his pocket with a grunt of satisfaction.* KATE *opens the door on the left and looks in—then rushes to* FREDA *and lifts her head up in her arms*)

KATE. (*gently*) Pore dearie! (*Looking at* JOE *angrily*) Been 'ittin' 'er agen, 'ave yer, yer cowardly swine!

JOE. Yus; an' I'll 'it you, too, if yer don't keep yer marf shut. Tike 'er aht of 'ere! (KATE *carries* FREDA *into the next room.* JOE *goes behind the bar. A moment later the outer door is opened and* DRISCOLL *and* COCKY *come in*)

DRISCOLL. Come on, Ollie. (*He suddenly sees that* OLSON *is not there, and turns to* JOE) Where is ut he's gone to?

JOE. (*with a meaning wink*) 'E an' Freda went aht t'gether 'bout five minutes past. 'E's fair gone on 'er, 'e is.

DRISCOLL. (*with a grin*) Oho, so that's ut, is ut? Who'd think Ollie'd be sich a divil wid the wimin? 'Tis lucky he's sober or she'd have him stripped to his last ha'penny. (*Turning to* COCKY, *who is blinking sleepily*) What'll ye have, ye little scut? (*To* JOE) Give me whiskey, *Irish* whiskey!

(*The Curtain Falls*)

IN THE ZONE

A Play in One Act

CHARACTERS

Smitty Davis Swanson Scotty Ivan Paul Jack Driscoll Cocky	*seamen on the British tramp steamer* Glencairn

IN THE ZONE

SCENE. *The seamen's forecastle. On the right above the bunks three or four portholes covered with black cloth can be seen. On the floor near the doorway is a pail with a tin dipper. A lantern in the middle of the floor, turned down very low, throws a dim light around the place. Five men,* SCOTTY, IVAN, SWANSON, SMITTY *and* PAUL, *are in their bunks apparently asleep. It is about ten minutes of twelve on a night in the fall of the year* 1915.

SMITTY *turns slowly in his bunk and, leaning out over the side, looks from one to another of the men as if to assure himself that they are asleep. Then he climbs carefully out of his bunk and stands in the middle of the forecastle fully dressed, but in his stocking feet, glancing around him suspiciously. Reassured, he leans down and cautiously pulls out a suit-case from under the bunks in front of him.*

Just at this moment DAVIS *appears in the doorway, carrying a large steaming coffee-pot in his hand. He stops short when he sees* SMITTY. *A puzzled expression comes over his face, followed by one of suspicion, and he retreats farther back in the alley-way, where he can watch* SMITTY *without being seen.*

All the latter's movements indicate a fear of discovery. He takes out a small bunch of keys and unlocks the suit-case, making a slight noise as he does so. SCOTTY *wakes up and peers at him over the side of the bunk.* SMITTY *opens the suit-case and takes out a small black tin box, carefully places this under his mattress, shoves the suit-case back under the bunk, climbs into his bunk again, closes his eyes and begins to snore loudly.*

DAVIS *enters the forecastle, places the coffee-pot beside the lantern, and goes from one to the other of the sleepers and shakes them vigorously, saying to each in a low voice:* Near eight bells, Scotty. Arise and shine, Swanson. Eight bells, Ivan. SMITTY *yawns loudly with a great pretense of having been dead asleep. All of the rest of the men tumble out of their bunks, stretching and gaping, and commence to pull on their shoes. They go one by one to the cupboard near the open door, take out their cups and spoons, and sit down together on the benches. The coffee-pot is passed around. They munch their biscuits and sip their coffee in dull silence.*

DAVIS. (*suddenly jumping to his feet—nervously*) Where's that air comin' from? (*All are startled and look at him wonderingly*)

SWANSON. (*a squat, surly-faced Swede—grumpily*) What air? I don't feel nothing.

DAVIS. (*excitedly*) I kin feel it—a draft. (*He stands on the bench and looks around—suddenly exploding*) Damn fool square-head! (*He leans over the upper bunk in which* PAUL *is sleeping and slams the porthole shut*) I got a good notion to report him. Serve him bloody well right! What's the use o' blindin' the ports when that thick-head goes an' leaves 'em open?

SWANSON. (*yawning—too sleepy to be aroused by anything—carelessly*) Dey don't see what little light go out yust one port.

SCOTTY. (*protestingly*) Dinna be a loon, Swanson! D'ye no ken the dangerr o' showin' a licht wi' a pack o' submarrines lyin' aboot?

IVAN. (*shaking his shaggy ox-like head in an emphatic affirmative*) Dot's right, Scotty. I don' li-ike blow up, no, by devil!

SMITTY. (*his manner slightly contemptuous*) I don't think there's much danger of meeting any of their submarines, not until we get into the war zone, at any rate.

DAVIS. (*he and* SCOTTY *look at* SMITTY *suspiciously—harshly*) You don't, eh? (*He lowers his voice and speaks slowly*) Well, we're in the war zone right this minit if you wants to know. (*The effect of this speech is instantaneous. All sit bolt upright on their benches and stare at* DAVIS)

SMITTY. How do you know, Davis?

DAVIS. (*angrily*) 'Cos Drisc heard the First send the Third below to wake the skipper when we fetched the zone—bout five bells, it was. Now whata y' got to say?

SMITTY. (*conciliatingly*) Oh, I wasn't doubting your word, Davis; but you know they're not pasting up bulletins to let the crew know when the zone is reached—especially on ammunition ships like this.

IVAN. (*decidedly*) I don't li-ike dees voyage. Next time I ship on windjammer Boston to River Plate, load with wood only so it float, by golly!

SWANSON. (*fretfully*) I hope British navy blow 'em to hell, those submarines, py damn!

SCOTTY. (*looking at* SMITTY, *who is staring at the doorway in a dream, his chin on his hands. Meaningly*) It is no the submarrines only we've to fear, I'm thinkin'.

DAVIS. (*assenting eagerly*) That's no lie, Scotty.

SWANSON. You mean the mines?

SCOTTY. I wasna thinkin' o' mines eitherr.

DAVIS. There's many a good ship blown up and at the bottom of the sea, what never hit no mine or torpedo.

SCOTTY. Did ye neverr read of the Gerrman spies and the dirrty work they're doin' all the war? (*He and* DAVIS *both glance at* SMITTY, *who is deep in thought and is not listening to the conversation*)

DAVIS. An' the clever way they fool you!

SWANSON. Sure; I read it in paper many time.

DAVIS. Well—(*he is about to speak, but hesitates and finishes lamely*) you got to watch out, that's all I says.

IVAN. (*drinking the last of his coffee and slamming his fist on the bench explosively*) I tell you dis rotten coffee give me belly-ache, yes! (*They all look at him in amused disgust*)

SCOTTY. (*sardonically*) Dinna fret about it, Ivan. If we blow up ye'll no be mindin' the pain in your middle. (JACK *enters. He is a young American with a tough, good-natured face. He wears dungarees and a heavy jersey*)

JACK. Eight bells, fellers.

IVAN. (*stupidly*) I don't hear bell ring.

JACK. No, and yuh won't hear any ring, yuh boob—(*lowering his voice unconsciously*) now we're in the war zone.

SWANSON. (*anxiously*) Is the boats all ready?

JACK. Sure; we can lower 'em in a second.

DAVIS. A lot o' good the boats'll do, with us loaded deep with all kinds o' dynamite and stuff the like o' that! If a torpedo hits this hooker we'll all be in hell b'fore you could wink your eye.

JACK. They ain't goin' to hit us, see? That's my dope. Whose wheel is it?

IVAN. (*sullenly*) My wheel. (*He lumbers out*)

JACK. And whose lookout?

SWANSON. Mine, I tink. (*He follows* IVAN)

JACK. (*scornfully*) A hell of a lot of use keepin' a lookout! We couldn't run away or fight if we wanted to. (*To* SCOTTY *and* SMITTY) Better look up the bo'sun or the Fourth, you two, and let 'em see you're awake. (SCOTTY *goes to the doorway and turns to wait for* SMITTY, *who is still in the same position, head on hands, seemingly unconscious of everything.* JACK *slaps him roughly on the shoulder and he comes to with a start*) Aft and report, Duke! What's the matter with yuh—in a dope dream? (SMITTY *goes out after* SCOTTY *without answering.* JACK *looks after him with a frown*) He's a queer guy. I can't figger him out.

DAVIS. Nor no one else. (*Lowering his voice—meaningly*) An' he's liable to turn out queerer than any of us think if we ain't careful.

JACK. (*suspiciously*) What d'yuh mean? (*They are interrupted by the entrance of* DRISCOLL *and* COCKY)

COCKY. (*protestingly*) Blimey if I don't fink I'll put in this 'ere watch ahtside on deck. (*He and* DRISCOLL *go over and get their cups*) I down't want to be caught in this 'ole if they 'its us. (*He pours out coffee*)

DRISCOLL. (*pouring his*) Divil a bit ut wud matther where ye arre. Ye'd be blown to smithereens b'fore ye cud say your name. (*He sits down, overturning as he does so the untouched cup of coffee which* SMITTY *had forgotten and left on the bench. They all jump nervously as the tin cup hits the floor with a bang.* DRISCOLL *flies into an unreasonable rage*) Who's the dirty scut left this cup where a man 'ud sit on ut?

DAVIS. It's Smitty's.

DRISCOLL. (*kicking the cup across the forecastle*) Does he think he's too much av a bloody gentleman to put his own away loike the rist av us? If he does I'm the bye'll beat that noshun out av his head.

COCKY. Be the airs 'e puts on you'd think 'e was the Prince of Wales. Wot's 'e doin' on a ship, I arsks yer? 'E ain't no good as a sailor, is 'e?—dawdlin' abaht on deck like a chicken wiv 'is 'ead cut orf!

JACK. (*good-naturedly*) Aw, the Duke's all right. S'posin' he did ferget his cup—what's the dif? (*He picks up the cup and puts it away—with a grin*) This war zone stuff's got yer goat, Drisc—and yours too, Cocky—and I ain't cheerin' much fur it myself, neither.

COCKY. (*with a sigh*) Blimey, it ain't no bleedin' joke, yer first trip, to know as there's a ship full of shells li'ble to go orf in under your bloomin' feet, as you might say, if we gets 'it be a torpedo or mine. (*With sudden savagery*) Calls theyselves 'uman bein's, too! Blarsted 'Uns!

DRISCOLL. (*gloomily*) 'Tis me last trip in the bloody zone, God help me. The divil take their twenty-foive per cent. bonus—and be drowned like a rat in a trap in the bargain, maybe.

DAVIS. Wouldn't be so bad if she wasn't carryin' ammunition. Them's the kind the subs is layin' for.

DRISCOLL. (*irritably*) Fur the love av hivin, don't be talkin' about ut. I'm sick wid thinkin' and jumpin' at iviry bit av a noise. (*There is a pause during which they all stare gloomily at the floor*)

JACK. Hey, Davis, what was you sayin' about Smitty when they come in?

DAVIS. (*with a great air of mystery*) I'll tell you in a minit. I want to wait an' see if he's comin' back. (*Impressively*) You won't be callin' him all right when you hears what I seen with my own eyes. (*He adds with an air of satisfaction*) An' you won't be feelin' no safer, neither. (*They all look at him with puzzled glances full of a vague apprehension*)

DRISCOLL. God blarst ut! (*He fills his pipe and lights it. The others, with an air of remembering something they had forgotten, do the same.* SCOTTY *enters*)

SCOTTY. (*in awed tones*) Mon, but it's clear outside the nicht! Like day.

DAVIS. (*in low tones*) Where's Smitty, Scotty?

SCOTTY. Out on the hatch starin' at the moon like a mon half-daft.

DAVIS. Kin you see him from the doorway?

SCOTTY. (*goes to doorway and carefully peeks out*) Aye; he's still there.

DAVIS. Keep your eyes on him for a moment. I've got something I want to tell the boys and I don't want him walkin' in in the middle of it. Give a shout if he starts this way.

SCOTTY. (*with suppressed excitement*) Aye, I'll watch him. And I've somethin' myself to tell aboot his Lordship.

DRISCOLL. (*impatiently*) Out wid ut! You're talkin' more than a pair av auld women wud be standin' in the road, and gittin' no further along.

DAVIS. Listen! You 'member when I went to git the coffee, Jack?

JACK. Sure, I do.

DAVIS. Well, I brings it down here same as usual and got as far as the door there when I sees him.

JACK. Smitty?

DAVIS. Yes, Smitty! He was standin' in the middle of the fo'c's'tle there. (*Pointing*) Lookin' around sneakin'-like at Ivan and Swanson and the rest 's if he wants to make certain they're asleep. (*He pauses significantly, looking from one to the other of his listeners.* SCOTTY *is nervously dividing his attention between* SMITTY *on the hatch outside and* DAVIS'S *story, fairly bursting to break in with his own revelations*)

JACK. (*impatiently*) What of it?

DAVIS. Listen! He was standin' right there—(*pointing again*) in his stockin' feet—no shoes on, mind, so he wouldn't make no noise!

JACK. (*spitting disgustedly*) Aw!

DAVIS. (*not heeding the interruption*) I seen right away somethin' on the queer was up so I slides back into the alleyway where I kin see him but he can't see me. After he makes sure they're all asleep he goes in under the bunks there—bein' careful not to raise a noise, mind!—an' takes out his bag there. (*By this time everyone,* JACK *included, is listening breathlessly to his story*) Then he fishes in his pocket an' takes out a bunch o' keys an' kneels down beside the bag an' opens it.

SCOTTY. (*unable to keep silent longer*) Mon, didn't I see him do that same thing wi' these two eyes. 'Twas just that moment I woke and spied him.

DAVIS. (*surprised, and a bit nettled to have to share his story with anyone*) Oh, you seen him, too, eh? (*To the others*) Then Scotty kin tell you if I'm lyin' or not.

DRISCOLL. An' what did he do whin he'd the bag opened?

DAVIS. He bends down and reaches out his hand sort o' scared-like, like it was somethin' dang'rous he was after, an' feels round in under his duds—hidden in under his duds an' wrapped up in 'em, it was—an' he brings out a black iron box!

COCKY. (*looking around him with a frightened glance*) Gawd blimey! (*The others likewise betray their uneasiness, shuffling their feet nervously*)

DAVIS. Ain't that right, Scotty?

SCOTTY. Right as rain, I'm tellin' ye'!

DAVIS. (*to the others with an air of satisfaction*) There you are! (*Lowering his voice*) An' then what d'you suppose he did? Sneaks to his bunk an' slips the black box in under his mattress—in under his mattress, mind!

JACK. And it's there now?

DAVIS. Course it is! (JACK *starts toward* SMITTY'S *bunk.* DRISCOLL *grabs him by the arm*)

DRISCOLL. Don't be touchin' ut, Jack!

JACK. Yuh needn't worry. I ain't goin' to touch it. (*He pulls up* SMITTY'S *mattress and looks down. The others stare at him, holding their breaths. He turns to them, trying hard to assume a careless tone*) It's there, aw right.

COCKY. (*miserably upset*) I'm gointer 'op it aht on deck. (*He gets up but* DRISCOLL *pulls him down again.* COCKY *protests*) It fair guvs me the trembles sittin' still in 'ere.

DRISCOLL. (*scornfully*) Are ye frightened, ye toad? 'Tis a hell av a thing fur grown men to be shiverin' loike childer at a bit av a black box. (*Scratching his head in uneasy perplexity*) Still, ut's damn queer, the looks av ut.

DAVIS. (*sarcastically*) A bit of a black box, eh? How big d'you think them—(*he hesitates*)—things has to be—big as this fo'c's'tle?

JACK. (*in a voice meant to be reassuring*) Aw, hell! I'll bet it ain't nothin' but some coin he's saved he's got locked up in there.

DAVIS. (*scornfully*) That's likely, ain't it? Then why does he act so s'picious? He's been on ship near two year, ain't he? He knows damn well there ain't no thiefs in this fo'c's'tle, don't he? An' you know's well's I do he didn't have no money when he came on board an' he ain't saved none since. Don't you? (JACK *doesn't answer*) Listen! D'you know what he done after he put that thing in under his mattress?—an' Scotty'll tell you if I ain't speakin' truth. He looks round to see if anyone's woke up——

SCOTTY. I clapped my eyes shut when he turned round.

DAVIS. An' then he crawls into his bunk an' shuts his eyes, an' starts in *snorin', pretendin'* he was asleep, mind!

SCOTTY. Aye, I could hear him.

DAVIS. An' when I goes to call him I don't even shake him. I just says, "Eight bells, Smitty," in almost a whisper-like, an' up he gets yawnin' an' stretchin' fit to kill hisself 's if he'd been dead asleep.

COCKY. Gawd blimey!

DRISCOLL. (*shaking his head*) Ut looks bad, divil a doubt av ut.

DAVIS. (*excitedly*) An' now I come to think of it, there's the porthole. How'd it come to git open, tell me that? I know'd well Paul never opened it. Ain't he grumblin' about bein' cold all the time?

SCOTTY. The mon that opened it meant no good to this ship, whoever he was.

JACK. (*sourly*) What porthole? What're yuh talkin' about?

DAVIS. (*pointing over* PAUL'S *bunk*) There. It was open when I come in. I felt the cold air on my neck an' shut it. It would'a been clear's a lighthouse to any sub that was watchin' —an' we s'posed to have all the ports blinded! Who'd do a dirty trick like that? It wasn't none of us, nor Scotty here, nor Swanson, nor Ivan. Who would it be, then?

COCKY. (*angrily*) Must'a been 'is bloody Lordship.

DAVIS. For all's we know he might'a been signalin' with it. They does it like that by winkin' a light. Ain't you read how they gets caught doin' it in London an' on the coast?

COCKY. (*firmly convinced now*) An' wots 'e doin' aht alone on the 'atch—keepin' 'isself clear of us like 'e was afraid?

DRISCOLL. Kape your eye on him, Scotty.

SCOTTY. There's no a move oot o' him.

JACK. (*in irritated perplexity*) But, hell, ain't he an Englishman? What'd he wanta——

DAVIS. English? How d'we know he's English? Cos he talks it? That ain't no proof. Ain't you read in the papers how all them German spies they been catchin' in England has been livin' there for ten, often as not twenty years, an' talks English as good's anyone? An' look here, ain't you noticed he don't talk natural? He talks it too damn good, that's what I mean. He don't talk exactly like a toff, does he, Cocky?

COCKY. Not like any toff as I ever met up wiv.

DAVIS. No; an' he don't talk it like us, that's certain. An' he don't look English. An' what d'we know about him when you come to look at it? Nothin'! He ain't ever said where he comes from or why. All we knows is he ships on here in London 'bout a year b'fore the war starts, as an A. B.—stole his papers most lik'ly—when he don't know how to box the compass, hardly. Ain't that queer in itself? An' was he ever open with us like a good shipmate? No; he's always had that sly air about him 's if he was hidin' somethin'.

DRISCOLL. (*slapping his thigh—angrily*) Divil take me if I don't think ye have the truth av ut, Davis.

COCKY. (*scornfully*) Lettin' on be 'is silly airs, and all, 'e's the son of a blarsted earl or somethink!

DAVIS. An' the name he calls hisself—Smith! I'd risk a quid of my next pay day that his real name is Schmidt, if the truth was known.

JACK. (*evidently fighting against his own conviction*) Aw, say, you guys give me a pain! What'd they want puttin' a spy on this old tub for?

DAVIS. (*shaking his head sagely*) They're deep ones, an' there's a lot o' things a sailor'll see in the ports he puts in ought to be useful to 'em. An' if he kin signal to 'em an' they blows us up it's one ship less, ain't it? (*Lowering his voice and indicating* SMITTY'S *bunk*) Or if he blows us up hisself.

SCOTTY. (*in alarmed tones*) Hush, mon! Here he comes! (SCOTTY *hurries over to a bench and sits down. A thick silence settles over the forecastle. The men look from one to another with uneasy glances.* SMITTY *enters and sits down beside his bunk. He is seemingly unaware of the dark glances of suspicion directed at him from all sides. He slides his hand back stealthily over his mattress and his fingers move, evidently feeling to make sure the box is still there. The others follow this movement carefully with quick looks out of the corners of their eyes. Their attitudes grow tense as if they were about to spring at him. Satisfied the box is safe,* SMITTY *draws his hand away slowly and utters a sigh of relief)*

SMITTY. *(in a casual tone which to them sounds sinister)* It's a good light night for the subs if there's any about. *(For a moment he sits staring in front of him. Finally he seems to sense the hostile atmosphere of the forecastle and looks from one to the other of the men in surprise. All of them avoid his eyes. He sighs with a puzzled expression and gets up and walks out of the doorway. There is silence for a moment after his departure and then a storm of excited talk breaks loose)*

DAVIS. Did you see him feelin' if it was there?

COCKY. 'E ain't arf a sly one wiv 'is talk of submarines, Gawd blind 'im!

SCOTTY. Did ye see the sneakin' looks he gave us?

DRISCOLL. If ivir I saw black shame on a man's face 'twas on his whin he sat there!

JACK. *(thoroughly convinced at last)* He looked bad to me. He's a crook, aw right.

DAVIS. *(excitedly)* What'll we do? We gotter do somethin' quick or—— *(He is interrupted by the sound of something hitting against the port side of the forecastle with a dull, heavy thud. The men start to their feet in wild-eyed terror and turn as if they were going to rush for the deck. They stand that way for a strained moment, scarcely breathing and listening intently)*

JACK. *(with a sickly smile)* Hell! It's on'y a piece of driftwood or a floatin' log. *(He sits down again)*

DAVIS. *(sarcastically)* Or a mine that didn't go off—that time—or a piece o' wreckage from some ship they've sent to Davy Jones.

COCKY. (*mopping his brow with a trembling hand*) Blimey! (*He sinks back weakly on a bench*)

DRISCOLL. (*furiously*) God blarst ut! No man at all cud be puttin' up wid the loike av this—an' I'm not wan to be fearin' anything or any man in the worrld'll stand up to me face to face; but this divil's trickery in the darrk—— (*He starts for* SMITTY'S *bunk*) I'll throw ut out wan av the portholes an' be done wid ut. (*He reaches toward the mattress*)

SCOTTY. (*grabbing his arm—wildly*) Arre ye daft, mon?

DAVIS. Don't monkey with it, Drisc. I knows what to do. Bring the bucket o' water here, Jack, will you? (JACK *gets it and brings it over to* DAVIS) An' you, Scotty, see if he's back on the hatch.

SCOTTY. (*cautiously peering out*) Aye, he's sittin' there the noo.

DAVIS. Sing out if he makes a move. Lift up the mattress, Drisc—careful now! (DRISCOLL *does so with infinite caution*) Take it out, Jack—careful—don't shake it now, for Christ's sake! Here—put it in the water—easy! There, that's fixed it! (*They all sit down with great sighs of relief*) The water'll git in and spoil it.

DRISCOLL. (*slapping* DAVIS *on the back*) Good wurrk for ye, Davis, ye scut! (*He spits on his hands aggressively*) An' now what's to be done wid that black-hearted thraitor?

COCKY. (*belligerently*) Guv 'im a shove in the marf and 'eave 'im over the side!

DAVIS. An' serve him right!

JACK. Aw, say, give him a chance. Yuh can't prove nothin' till yuh find out what's in there.

DRISCOLL. (*heatedly*) Is ut more proof ye'd be needin'

afther what we've seen an' heard? Then listen to me—an' ut's Driscoll talkin'—if there's divilmint in that box an' we see plain 'twas his plan to murrdher his own shipmates that have served him fair—— (*He raises his fist*) I'll choke his rotten hearrt out wid me own hands, an' over the side wid him, and one man missin' in the mornin'.

DAVIS. An' no one the wiser. He's the balmy kind what commits suicide.

COCKY. They 'angs spies ashore.

JACK. (*resentfully*) If he's done what yuh think I'll croak him myself. Is that good enough for yuh?

DRISCOLL. (*looking down at the box*) How'll we be openin' this, I wonder?

SCOTTY. (*from the doorway—warningly*) He's standin' up.

DAVIS. We'll take his keys away from him when he comes in. Quick, Drisc! You an' Jack get beside the door and grab him. (*They get on either side of the door.* DAVIS *snatches a small coil of rope from one of the upper bunks*) This'll do for me an' Scotty to tie him.

SCOTTY. He's turrnin' this way—he's comin'! (*He moves away from door*)

DAVIS. Stand by to lend a hand, Cocky.

COCKY. Righto. (*As* SMITTY *enters the forecastle he is seized roughly from both sides and his arms pinned behind him. At first he struggles fiercely, but seeing the uselessness of this, he finally stands calmly and allows* DAVIS *and* SCOTTY *to tie up his arms*)

SMITTY. (*when they have finished—with cold contempt*) If this is your idea of a joke I'll have to confess it's a bit too thick for me to enjoy

COCKY. (*angrily*) Shut yer marf, 'ear!

DRISCOLL. (*roughly*) Ye'll find ut's no joke, me bucko, b'fore we're done wid you. (*To* SCOTTY) Kape your eye peeled, Scotty, and sing out if anyone's comin'. (SCOTTY *resumes his post at the door*)

SMITTY. (*with the same icy contempt*) If you'd be good enough to explain——

DRISCOLL. (*furiously*) Explain, is ut? 'Tis you'll do the explainin'—an' damn quick, or we'll know the reason why. (*To* JACK *and* DAVIS) Bring him here, now. (*They push* SMITTY *over to the bucket*) Look here, ye murrdherin' swab. D'you see ut? (SMITTY *looks down with an expression of amazement which rapidly changes to one of anguish*)

DAVIS. (*with a sneer*) Look at him! S'prised, ain't you? If you wants to try your dirty spyin' tricks on us you've gotter git up earlier in the mornin'.

COCKY. Thorght yer weren't 'arf a fox, didn't yer?

SMITTY. (*trying to restrain his growing rage*) What—what do you mean? That's only—How dare—What are you doing with my private belongings?

COCKY. (*sarcastically*) Ho yus! Private b'longings!

DRISCOLL. (*shouting*) What is ut, ye swine? Will you tell us to our faces? What's in ut?

SMITTY. (*biting his lips—holding himself in check with a great effort*) Nothing but—— That's my business. You'll please attend to your own.

DRISCOLL. Oho, ut is, is ut? (*Shaking his fist in* SMITTY'S *face*) Talk aisy now if ye know what's best for you. Your business. Your business, indade! Then we'll be makin' ut ours,

I'm thinkin'. (*To* JACK *and* DAVIS) Take his keys away from him an' we'll see if there's one'll open ut, maybe. (*They start in searching* SMITTY, *who tries to resist and kicks out at the bucket.* DRISCOLL *leaps forward and helps them push him away*) Try to kick ut over, wud ye? Did ye see him then? Tryin' to murrdher us all, the scut! Take that pail out av his way, Cocky. (SMITTY *struggles with all of his strength and keeps them busy for a few seconds. As* COCKY *grabs the pail* SMITTY *makes a final effort and, lunging forward, kicks again at the bucket but only succeeds in hitting* COCKY *on the shin.* COCKY *immediately sets down the pail with a bang and, clutching his knee in both hands, starts hopping around the forecastle, groaning and swearing*)

COCKY. Ooow! Gawd strike me pink! Kicked me, 'e did! Bloody, bleedin', rotten Dutch 'og! (*Approaching* SMITTY, *who has given up the fight and is pushed back against the wall near the doorway with* JACK *and* DAVIS *holding him on either side—wrathfully, at the top of his lungs*) Kick me, will yer? I'll show yer what for, yer bleedin' sneak! (*He draws back his fist.* DRISCOLL *pushes him to one side*)

DRISCOLL. Shut your mouth! D'you want to wake the whole ship? (COCKY *grumbles and retires to a bench, nursing his sore shin*)

JACK. (*taking a small bunch of keys from* SMITTY'*s pocket*) Here yuh are, Drisc.

DRISCOLL. (*taking them*) We'll soon be knowin'. (*He takes the pail and sits down, placing it on the floor between his feet.* SMITTY *again tries to break loose but he is too tired and is easily held back against the wall*)

SMITTY. (*breathing heavily and very pale*) Cowards!

JACK. (*with a growl*) Nix on the rough talk, see! That don't git yuh nothin'.

DRISCOLL. (*looking at the lock on the box in the water and then scrutinizing the keys in his hand*) This'll be ut, I'm thinkin'. (*He selects one and gingerly reaches his hand in the water*)

SMITTY. (*his face grown livid—chokingly*) Don't you open that box, Driscoll. If you do, so help me God, I'll kill you if I hang for it.

DRISCOLL. (*pausing—his hand in the water*) Whin I open this box I'll not be the wan to be kilt, me sonny bye! I'm no dirty spy.

SMITTY. (*his voice trembling with rage. His eyes are fixed on* DRISCOLL'S *hand*) Spy? What are you talking about? I only put that box there so I could get it quick in case we were torpedoed. Are you all mad? Do you think I'm—— (*Chokingly*) You stupid curs! You cowardly dolts! (DAVIS *claps his hand over* SMITTY'S *mouth*)

DAVIS. That'll be enough from you! (DRISCOLL *takes the dripping box from the water and starts to fit in the key.* SMITTY *springs forward furiously, almost escaping from their grasps, and drags them after him half-way across the forecastle*)

DRISCOLL. Hold him, ye divils! (*He puts the box back in the water and jumps to their aid.* COCKY *hovers on the outskirts of the battle, mindful of the kick he received*)

SMITTY. (*raging*) Cowards! Damn you! Rotten curs! (*He is thrown to the floor and held there*) Cowards! Cowards!

DRISCOLL. I'll shut your dirty mouth for you. (*He goes to his bunk and pulls out a big wad of waste and comes back to* SMITTY)

SMITTY. Cowards! Cowards!

DRISCOLL. (*with no gentle hand slaps the waste over* SMITTY'S *mouth*) That'll teach you to be misnamin' a man, ye sneak. Have ye a handkerchief, Jack? (JACK *hands him one and he ties it tightly around* SMITTY'S *head over the waste*) That'll fix your gab. Stand him up, now, and tie his feet, too, so he'll not be movin'. (*They do so and leave him with his back against the wall near* SCOTTY. *Then they all sit down beside* DRISCOLL, *who again lifts the box out of the water and sets it carefully on his knees. He picks out the key, then hesitates, looking from one to the other uncertainly*) We'd best be takin' this to the skipper, d'you think, maybe?

JACK. (*irritably*) To hell with the Old Man. This is our game and we c'n play it without no help.

COCKY. No bleedin' horficers, I says!

DAVIS. They'd only be takin' all the credit and makin' heroes of themselves.

DRISCOLL. (*boldly*) Here goes, thin! (*He slowly turns the key in the lock. The others instinctively turn away. He carefully pushes the cover back on its hinges and looks at what he sees inside with an expression of puzzled astonishment. The others crowd up close. Even* SCOTTY *leaves his post to take a look*) What is ut, Davis?

DAVIS. (*mystified*) Looks funny, don't it? Somethin' square tied up in a rubber bag. Maybe it's dynamite—or somethin'—you can't never tell.

JACK. Aw, it ain't got no works, so it ain't no bomb, I'll bet.

DAVIS. (*dubiously*) They makes them all kinds, they do.

JACK. Open it up, Drisc.

DAVIS. Careful now! (DRISCOLL *takes a black rubber bag re-*

sembling a large tobacco pouch from the box and unties the string which is wound tightly around the top. He opens it and takes out a small packet of letters also tied up with string. He turns these over in his hands and looks at the others questioningly)

JACK. *(with a broad grin)* On'y letters! *(Slapping* DAVIS *on the back)* Yuh're a hell of a Sherlock Holmes, ain't yuh? Letters from his best girl too, I'll bet. Let's turn the Duke loose, what d'yuh say? *(He starts to get up)*

DAVIS. *(fixing him with a withering look)* Don't be so damn smart, Jack. Letters, you says, 's if there never was no harm in 'em. How d'you s'pose spies gets their orders and sends back what they finds out if it ain't by letters and such things? There's many a letter is worser'n any bomb.

COCKY. Righto! They ain't as innercent as they looks, I'll take me oath, when you read 'em. *(Pointing at* SMITTY*)* Not 'is Lordship's letters; not be no means!

JACK. *(sitting down again)* Well, read 'em and find out. *(*DRISCOLL *commences untying the packet. There is a muffled groan of rage and protest from* SMITTY*)*

DAVIS. *(triumphantly)* There! Listen to him! Look at him tryin' to git loose! Ain't that proof enough? He knows well we're findin' him out. Listen to me! Love letters, you says, Jack, 's if they couldn't harm nothin'. Listen! I was readin' in some magazine in New York on'y two weeks back how some German spy in Paris was writin' love letters to some woman spy in Switzerland who sent 'em on to Berlin, Germany. To read 'em you wouldn't s'pect nothin'—just mush and all. *(Impressively)* But they had a way o' doin' it—a damn sneakin' way. They had a piece o' plain paper with pieces cut out of it an' when they puts it on top o' the letter they sees on'y the words what tells them what they wants to know. An' the Frenchies gets beat in a fight all on account o' that letter.

COCKY. (*awed*) Gawd blimey! They ain't 'arf smart bleeders!

DAVIS. (*seeing his audience is again all with him*) An' even if these letters of his do sound all right they may have what they calls a code. You can't never tell. (*To* DRISCOLL, *who has finished untying the packet*) Read one of 'em, Drisc. My eyes is weak.

DRISCOLL. (*takes the first one out of its envelope and bends down to the lantern with it. He turns up the wick to give him a better light*) I'm no hand to be readin' but I'll try ut. (*Again there is a muffled groan from* SMITTY *as he strains at his bonds*)

DAVIS. (*gloatingly*) Listen to him! He knows. Go ahead, Drisc!

DRISCOLL. (*his brow furrowed with concentration*) Ut begins: Dearest Man—— (*His eyes travel down the page*) An' thin there's a lot av blarney tellin' him how much she misses him now she's gone away to singin' school—an' how she hopes he'll settle down to rale worrk an' not be skylarkin' around now that she's away loike he used to before she met up wid him—and ut ends: "I love you betther than anythin' in the worrld. You know that, don't you, dear? But b'fore I can agree to live out my life wid you, you must prove to me that the black shadow—I won't menshun uts hateful name but you know what I mean—which might wreck both our lives, does not exist for you. You can do that, can't you, dear? Don't you see you must for my sake?" (*He pauses for a moment—then adds gruffly*) Ut's signed: "Edith." (*At the sound of the name* SMITTY, *who has stood tensely with his eyes shut as if he were undergoing torture during the reading, makes a muffled sound like a sob and half turns his face to the wall*)

JACK. (*sympathetically*) Hell! What's the use of readin' that stuff even if——

DAVIS. (*interrupting him sharply*) Wait! What's that letter from, Drisc?

DRISCOLL. There's no address on the top av ut.

DAVIS. (*meaningly*) What'd I tell you? Look at the post-mark, Drisc—on the envelope.

DRISCOLL. The name that's written is Sidney Davidson, wan hundred an'——

DAVIS. Never mind that. O' course it's a false name. Look at the postmark.

DRISCOLL. There's a furrin' stamp on ut by the looks av ut. The mark's blurred so it's hard to read. (*He spells it out laboriously*) B-e-r—the nixt is an l, I think—i—an' an n.

DAVIS. (*excitedly*) Berlin! What did I tell you? I knew them letters was from Germany.

COCKY. (*shaking his fist in* SMITTY'S *direction*) Rotten 'ound! (*The others look at* SMITTY *as if this last fact had utterly condemned him in their eyes*)

DAVIS. Give me the letter, Drisc. Maybe I kin make somethin' out of it. (DRISCOLL *hands the letter to him*) You go through the others, Drisc, and sing out if you sees anythin' queer. (*He bends over the first letter as if he were determined to figure out its secret meaning.* JACK, COCKY *and* SCOTTY *look over his shoulder with eager curiosity.* DRISCOLL *takes out some of the other letters, running his eyes quickly down the pages.*

He looks curiously over at SMITTY *from time to time, and sighs frequently with a puzzled frown*)

DAVIS. (*disappointingly*) I gotter give it up. It's too deep for me, but we'll turn 'em over to the perlice when we docks at Liverpool to look through. This one I got was written a year before the war started anyway. Find anythin' in yours, Drisc?

DRISCOLL. They're all the same as the first—lovin' blarney, an' how her singin' is doin', and the great things the Dutch teacher says about her voice, an' how glad she is that her Sidney bye is worrkin' harrd an' makin' a man av himself for her sake. (SMITTY *turns his face completely to the wall*)

DAVIS. (*disgustedly*) If we on'y had the code!

DRISCOLL. (*taking up the bottom letter*) Hullo! Here's wan addressed to this ship—s. s. *Glencairn,* ut says—whin we was in Cape Town sivin months ago—— (*Looking at the postmark*) Ut's from London.

DAVIS. (*eagerly*) Read it. (*There is another choking groan from* SMITTY)

DRISCOLL. (*reads slowly—his voice becomes lower and lower as he goes on*) Ut begins wid simply the name Sidney Davidson—no dearest or sweetheart to this wan. "Ut is only from your chance meetin' with Harry—whin you were drunk—that I happen to know where to reach you. So you have run away to sea loike the coward you are because you knew I had found out the truth—the truth you have covered over with your mean little lies all the time I was away in Berlin and blindly trusted you. Very well, you have chosen. You have shown that your drunkenness means more to you than any love or faith av mine. I am sorry —for I loved you, Sidney Davidson—but this is the end. I lave you—the mem'ries; an' if ut is any satisfaction to you I lave you the real-i-zation that you have wrecked my loife as you have wrecked your own. My one remainin' hope is that nivir in God's worrld will I ivir see your face again. Good-by. Edith." (*As he finishes there is a deep silence, broken only by* SMITTY'S *muffled sobbing. The men cannot look at each other.* DRISCOLL *holds the rubber bag limply in his hand and some small white object falls out of it and drops noiselessly on the floor. Mechanically* DRISCOLL *leans over and picks it up, and looks at it wonderingly*).

DAVIS. (*in a dull voice*) What's that?

DRISCOLL. (*slowly*) A bit av a dried-up flower—a rose, maybe. (*He drops it into the bag and gathers up the letters and puts them back. He replaces the bag in the box, and locks it and puts it back under* SMITTY'S *mattress. The others follow him with their eyes. He steps softly over to* SMITTY *and cuts the ropes about his arms and ankles with his sheath-knife, and unties the handkerchief over the gag.* SMITTY *does not turn around but covers his face with his hands and leans his head against the wall. His shoulders continue to heave spasmodically but he makes no further sound*)

DRISCOLL. (*stalks back to the others—there is a moment of silence, in which each man is in agony with the hopelessness of finding a word he can say—then* DRISCOLL *explodes*) God stiffen us, are we never goin' to turn in fur a wink av sleep? (*They all start as if awakening from a bad dream and gratefully crawl into their bunks, shoes and all, turning their faces to the wall, and pulling their blankets up over their shoulders.* SCOTTY *tiptoes past* SMITTY *out into the darkness. . . .* DRISCOLL *turns down the light and crawls into his bunk as*

The Curtain Falls)

ILE

A Play in One Act

CHARACTERS

BEN, *the cabin boy*

THE STEWARD

CAPTAIN KEENEY

SLOCUM, *second mate*

MRS. KEENEY

JOE, *a harpooner*

Members of the crew of the steam whaler Atlantic Queen

ILE

SCENE. CAPTAIN KEENEY's *cabin on board the steam whaling ship* Atlantic Queen—*a small, square compartment about eight feet high with a skylight in the center looking out on the poop deck. On the left (the stern of the ship) a long bench with rough cushions is built in against the wall. In front of the bench, a table. Over the bench, several curtained portholes.*

In the rear, left, a door leading to the CAPTAIN'S *sleeping quarters. To the right of the door a small organ, looking as if it were brand-new, is placed against the wall.*

On the right, to the rear, a marble-topped sideboard. On the sideboard, a woman's sewing basket. Farther forward, a doorway leading to the companionway, and past the officers' quarters to the main deck.

In the center of the room, a stove. From the middle of the ceiling a hanging lamp is suspended. The walls of the cabin are painted white.

There is no rolling of the ship, and the light which comes through the skylight is sickly and faint, indicating one of those gray days of calm when ocean and sky are alike dead. The silence is unbroken except for the measured tread of someone walking up and down on the poop deck overhead.

It is nearing two bells—one o'clock—in the afternoon of a day in the year 1895.

At the rise of the curtain there is a moment of intense silence. Then the STEWARD *enters and commences to clear the table of the few dishes which still remain on it after the* CAPTAIN'S *dinner. He is an old, grizzled man dressed in dungaree pants, a sweater, and a woolen cap with ear-flaps. His manner is sullen and angry. He stops stacking up the plates and casts a quick glance upward at the skylight; then tiptoes over to the closed door in rear and listens with his ear pressed to the crack. What he hears makes his face darken and he mutters a furious curse. There is a noise from the doorway on the right and he darts back to the table.*

BEN *enters. He is an overgrown, gawky boy with a long, pinched face. He is dressed in sweater, fur cap, etc. His teeth are chattering with the cold and he hurries to the stove, where he stands for a moment shivering, blowing on his hands, slapping them against his sides, on the verge of crying.*

THE STEWARD. (*in relieved tones—seeing who it is*) Oh, 'tis you, is it? What're ye shiverin' 'bout? Stay by the stove where ye belong and ye'll find no need of chatterin'.

BEN. It's c-c-cold. (*Trying to control his chattering teeth —derisively*) Who d'ye think it were—the Old Man?

THE STEWARD. (*makes a threatening move—*BEN *shrinks away*) None o' your lip, young un, or I'll learn ye. (*More kindly*) Where was it ye've been all o' the time—the fo'c's'tle?

BEN. Yes.

THE STEWARD. Let the Old Man see ye up for'ard monkeyshinin' with the hands and ye'll get a hidin' ye'll not forget in a hurry.

BEN. Aw, he don't see nothin'. (*A trace of awe in his tones —he glances upward*) He just walks up and down like he didn't notice nobody—and stares at the ice to the no'the'ard.

THE STEWARD. (*the same tone of awe creeping into his voice*) He's always starin' at the ice. (*In a sudden rage, shaking his fist at the skylight*) Ice, ice, ice! Damn him and damn the ice! Holdin' us in for nigh on a year—nothin' to see but ice —stuck in it like a fly in molasses!

BEN. (*apprehensively*) Ssshh! He'll hear ye.

THE STEWARD. (*raging*) Aye, damn him, and damn the Arctic seas, and damn this stinkin' whalin' ship of his, and damn me for a fool to ever ship on it! (*Subsiding as if realizing the uselessness of this outburst—shaking his head—slowly, with deep conviction*) He's a hard man—as hard a man as ever sailed the seas.

BEN. (*solemnly*) Aye.

THE STEWARD. The two years we all signed up for are done this day. Blessed Christ! Two years o' this dog's life, and no luck in the fishin', and the hands half starved with the food runnin' low, rotten as it is; and not a sign of him turnin' back for home! (*Bitterly*) Home! I begin to doubt if ever I'll set foot on land again. (*Excitedly*) What is it he thinks he's goin' to do? Keep us all up here after our time is worked out till the last man of us is starved to death or frozen? We've grub enough hardly to last out the voyage back if we started now. What are the men goin' to do' bout it? Did ye hear any talk in the fo'c's'tle?

BEN. (*going over to him—in a half-whisper*) They said if he don't put back south for home today they're goin' to mutiny.

THE STEWARD. (*with grim satisfaction*) Mutiny? Aye, 'tis

the only thing they can do; and serve him right after the manner he's treated them—'s if they weren't no better nor dogs.

BEN. The ice is all broke up to s'uth'ard. They's clear water 's far 's you can see. He ain't got no excuse for not turnin' back for home, the men says.

THE STEWARD. (*bitterly*) He won't look nowheres but no'the'ard where they's only the ice to see. He don't want to see no clear water. All he thinks on is gittin' the ile—'s if it was our fault he ain't had good luck with the whales. (*Shaking his head*) I think the man's mighty nigh losin' his senses.

BEN. (*awed*) D'you really think he's crazy?

THE STEWARD. Aye, it's the punishment o' God on him. Did ye ever hear of a man who wasn't crazy do the things he does? (*Pointing to the door in rear*) Who but a man that's mad would take his woman—and as sweet a woman as ever was—on a stinkin' whalin' ship to the Arctic seas to be locked in by the rotten ice for nigh on a year, and maybe lose her senses forever—for it's sure she'll never be the same again.

BEN. (*sadly*) She useter be awful nice to me before—(*his eyes grow wide and frightened*)—she got—like she is.

THE STEWARD. Aye, she was good to all of us. 'Twould have been hell on board without her; for he's a hard man—a hard, hard man—a driver if there ever was one. (*With a grim laugh*) I hope he's satisfied now—drivin' her on till she's near lost her mind. And who could blame her? 'Tis a God's wonder we're not a ship full of crazed people—with the damned ice all the time, and the quiet so thick you're afraid to hear your own voice.

BEN. (*with a frightened glance toward the door on right*) She don't never speak to me no more—jest looks at me 's if she didn't know me.

THE STEWARD. She don't know no one—but him. She talks to him—when she does talk—right enough.

BEN. She does nothin' all day long now but sit and sew—and then she cries to herself without makin' no noise. I've seen her.

THE STEWARD. Aye, I could hear her through the door a while back.

BEN. (*tiptoes over to the door and listens*) She's cryin' now.

THE STEWARD. (*furiously—shaking his fist*) God send his soul to hell for the devil he is! (*There is the noise of someone coming slowly down the companionway stairs.* THE STEWARD *hurries to his stacked-up dishes. He is so nervous from fright that he knocks off the top one, which falls and breaks on the floor. He stands aghast, trembling with dread.* BEN *is violently rubbing off the organ with a piece of cloth which he has snatched from his pocket.* CAPTAIN KEENEY *appears in the doorway on right and comes into the cabin, removing his fur cap as he does so. He is a man of about forty, around five-ten in height but looking much shorter on account of the enormous proportions of his shoulders and chest. His face is massive and deeply lined, with gray-blue eyes of a bleak hardness, and a tightly clenched, thin-lipped mouth. His thick hair is long and gray. He is dressed in a heavy blue jacket and blue pants stuffed into his sea-boots.*

He is followed into the cabin by the SECOND MATE, *a rangy six-footer with a lean weather-beaten face. The* MATE *is dressed about the same as the* CAPTAIN. *He is a man of thirty or so*)

KEENEY. (*comes toward* THE STEWARD*—with a stern look on his face.* THE STEWARD *is visibly frightened and the stack of* *dishes rattle in his trembling hands.* KEENEY *draws back his fist and* THE STEWARD *shrinks away. The fist is gradually lowered and* KEENEY *speaks slowly)* 'Twould be like hitting a worm. It is nigh on two bells, Mr. Steward, and this truck not cleared yet.

THE STEWARD. *(stammering)* Y-y-yes, sir.

KEENEY. Instead of doin' your rightful work ye've been below here gossipin' old woman's talk with that boy. *(To* BEN, *fiercely)* Get out o' this, you! Clean up the chart-room. *(*BEN *darts past the* MATE *to the open doorway.)* Pick up that dish, Mr. Steward!

THE STEWARD. *(doing so with difficulty)* Yes, sir.

KEENEY. The next dish you break, Mr. Steward, you take a bath in the Bering Sea at the end of a rope.

THE STEWARD. *(tremblingly)* Yes, sir. *(He hurries out. The* SECOND MATE *walks slowly over to the* CAPTAIN*)*

MATE. I warn't 'specially anxious the man at the wheel should catch what I wanted to say to you, sir. That's why I asked you to come below.

KEENEY. *(impatiently)* Speak your say, Mr. Slocum.

MATE. *(unconsciously lowering his voice)* I'm afeard there'll be trouble with the hands by the look o' things. They'll likely turn ugly, every blessed one o' them, if you don't put back. The two years they signed up for is up today.

KEENEY. And d'you think you're tellin' me somethin' new, Mr. Slocum? I've felt it in the air this long time past. D'you think I've not seen their ugly looks and the grudgin' way they worked? *(The door in rear is opened and* MRS. KEENEY *stands in the doorway. She is a slight, sweet-faced little woman primly dressed in black. Her eyes are red from weeping and her face drawn and pale. She takes in the cabin with a frightened glance and stands as if fixed to the spot by some nameless dread, clasping and unclasping her hands nervously. The two men turn and look at her)*

KEENEY. *(with rough tenderness)* Well, Annie?

MRS. KEENEY. *(as if awakening from a dream)* David, I—— *(She is silent. The* MATE *starts for the doorway)*

KEENEY. *(turning to him—sharply)* Wait!

MATE. Yes, sir.

KEENEY. D'you want anything, Annie?

MRS. KEENEY. *(after a pause, during which she seems to be endeavoring to collect her thoughts)* I thought maybe—I'd go on deck, David, to get a breath of fresh air. *(She stands humbly awaiting his permission. He and the* MATE *exchange a significant glance)*

KEENEY. It's too cold, Annie. You'd best stay below today. There's nothing to look at on deck—but ice.

MRS. KEENEY. *(monotonously)* I know—ice, ice, ice! But there's nothing to see down here but these walls. *(She makes a gesture of loathing)*

KEENEY. You can play the organ, Annie.

MRS. KEENEY. *(dully)* I hate the organ. It puts me in mind of home.

KEENEY. *(a touch of resentment in his voice)* I got it jest for you.

MRS. KEENEY. *(dully)* I know. *(She turns away from them and walks slowly to the bench on left. She lifts up one of the curtains and looks through a porthole; then utters an exclamation of joy)* Ah, water! Clear water! As far as I can see! How good it looks after all these months of ice! *(She turns round to them, her face transfigured with joy)* Ah, now I must go up on the deck and look at it, David.

KEENEY. *(frowning)* Best not today, Annie. Best wait for a day when the sun shines.

MRS. KEENEY. *(desperately)* But the sun never shines in this terrible place.

KEENEY. *(a tone of command in his voice)* Best not today, Annie.

MRS. KEENEY. *(crumbling before this command—abjectly)* Very well, David. *(She stands there staring straight before her as if in a daze. The two men look at her uneasily)*

KEENEY. *(sharply)* Annie!

MRS. KEENEY. *(dully)* Yes, David.

KEENEY. Me and Mr. Slocum has business to talk about—ship's business.

MRS. KEENEY. Very well, David. *(She goes slowly out, rear, and leaves the door three-quarters shut behind her)*

KEENEY. Best not have her on deck if they's goin' to be any trouble.

MATE. Yes, sir.

KEENEY. And trouble they's going to be. I feel it in my bones. *(Takes a revolver from the pocket of his coat and examines it)* Got your'n?

MATE. Yes, sir.

KEENEY. Not that we'll have to use 'em—not if I know their breed of dog—jest to frighten 'em up a bit. *(Grimly)* I ain't never been forced to use one yit; and trouble I've had by land and by sea 's long as I kin remember, and will have till my dyin' day, I reckon.

MATE. *(hesitatingly)* Then you ain't goin'—to turn back?

KEENEY. Turn back? Mr. Slocum, did you ever hear o' me pointin' s'uth for home with only a measly four hundred barrel of ile in the hold?

MATE. (*hastily*) No, sir—but the grub's gittin' low.

KEENEY. They's enough to last a long time yit, if they're careful with it; and they's plenty o' water.

MATE. They say it's not fit to eat—what's left; and the two years they signed on fur is up today. They might make trouble for you in the courts when we git home.

KEENEY. To hell with 'em! Let them make what law trouble they kin. I don't give a damn 'bout the money. I've got to git the ile! (*Glancing sharply at the* MATE) You ain't turnin' no damned sea-lawyer, be you, Mr. Slocum?

MATE. (*flushing*) Not by a hell of a sight, sir.

KEENEY. What do the fools want to go home fur now? Their share o' the four hundred barrel wouldn't keep 'em in chewin' terbacco.

MATE. (*slowly*) They wants to git back to their folks an' things, I s'pose.

KEENEY. (*looking at him searchingly*) 'N you want to turn back, too. (*The* MATE *looks down confusedly before his sharp gaze*) Don't lie, Mr. Slocum. It's writ down plain in your eyes. (*With grim sarcasm*) I hope, Mr. Slocum, you ain't agoin' to jine the men agin me.

MATE. (*indignantly*) That ain't fair, sir, to say sich things.

KEENEY (*with satisfaction*) I warn't much afeard o' that, Tom. You been with me nigh on ten year and I've learned ye whalin'. No man kin say I ain't a good master, if I be a hard one.

MATE. I warn't thinkin' of myself, sir—'bout turnin' home,

I mean. (*Desperately*) But Mrs. Keeney, sir—seems like she ain't jest satisfied up here, ailin' like—what with the cold an' bad luck an' the ice an' all.

KEENEY. (*his face clouding—rebukingly but not severely*) That's my business, Mr. Slocum. I'll thank you to steer a clear course o' that. (*A pause*) The ice'll break up soon to no'th'ard. I could see it startin' today. And when it goes and we git some sun Annie'll perk up. (*Another pause—then he bursts forth*) It ain't the damned money what's keepin' me up in the Northern seas, Tom. But I can't go back to Homeport with a measly four hundred barrel of ile. I'd die fust. I ain't never come back home in all my days without a full ship. Ain't that truth?

MATE. Yes, sir; but this voyage you been icebound, an'——

KEENEY. (*scornfully*) And d'you s'pose any of 'em would believe that—any o' them skippers I've beaten voyage after voyage? Can't you hear 'em laughin' and sneerin'—Tibbots 'n' Harris 'n' Simms and the rest—and all o' Homeport makin' fun o' me? "Dave Keeney what boasts he's the best whalin' skipper out o' Homeport comin' back with a measly four hundred barrel of ile?" (*The thought of this drives him into a frenzy, and he smashes his fist down on the marble top of the sideboard*) Hell! I got to git the ile, I tell you. How could I figger on this ice? It's never been so bad before in the thirty year I been acomin' here. And now it's breakin' up. In a couple o' days it'll be all gone. And they's whale here, plenty of 'em. I know they is and I ain't never gone wrong yit. I got to git the ile! I got to git in in spite of all hell, and by God, I ain't agoin' home till I do git it! (*There is the sound of subdued sobbing from the door in the rear. The two men stand silent for a moment, listening. Then* KEENEY *goes over to the door and looks in. He hesitates for a moment as if he were going to enter—then closes the door softly.* JOE, *the harpooner, an enormous six-footer with a battered, ugly face, enters from right and stands waiting for the captain to notice him)*

KEENEY. *(turning and seeing him)* Don't be standin' there like a gawk, Harpooner. Speak up!

JOE. *(confusedly)* We want—the men, sir—they wants to send a depitation aft to have a word with you.

KEENEY. *(furiously)* Tell 'em to go to—— *(Checks himself and continues grimly)* Tell 'em to come. I'll see 'em.

JOE. Aye, aye, sir. *(He goes out)*

KEENEY. *(with a grim smile)* Here it comes, the trouble you spoke of, Mr. Slocum, and we'll make short shift of it. It's better to crush such things at the start than let them make headway.

MATE. *(worriedly)* Shall I wake up the First and Fourth, sir? We might need their help.

KEENEY. No, let them sleep. I'm well able to handle this alone, Mr. Slocum. *(There is the shuffling of footsteps from outside and five of the crew crowd into the cabin, led by* JOE. *All are dressed alike—sweaters, sea-boots, etc. They glance uneasily at the* CAPTAIN, *twirling their fur caps in their hands)*

KEENEY. *(after a pause)* Well? Who's to speak fur ye?

JOE. *(stepping forward with an air of bravado)* I be.

KEENEY. *(eyeing him up and down coldly)* So you be. Then speak your say and be quick about it.

JOE. *(trying not to wilt before the* CAPTAIN'S *glance and avoiding his eyes)* The time we signed up for is done today.

KEENEY. *(icily)* You're tellin' me nothin' I don't know.

JOE. You ain't pintin' fur home yit, far 's we kin see.

KEENEY. No, and I ain't agoin' to till this ship is full of ile.

JOE. You can't go no further no'the with the ice afore ye.

KEENEY. The ice is breaking up.

JOE. (*after a slight pause during which the others mumble angrily to one another*) The grub we're gittin' now is rotten.

KEENEY. It's good enough fur ye. Better men than ye are have eaten worse. (*There is a chorus of angry exclamations from the crowd*)

JOE. (*encouraged by this support*) We ain't agoin' to work no more 'less you puts back for home.

KEENEY. (*fiercely*) You ain't, ain't you?

JOE. No; and the law courts'll say we was right.

KEENEY. To hell with your law courts! We're at sea now and I'm the law on this ship. (*Edging up toward the harpooner*) And every mother's son of you what don't obey orders goes in irons. (*There are more angry exclamations from the crew.* MRS. KEENEY *appears in the doorway in rear and looks on with startled eyes. None of the men notice her*).

JOE. (*with bravado*) Then we're agoin' to mutiny and take the old hooker home ourselves. Ain't we, boys? (*As he turns his head to look at the others,* KEENEY'S *fist shoots out to the side of his jaw.* JOE *goes down in a heap and lies there.* MRS. KEENEY *gives a shriek and hides her face in her hands. The men pull out their sheath-knives and start a rush, but stop when they find themselves confronted by the revolvers of* KEENEY *and the* MATE)

KEENEY. (*his eyes and voice snapping*) Hold still! (*The men stand huddled together in a sullen silence.* KEENEY'S *voice is full of mockery*) You've found out it ain't safe to mutiny on this ship, ain't you? And now git for'ard where ye belong, and—— (*He gives* JOE'*s body a contemptuous kick*) Drag him with you. And remember the first man of ye I see shirkin' I'll shoot dead as sure as there's a sea under us, and you can tell the rest the same. Git for'ard now! Quick! (*The men leave in cowed silence, carrying* JOE *with them.* KEENEY *turns to the* MATE *with a short laugh and puts his revolver back in his pocket*) Best get up on deck, Mr. Slocum, and see to it they don't try none of their skulkin' tricks. We'll have to keep an eye peeled from now on. I know 'em.

MATE. Yes, sir. (*He goes out, right.* KEENEY *hears his wife's hysterical weeping and turns around in surprise—then walks slowly to her side*)

KEENEY. (*putting an arm around her shoulder—with gruff tenderness*) There, there, Annie. Don't be afeard. It's all past and gone.

MRS. KEENEY. (*shrinking away from him*) Oh, I can't bear it! I can't bear it any longer!

KEENEY. (*gently*) Can't bear what, Annie?

MRS. KEENEY. (*hysterically*) All this horrible brutality, and these brutes of men, and this terrible ship, and this prison cell of a room, and the ice all around, and the silence. (*After this outburst she calms down and wipes her eyes with her handkerchief*)

KEENEY. (*after a pause during which he looks down at her with a puzzled frown*) Remember, I warn't hankerin' to have you come on this voyage, Annie.

MRS. KEENEY. I wanted to be with you, David, don't you see? I didn't want to wait back there in the house all alone as I've been doing these last six years since we were married—waiting, and watching, and fearing—with nothing to keep my mind occupied—not able to go back teaching school on account of being Dave Keeney's wife. I used to dream of sailing on the great, wide, glorious ocean. I wanted to be by your side in the danger and vigorous life of it all. I wanted to see you the hero they make you out to be in Homeport. And instead—— (*Her voice grows tremulous*) All I find is ice and cold—and brutality! (*Her voice breaks*)

KEENEY. I warned you what it'd be, Annie. "Whalin' ain't no ladies' tea-party," I says to you, and "you better stay to home where you've got all your woman's comforts." (*Shaking his head*) But you was so set on it.

MRS. KEENEY. (*wearily*) Oh, I know it isn't your fault, David. You see, I didn't believe you. I guess I was dreaming about the old Vikings in the story-books and I thought you were one of them.

KEENEY. (*protestingly*) I done my best to make it as cozy and comfortable as could be. (MRS. KEENEY *looks around her in wild scorn*) I even sent to the city for that organ for ye, thinkin' it might be soothin' to ye to be playin' it times when they was calms and things was dull-like.

MRS. KEENEY. (*wearily*) Yes, you were very kind, David. I know that. (*She goes to left and lifts the curtains from the porthole and looks out—then suddenly bursts forth*) I won't stand it—I can't stand it—pent up by these walls like a prisoner. (*She runs over to him and throws her arms around him, weeping. He puts his arm protectingly over her shoulders*) Take me away from here, David! If I don't get away from here, out of this terrible ship, I'll go mad! Take me home, David! I can't think any more. I feel as if the cold and the silence were crushing down on my brain. I'm afraid. Take me home!

KEENEY. (*holds her at arm's length and looks at her anxiously*) Best go to bed, Annie. You ain't yourself. You got fever. Your eyes look so strange-like. I ain't never seen you look this way before.

MRS. KEENEY. (*laughing hysterically*) It's the ice and the cold and the silence—they'd make anyone look strange.

KEENEY. (*soothingly*) In a month or two, with good luck, three at the most, I'll have her filled with ile and then we'll give her everything she'll stand and pint for home.

MRS. KEENEY. But we can't wait for that—I can't wait. I want to get home. And the men won't wait. They want to get home. It's cruel, it's brutal for you to keep them. You must sail back. You've got no excuse. There's clear water to the south now. If you've a heart at all you've got to turn back.

KEENEY. (*harshly*) I can't, Annie.

MRS. KEENEY. Why can't you?

KEENEY. A woman couldn't rightly understand my reason.

MRS. KEENEY. (*wildly*) Because it's a stupid, stubborn reason. Oh, I heard you talking with the second mate. You're afraid the other captains will sneer at you because you didn't come back with a full ship. You want to live up to your silly reputation even if you do have to beat and starve men and drive me mad to do it.

KEENEY. (*his jaw set stubbornly*) It ain't that, Annie. Them skippers would never dare sneer to my face. It ain't so much what anyone'd say—but—— (*He hesitates, struggling to express his meaning*) You see—I've always done it—since my first voyage as skipper. I always come back—with a full ship—and—it don't seem right not to—somehow. I been always first whalin' skipper out o' Homeport, and—— Don't you see my meanin', Annie? (*He glances at her. She is not looking at him but staring dully in front of her, not hearing a word he is saying*) Annie! (*She comes to herself with a start*) Best turn in, Annie, there's a good woman. You ain't well.

MRS. KEENEY. (*resisting his attempts to guide her to the door in rear*) David! Won't you please turn back?

KEENEY. (*gently*) I can't, Annie—not yet awhile. You don't see my meanin'. I got to git the ile.

MRS. KEENEY. It'd be different if you needed the money, but you don't. You've got more than plenty.

KEENEY. (*impatiently*) It ain't the money I'm thinkin' of. D'you think I'm as mean as that?

MRS. KEENEY. (*dully*) No—I don't know—I can't understand—— (*Intensely*) Oh, I want to be home in the old house once more and see my own kitchen again, and hear a woman's voice talking to me and be able to talk to her. Two years! It seems so long ago—as if I'd been dead and could never go back.

KEENEY. (*worried by her strange tone and the far-away look in her eyes*) Best go to bed, Annie. You ain't well.

MRS. KEENEY. (*not appearing to hear him*) I used to be lonely when you were away. I used to think Homeport was a stupid, monotonous place. Then I used to go down on the beach, especially when it was windy and the breakers were rolling in, and I'd dream of the fine free life you must be leading. (*She gives a laugh which is half a sob*) I used to love the sea then. (*She pauses; then continues with slow intensity*) But now—I don't ever want to see the sea again.

KEENEY. (*thinking to humor her*) 'Tis no fit place for a woman, that's sure. I was a fool to bring ye.

MRS. KEENEY. (*after a pause—passing her hand over her eyes with a gesture of pathetic weariness*) How long would it take us to reach home—if we started now?

KEENEY. (*frowning*) 'Bout two months, I reckon, Annie, with fair luck.

MRS. KEENEY. (*counts on her fingers—then murmurs with a rapt smile*) That would be August, the latter part of August, wouldn't it? It was on the twenty-fifth of August we were married, David, wasn't it?

KEENEY. (*trying to conceal the fact that her memories have moved him—gruffly*) Don't *you* remember?

MRS. KEENEY. (*vaguely—again passes her hand over her eyes*) My memory is leaving me—up here in the ice. It was so long ago. (*A pause—then she smiles dreamily*) It's June now. The lilacs will be all in bloom in the front yard—and the climbing roses on the trellis to the side of the house—they're budding. (*She suddenly covers her face with her hands and commences to sob*)

KEENEY. (*disturbed*) Go in and rest, Annie. You're all wore out cryin' over what can't be helped.

MRS. KEENEY. (*suddenly throwing her arms around his neck and clinging to him*) You love me, don't you, David?

KEENEY. (*in amazed embarrassment at this outburst*) Love you? Why d'you ask me such a question, Annie?

MRS. KEENEY. (*shaking him—fiercely*) But you do, don't you, David? Tell me!

KEENEY. I'm your husband, Annie, and you're my wife. Could there be aught but love between us after all these years?

MRS. KEENEY. (*shaking him again—still more fiercely*) Then you do love me. Say it!

KEENEY. (*simply*) I do, Annie!

MRS. KEENEY. (*gives a sigh of relief—her hands drop to her sides.* KEENEY *regards her anxiously. She passes her hand across her eyes and murmurs half to herself*) I sometimes think if we could only have had a child. (KEENEY *turns away from her, deeply moved. She grabs his arm and turns him around to face her—intensely*) And I've always been a good wife to you, haven't I, David?

KEENEY. (*his voice betraying his emotion*) No man has ever had a better, Annie.

MRS. KEENEY. And I've never asked for much from you, have I, David? Have I?

KEENEY. You know you could have all I got the power to give ye, Annie.

MRS. KEENEY. (*wildly*) Then do this this once for my sake, for God's sake—take me home! It's killing me, this life—the brutality and cold and horror of it. I'm going mad. I can feel the threat in the air. I can hear the silence threatening me—day after gray day and every day the same. I can't bear it. (*Sobbing*) I'll go mad, I know I will. Take me home, David, if you love me as you say. I'm afraid. For the love of God, take me home! (*She throws her arms around him, weeping against his shoulder. His face betrays the tremendous struggle going on within him. He holds her out at arm's length, his expression softening. For a moment his shoulders sag, he becomes old, his iron spirit weakens as he looks at her tear-stained face*)

KEENEY. (*dragging out the words with an effort*) I'll do it, Annie—for your sake—if you say it's needful for ye.

MRS. KEENEY. (*with wild joy—kissing him*) God bless you for that, David! (*He turns away from her silently and walks toward the companionway. Just at that moment there is a clatter of footsteps on the stairs and the* SECOND MATE *enters the cabin*)

MATE. (*excitedly*) The ice is breakin' up to no'the'ard, sir. There's a clear passage through the floe, and clear water beyond, the lookout says. (KEENEY *straightens himself like a man coming out of a trance.* MRS. KEENEY *looks at the* MATE *with terrified eyes*)

KEENEY. (*dazedly—trying to collect his thoughts*) A clear passage? To no'the'ard?

MATE. Yes, sir.

KEENEY. (*his voice suddenly grim with determination*) Then get her ready and we'll drive her through.

MATE. Aye, aye, sir.

MRS. KEENEY. (*appealingly*) David!

KEENEY. (*not heeding her*) Will the men turn to willin' or must we drag 'em out?

MATE. They'll turn to willin' enough. You put the fear o' God into 'em, sir. They're meek as lambs.

KEENEY. Then drive 'em—both watches. (*With grim determination*) They's whale t'other side o' this floe and we're going to git 'em.

MATE. Aye, aye, sir. (*He goes out hurriedly. A moment later there is the sound of scuffling feet from the deck outside and the* MATE'*s voice shouting orders*)

KEENEY. (*speaking aloud to himself—derisively*) And I was agoin' home like a yaller dog!

MRS. KEENEY. (*imploringly*) David!

KEENEY. (*sternly*) Woman, you ain't adoin' right when you meddle in men's business and weaken 'em. You can't know my feelin's. I got to prove a man to be a good husband for ye to take pride in. I got to git the ile, I tell ye.

MRS. KEENEY. (*supplicatingly*) David! Aren't you going home?

KEENEY. (*ignoring this question—commandingly*) You ain't well. Go and lay down a mite. (*He starts for the door*) I got to git on deck. (*He goes out. She cries after him in anguish*) David! (*A pause. She passes her hand across her eyes—then commences to laugh hysterically and goes to the organ. She sits down and starts to play wildly an old hymn.* KEENEY *reënters from the doorway to the deck and stands looking at her angrily. He comes over and grabs her roughly by the shoulder*)

KEENEY. Woman, what foolish mockin' is this? (*She laughs wildly and he starts back from her in alarm*) Annie! What is it? (*She doesn't answer him.* KEENEY's *voice trembles*) Don't you know me, Annie? (*He puts both hands on her shoulders and turns her around so that he can look into her eyes. She stares up at him with a stupid expression, a vague smile on her lips. He stumbles away from her, and she commences softly to play the organ again*)

KEENEY. (*swallowing hard—in a hoarse whisper, as if he had difficulty in speaking*) You said—you was agoin' mad—God! (*A long wail is heard from the deck above*) Ah bl-o-o-o-ow! (*A moment later the* MATE's *face appears through the skylight. He cannot see* MRS. KEENEY)

MATE. (*in great excitement*) Whales, sir—a whole school of 'em—off the star'b'd quarter 'bout five miles away—big ones!

KEENEY. (*galvanized into action*) Are you lowerin' the boats?

MATE. Yes, sir.

KEENEY. (*with grim decision*) I'm acomin' with ye.

MATE. Aye, aye, sir. (*Jubilantly*) You'll git the ile now right enough, sir. (*His head is withdrawn and he can be heard shouting orders*)

KEENEY. (*turning to his wife*) Annie! Did you hear him? I'll git the ile. (*She doesn't answer or seem to know he is there. He gives a hard laugh, which is almost a groan*) I know you're foolin' me. Annie. You ain't out of your mind—(*anxiously*) be you? I'll git the ile now right enough—jest a little while longer, Annie—then we'll turn hom'ard. I can't turn back now, you see that, don't ye? I've got to git the ile. (*In sudden terror*) Answer me! You ain't mad, be you? (*She keeps on playing the organ, but makes no reply. The* MATE'*s face appears again through the skylight*)

MATE. All ready, sir. (KEENEY *turns his back on his wife and strides to the doorway, where he stands for a moment and looks back at her in anguish, fighting to control his feelings*)

MATE. Comin', sir?

KEENEY. (*his face suddenly grown hard with determination*) Aye. (*He turns abruptly and goes out.* MRS. KEENEY *does not appear to notice his departure. Her whole attention seems centered in the organ. She sits with half-closed eyes, her body swaying a little from side to side to the rhythm of the hymn. Her fingers move faster and faster and she is playing wildly and discordantly as*

The Curtain Falls)

WHERE THE CROSS IS MADE

A Play in One Act

CHARACTERS

CAPTAIN ISAIAH BARTLETT
NAT BARTLETT, *his son*
SUE BARTLETT, *his daughter*
DOCTOR HIGGINS
SILAS HORNE, *mate*
CATES, *bo'sun*
JIMMY KANAKA, *harpooner*

(Silas Horne, Cates and Jimmy Kanaka: *of the schooner* Mary Allen)

WHERE THE CROSS IS MADE

SCENE. *Captain Bartlett's "cabin"—a room erected as a lookout post at the top of his house situated on a high point of land on the California coast. The inside of the compartment is fitted up like the captain's cabin of a deep-sea sailing vessel. On the left, forward, a porthole. Farther back, the stairs of the companionway. Still farther, two more portholes. In the rear, left, a marble-topped sideboard with a ship's lantern on it. In the rear, center, a door opening on stairs which lead to the lower house. A cot with a blanket is placed against the wall to the right of the door. In the right wall, five portholes. Directly under them, a wooden bench. In front of the bench, a long table with two straight-backed chairs, one in front, the other to the left of it. A cheap, dark-colored rug is on the floor. In the ceiling, midway from front to rear, a skylight extending from opposite the door to above the left edge of the table. In the right extremity of the skylight is placed a floating ship's compass. The light from the binnacle sheds over this from above and seeps down into the room, casting a vague globular shadow of the compass on the floor.*

The time is an early hour of a clear windy night in the fall of the year 1900. Moonlight, winnowed by the wind which moans in the stubborn angles of the old house, creeps wearily in through the portholes and rests like tired dust in circular patches upon the floor and table. An insistent monotone of thundering surf, muffled and far-off, is borne upward from the beach below.

After the curtain rises the door in the rear is opened slowly and the head and shoulders of NAT BARTLETT *appear over the sill. He casts a quick glance about the room, and seeing no one there, ascends the remaining steps and enters. He makes a sign to someone in the darkness beneath: "All right, Doctor."* DOCTOR HIGGINS *follows him into the room and, closing the door, stands looking with great curiosity around him. He is a slight, medium-sized professional-looking man of about thirty-five.* NAT BARTLETT *is very tall, gaunt, and loose-framed. His right arm has been amputated at the shoulder and the sleeve on that side of the heavy mackinaw he wears hangs flabbily or flaps against his body as he moves. He appears much older than his thirty years. His shoulders have a weary stoop as if worn down by the burden of his massive head with its heavy shock of tangled black hair. His face is long, bony, and sallow, with deep-set black eyes, a large aquiline nose, a wide thin-lipped mouth shadowed by an unkempt bristle of mustache. His voice is low and deep with a penetrating, hollow, metallic quality. In addition to the mackinaw, he wears corduroy trousers stuffed down into high laced boots.*

NAT. Can you see, Doctor?

HIGGINS. (*in the too-casual tones which betray an inward uneasiness*) Yes—perfectly—don't trouble. The moonlight is so bright——

NAT. Luckily. (*Walking slowly toward the table*) He doesn't want any light—lately—only the one from the binnacle there.

HIGGINS. He? Ah—you mean your father?

NAT. (*impatiently*) Who else?

HIGGINS. (*a bit startled—gazing around him in embarrass-*

ment) I suppose this is all meant to be like a ship's cabin?

NAT. Yes—as I warned you.

HIGGINS. (*in surprise*) Warned me? Why, warned? I think it's very natural—and interesting—this whim of his.

NAT. (*meaningly*) Interesting, it may be.

HIGGINS. And he lives up here, you said—never comes down?

NAT. Never—for the past three years. My sister brings his food up to him. (*He sits down in the chair to the left of the table*) There's a lantern on the sideboard there, Doctor. Bring it over and sit down. We'll make a light. I'll ask your pardon for bringing you to this room on the roof—but—no one'll hear us here; and by seeing for yourself the mad way he lives—— Understand that I want you to get all the facts—just that, facts! —and for that light is necessary. Without that—they become dreams up here—dreams, Doctor.

HIGGINS. (*with a relieved smile carries over the lantern*) It is a trifle spooky.

NAT. (*not seeming to notice this remark*) He won't take any note of this light. His eyes are too busy—out there. (*He flings his left arm in a wide gesture seaward*) And if he does notice—well, let him come down. You're bound to see him sooner or later. (*He scratches a match and lights the lantern*)

HIGGINS. Where is—he?

NAT. (*pointing upward*) Up on the poop. Sit down, man! He'll not come—yet awhile.

HIGGINS. (*sitting gingerly on the chair in front of table*) Then he has the roof too rigged up like a ship?

NAT. I told you he had. Like a deck, yes. A wheel, compass, binnacle light, the companionway there (*he points*), a bridge to pace up and down on—*and keep watch.* If the wind wasn't so high you'd hear him now—back and forth—all the live-long night. (*With a sudden harshness*) Didn't I tell you he's mad?

HIGGINS. (*with a professional air*) That was nothing new. I've heard that about him from all sides since I first came to the asylum yonder. You say he only walks at night—up there?

NAT. Only at night, yes. (*Grimly*) The things he wants to see can't be made out in daylight—dreams and such.

HIGGINS. But just what is he trying to see? Does anyone know? Does he tell?

NAT. (*impatiently*) Why, everyone knows what Father looks for, man! The ship, of course.

HIGGINS. What ship?

NAT. His ship—the Mary Allen—named for my dead mother.

HIGGINS. But—I don't understand—— Is the ship long overdue—or what?

NAT. Lost in a hurricane off the Celebes with all on board—three years ago!

HIGGINS. (*wonderingly*) Ah. (*After a pause*) But your father still clings to a doubt——

NAT. There is no doubt for him or anyone else to cling to. She was sighted bottom up, a complete wreck, by the whaler John Slocum. That was two weeks after the storm. They sent a boat out to read her name.

HIGGINS. And hasn't your father ever heard——

NAT. He was the first to hear, naturally. Oh, he *knows* right enough, if that's what you're driving at. (*He bends toward the doctor—intensely*) He *knows*, Doctor, he *knows*—but he won't *believe*. He can't—and keep living.

HIGGINS. (*impatiently*) Come, Mr. Bartlett, let's get down to brass tacks. You didn't drag me up here to make things more obscure, did you? Let's have the facts you spoke of. I'll need them to give sympathetic treatment to his case when we get him to the asylum.

NAT. (*anxiously—lowering his voice*) And you'll come to take him away tonight—for sure?

HIGGINS. Twenty minutes after I leave here I'll be back in the car. That's positive.

NAT. And you know your way through the house?

HIGGINS. Certainly, I remember—but I don't see——

NAT. The outside door will be left open for you. You must come right up. My sister and I will be here—with him. And you understand—— Neither of us knows anything about this. The authorities have been complained to—not by us, mind—but by someone. He must never know——

HIGGINS. Yes, yes—but still I don't—— Is he liable to prove violent?

NAT. No—no. He's quiet always—too quiet; but he might do something—anything—if he knows——

HIGGINS. Rely on me not to tell him, then; but I'll bring along two attendants in case—— (*He breaks off and continues in matter-of-fact tones*) And now for the facts in this case, if you don't mind, Mr. Bartlett.

NAT. (*shaking his head—moodily*) There are cases where facts—— Well, here goes—the brass tacks. My father was a whaling captain as his father before him. The last trip he made was seven years ago. He expected to be gone two years. It was four before we saw him again. His ship had been wrecked in the Indian Ocean. He and six others managed to reach a small island on the fringe of the Archipelago—an island barren as hell, Doctor—after seven days in an open boat. The rest of the whaling crew never were heard from again—gone to the sharks. Of the six who reached the island with my father only three were alive when a fleet of Malay canoes picked them up, mad from thirst and starvation, the four of them. These four men finally reached Frisco. (*With great emphasis*) They were my father; Silas Horne, the mate; Cates, the bo'sun, and Jimmy Kanaka, a Hawaiian harpooner. Those four! (*With a forced laugh*) There are facts for you. It was all in the papers at the time—my father's story.

HIGGINS. But what of the other three who were on the island?

NAT. (*harshly*) Died of exposure, perhaps. Mad and jumped into the sea, perhaps. That was the told story. Another was whispered—killed and eaten, perhaps! But gone—vanished—that, undeniably. That was the fact. For the rest—who knows? And what does it matter?

HIGGINS. (*with a shudder*) I should think it would matter—a lot.

NAT. (*fiercely*) We're dealing with facts, Doctor! (*With a laugh*) And here are some more for you. My father brought the three down to this house with him—Horne and Cates and Jimmy Kanaka. We hardly recognized my father. He had been through hell and looked it. His hair was white. But you'll see for yourself—soon. And the others—they were all a bit queer, too—mad, if you will. (*He laughs again*) So much for the facts, Doctor. They leave off there and the dreams begin.

HIGGINS. (*doubtfully*) It would seem—the facts are enough.

NAT. Wait. (*He resumes deliberately*) One day my father sent for me and in the presence of the others told me the dream. I was to be heir to the secret. Their second day on the island, he said, they discovered in a sheltered inlet the rotten, water-logged hulk of a Malay prau—a proper war-prau such as the pirates used to use. She had been there rotting—God knows how long. The crew had vanished—God knows where, for there was no sign on the island that man had ever touched there. The Kanakas went over the prau—they're devils for staying under water, you know—and they found—in two chests—— (*He leans back in his chair and smiles ironically*) Guess what, Doctor?

HIGGINS. (*with an answering smile*) Treasure, of course.

NAT. (*leaning forward and pointing his finger accusingly at the other*) You see! The root of belief is in you, too! (*Then he leans back with a hollow chuckle*) Why, yes. Treasure, to be sure. What else? They landed it and—you can guess the rest, too—diamonds, emeralds, gold ornaments—innumerable, of course. Why limit the stuff of dreams? Ha-ha! (*He laughs sardonically as if mocking himself*)

HIGGINS. (*deeply interested*) And then?

NAT. They began to go mad—hunger, thirst, and the rest—and they began to forget. Oh, they forgot a lot, and lucky for them they did, probably. But my father realizing, as he told me, what was happening to them, insisted that while they still knew what they were doing they should—guess again now, Doctor. Ha-ha!

HIGGINS. Bury the treasure?

NAT. (*ironically*) Simple, isn't it? Ha-ha. And then they made a map—the same old dream, you see—with a charred stick, and my father had care of it. They were picked up soon after, mad as hatters, as I have told you, by some Malays. (*He drops his mocking and adopts a calm, deliberate tone again*)

But the map isn't a dream, Doctor. We're coming back to facts again. (*He reaches into the pocket of his mackinaw and pulls out a crumpled paper*) Here. (*He spreads it out on the table*)

HIGGINS. (*craning his neck eagerly*) Dammit! This is interesting. The treasure, I suppose, is where——

NAT. Where the cross is made.

HIGGINS. And here are the signatures, I see. And that sign?

NAT. Jimmy Kanaka's. He couldn't write.

HIGGINS. And below? That's yours, isn't it?

NAT. As heir to the secret, yes. We all signed it here the morning the Mary Allen, the schooner my father had mortgaged this house to fit out, set sail to bring back the treasure. Ha-ha.

HIGGINS. The ship he's still looking for—that was lost three years ago?

NAT. The Mary Allen, yes. The other three men sailed away on her. Only father and the mate knew the approximate location of the island—and I—as heir. It's—— (*He hesitates, frowning*) No matter. I'll keep the mad secret. My father wanted to go with them—but my mother was dying. I dared not go either.

HIGGINS. Then you wanted to go? You believed in the treasure then?

NAT. Of course. Ha-ha. How could I help it? I believed until my mother's death. Then *he* became mad, entirely mad. He built this cabin—to wait in—and he suspected my growing doubt as time went on. So, as final proof, he gave me a thing he had kept hidden from them all—a sample of the richest of the treasure. Ha-ha. Behold! (*He takes from his pocket a heavy bracelet thickly studded with stones and throws it on the table near the lantern)*

HIGGINS. *(picking it up with eager curiosity—as if in spite of himself)* Real jewels?

NAT. Ha-ha! You want to believe, too. No—paste and brass—Malay ornaments.

HIGGINS. You had it looked over?

NAT. Like a fool, yes. *(He puts it back in his pocket and shakes his head as if throwing off a burden)* Now you know why he's mad—waiting for that ship—and why in the end I had to ask you to take him away where he'll be safe. The mortgage—the price of that ship—is to be foreclosed. We have to move, my sister and I. We can't take him with us. She is to be married soon. Perhaps away from the sight of the sea he may——

HIGGINS. *(perfunctorily)* Let's hope for the best. And I fully appreciate your position. *(He gets up, smiling)* And thank you for the interesting story. I'll know how to humor him when he raves about treasure.

NAT. *(somberly)* He is quiet always—too quiet. He only walks to and fro—watching——

HIGGINS Well, I must go. You think it's best to take him tonight?

NAT. *(persuasively)* Yes, Doctor. The neighbors—they're far away but—for my sister's sake—you understand.

HIGGINS. I see. It must be hard on her—this sort of thing—Well—*(he goes to the door, which* NAT *opens for him)* I'll return presently. *(He starts to descend)*

NAT. *(urgently)* Don't fail us, Doctor. And come right up. He'll be here.

(*He closes the door and tiptoes carefully to the companionway. He ascends it a few steps and remains for a moment listening for some sound from above. Then he goes over to the table, turning the lantern very low, and sits down, resting his elbows, his chin on his hands, staring somberly before him. The door in the rear is slowly opened. It creaks slightly and* NAT *jumps to his feet—in a thick voice of terror*) Who's there? (*The door swings wide open, revealing* SUE BARTLETT. *She ascends into the room and shuts the door behind her. She is a tall, slender woman of twenty-five, with a pale, sad face framed in a mass of dark red hair. This hair furnishes the only touch of color about her. Her full lips are pale; the blue of her wistful wide eyes is fading into a twilight gray. Her voice is low and melancholy. She wears a dark wrapper and slippers*)

SUE. (*stands and looks at her brother accusingly*) It's only I. What are you afraid of?

NAT. (*averts his eyes and sinks back on his chair again*) Nothing. I didn't know—I thought you were in your room.

SUE. (*comes to the table*) I was reading. Then I heard someone come down the stairs and go out. Who was it? (*With sudden terror*) It wasn't—Father?

NAT. No. He's up there—watching—as he always is.

SUE. (*sitting down—insistently*) Who was it?

NAT. (*evasively*) A man—I know.

SUE. What man? What is he? You're holding something back. Tell me.

NAT. (*raising his eyes defiantly*) A doctor.

SUE. (*alarmed*) Oh! (*With quick intuition*) You brought him up here—so that I wouldn't know!

NAT. (*doggedly*) No. I took him up here to see how things were—to ask him about Father.

SUE. (*as if afraid of the answer she will get*) Is he one of them—from the asylum? Oh, Nat, you haven't——

NAT. (*interrupting her—hoarsely*) No, no! Be still.

SUE. That would be—the last horror.

NAT. (*defiantly*) Why? You always say that. What could be more horrible than things as they are? I believe—it would be better for him—away—where he couldn't see the sea. He'll forget his mad idea of waiting for a lost ship and a treasure that never was. (*As if trying to convince himself—vehemently*) I believe this!

SUE. (*reproachfully*) You don't, Nat. You know he'd die if he hadn't the sea to live with.

NAT. (*bitterly*) And you know old Smith will foreclose the mortgage. Is that nothing? We cannot pay. He came yesterday and talked with me. He knows the place is his—to all purposes. He talked as if we were merely his tenants, curse him! And he swore he'd foreclose immediately unless——

SUE. (*eagerly*) What?

NAT. (*in a hard voice*) Unless we have—Father—taken away.

SUE. (*in anguish*) Oh! But why, why? What is Father to him?

NAT. The value of the property—our home which is his, Smith's. The neighbors are afraid. They pass by on the road at nights coming back to their farms from the town. They see *him* up there walking back and forth—waving his arms against the sky. They're afraid. They talk of a complaint. They say for his own good he must be taken away. They even whisper the house is haunted. Old Smith is afraid of his property. He thinks that *he* may set fire to the house—do anything——

SUE. (*despairingly*) But you told him how foolish that was, didn't you? That Father is quiet, always quiet.

NAT. What's the use of telling—when they believe—when they're afraid? (SUE *hides her face in her hands—a pause—* NAT *whispers hoarsely*) I've been afraid myself—at times.

SUE. Oh, Nat! Of what?

NAT. (*violently*) Oh, him and the sea he calls to! Of the damned sea he forced me on as a boy—the sea that robbed me of my arm and made me the broken thing I am!

SUE. (*pleadingly*) You can't blame Father—for your misfortune.

NAT. He took me from school and forced me on his ship, didn't he? What would I have been now but an ignorant sailor like him if he had had his way? No. It's the sea I should not blame, that foiled him by taking my arm and then throwing me ashore—another one of *his* wrecks!

SUE. (*with a sob*) You're bitter, Nat—and hard. It was so long ago. Why can't you forget?

NAT. (*bitterly*) Forget! You can talk! When Tom comes from this voyage you'll be married and out of this with life before you—a captain's wife as our mother was. I wish you joy.

SUE. (*supplicatingly*) And you'll come with us, Nat—and father, too—and then——

NAT. Would you saddle your young husband with a madman and a cripple? (*Fiercely*) No, no, not I! (*Vindictively*) And not him, either! (*With sudden meaning—deliberately*) I've got to stay here. My book is three-fourths done—my book that will set me free! But I know, I feel, as sure as I stand here living before you, that I must finish it here. It could not live for me outside of this house where it was born. (*Staring at her fixedly*) So I will stay—in spite of hell! (SUE *sobs hopelessly. After a pause he continues*) Old Smith told me I could live here indefinitely without paying—as caretaker—if——

SUE. (*fearfully—like a whispered echo*) If?

NAT. (*staring at her—in a hard voice*) If I have *him* sent —where he'll no longer harm himself—nor others.

SUE. (*with horrified dread*) No—no, Nat! For our dead mother's sake.

NAT. (*struggling*) Did I say I had? Why do you look at me—like that?

SUE. Nat! Nat! For our mother's sake!

NAT. (*in terror*) Stop! Stop! She's dead—and at peace. Would you bring her tired soul back to him again to be bruised and wounded?

SUE. Nat!

NAT. (*clutching at his throat as though to strangle something within him—hoarsely*) Sue! Have mercy! (*His sister stares at him with dread foreboding.* NAT *calms himself with an effort and continues deliberately*) Smith said he would give two thousand cash if I would sell the place to him—and he would let me stay, rent-free, as caretaker.

SUE. (*scornfully*) Two thousand! Why, over and above the mortgage it's worth——

NAT. It's not what it's worth. It's what one can get, cash— for my book—for freedom!

SUE. So that's why he wants Father sent away, the wretch! He must know the will Father made——

NAT. Gives the place to me. Yes, he knows. I told him.

SUE. (*dully*) Ah, how vile men are!

NAT. (*persuasively*) If it were to be done—if it were, I say—there'd be half for you for your wedding portion. That's fair.

SUE. (*horrified*) Blood-money! Do you think I could touch it?

NAT. (*persuasively*) It would be only fair. I'd give it you.

SUE. My God, Nat, are you trying to bribe me?

NAT. No. It's yours in all fairness. (*With a twisted smile*) You forget I'm heir to the treasure, too, and can afford to be generous. Ha-ha.

SUE. (*alarmed*) Nat! You're so strange. You're sick, Nat. You couldn't talk this way if you were yourself. Oh, we must go away from here—you and father and I! Let Smith foreclose. There'll be something over the mortgage; and we'll move to some little house—by the sea so that father——

NAT. (*fiercely*) Can keep up his mad game with me—whispering dreams in my ear—pointing out to sea—mocking me with stuff like this! (*He takes the bracelet from his pocket. The sight of it infuriates him and he hurls it into a corner, exclaiming in a terrible voice*) No! No! It's too late for dreams now. It's too late; I've put them behind me tonight—forever!

SUE. (*looks at him and suddenly understands that what she dreads has come to pass—letting her head fall on her outstretched arms with a long moan*) Then—you've done it! You've sold him! Oh, Nat, you're cursed!

NAT. (*with a terrified glance at the roof above*) Ssshh! What are you saying? He'll be better off—away from the sea.

SUE. (*dully*) You've sold him.

NAT. (*wildly*) No! No! (*He takes the map from his pocket*) Listen, Sue! For God's sake, listen to me! See! The map of the island. (*He spreads it out on the table*) And the treasure—where the cross is made. (*He gulps and his words pour out incoherently*) I've carried it about for years. Is that nothing? You don't know what it means. It stands between me and my book. It's stood between me and life—driving me mad! *He* taught me to wait and hope with him—wait and hope—day after day. He made me doubt my brain and give the lie to my eyes—when hope was dead—when I knew it was all a dream—I couldn't kill it! (*His eyes starting from his head*) God forgive me, I still believe! And that's mad—mad, do you hear?

SUE. (*looking at him with horror*) And that is why—you hate him!

NAT. No, I don't—— (*Then in a sudden frenzy*) Yes! I do hate him! He's stolen my brain! I've got to free myself, can't you see, from him—and his madness.

SUE. (*terrified—appealingly*) Nat! Don't! You talk as if——

NAT. (*with a wild laugh*) As if I were mad? You're right—but I'll be mad no more! See! (*He opens the lantern and sets fire to the map in his hand. When he shuts the lantern again it flickers and goes out. They watch the paper burn with fascinated eyes as he talks*) See how I free myself and become sane. And now for facts, as the doctor said. I lied to you about him. He was a doctor from the asylum. See how it burns! It must all be destroyed—this poisonous madness. Yes, I lied to you—see—it's gone—the last speck—and the only other map is the one Silas Horne took to the bottom of the sea with him. (*He lets the ash fall to the floor and crushes it with his foot*) Gone! I'm free of it—at last! (*His face is very pale, but he goes on calmly*) Yes, I sold him, if you will—to save my soul. They're coming from the asylum to get him—— (*There is a loud, muffled cry from above, which sounds like "Sail-ho," and a stamping of feet. The slide to the companionway above is slid back with a bang. A gust of air tears down into the room.* NAT *and* SUE *have jumped to their feet and stand petrified.* CAPTAIN BARTLETT *tramps down the stairs*)

NAT. (*with a shudder*) God! Did he hear?

SUE. Ssshh! (CAPTAIN BARTLETT *comes into the room. He bears a striking resemblance to his son, but his face is more stern and formidable, his form more robust, erect and muscular. His mass of hair is pure white, his bristly mustache the same, contrasting with the weather-beaten leather color of his furrowed face. Bushy gray brows overhang the obsessed glare of his fierce dark eyes. He wears a heavy, double-breasted blue coat, pants of the same material, and rubber boots turned down from the knee*)

BARTLETT. (*in a state of mad exultation strides toward his son and points an accusing finger at him.* NAT *shrinks backward a step*) Bin thinkin' me mad, did ye? Thinkin' it for the past three years, ye bin—ever since them fools on the Slocum tattled their damn lie o' the Mary Allen bein' a wreck.

NAT. (*swallowing hard—chokingly*) No—— Father—I——

BARTLETT. Don't lie, ye whelp! You that I'd made my heir

—aimin' to git me out o' the way! Aimin' to put me behind the bars o' the jail for mad folk!

SUE. Father—no!

BARTLETT (*waving his hand for her to be silent*) Not you, girl, not you. You're your mother.

NAT. (*very pale*) Father—do you think—I——

BARTLETT (*fiercely*) A lie in your eyes! I bin a-readin' 'em. My curse on you!

SUE. Father! Don't!

BARTLETT. Leave me be, girl. He believed, didn't he? And ain't he turned traitor—mockin' at me and sayin' it's all a lie—mockin' at himself, too, for bein' a fool to believe in dreams, as he calls 'em.

NAT. (*placatingly*) You're wrong, Father. I do believe.

BARTLETT. (*triumphantly*) Aye, now ye do! Who wouldn't credit their own eyes?

NAT. (*mystified*) Eyes?

BARTLETT. Have ye not seen her, then? Did ye not hear me hail?

NAT. (*confusedly*) Hail? I heard a shout. But—hail what? —seen what?

BARTLETT. (*grimly*) Aye, now's your punishment, Judas. (*Explosively*) The Mary Allen, ye blind fool, come back from the Southern Seas—come back as I swore she must!

SUE. (*trying to soothe him*) Father! Be quiet. It's nothing.

BARTLETT. (*not heeding her—his eyes fixed hypnotically on his son's*) Turned the pint a half-hour back—the Mary Allen loaded with gold as I swore she would be—carryin' her lowers—

not a reef in 'em—makin' port, boy, as I swore she must—too late for traitors, boy, too late!—droppin' her anchor just when I hailed her.

NAT. (*a haunted, fascinated look in his eyes, which are fixed immovably on his father's*) The Mary Allen! But how do you know?

BARTLETT. Not know my own ship! 'Tis you 're mad!

NAT. But at night—some other schooner——

BARTLETT. No other, I say! The Mary Allen—clear in the moonlight. And heed this: D'you call to mind the signal I gave to Silas Horne if he made this port o' a night?

NAT. (*slowly*) A red and a green light at the mainmast-head.

BARTLETT (*triumphantly*) Then look out if ye dare! (*He goes to the porthole, left forward*) Ye can see it plain from here. (*Commandingly*) Will ye believe your eyes? Look—and then call me mad! (NAT *peers through the porthole and starts back, a dumbfounded expression on his face*)

NAT. (*slowly*) A red and a green at the mainmast-head. Yes—clear as day.

SUE. (*with a worried look at him*) Let me see. (*She goes to the porthole*)

BARTLETT. (*to his son with fierce satisfaction*) Aye, ye see now clear enough—too late for you. (NAT *stares at him spell-bound*) And from above I saw Horne and Cates and Jimmy Kanaka plain on the deck in the moonlight lookin' up at me. Come! (*He strides to the companionway, followed by* NAT. *The two of them ascend.* SUE *turns from the porthole, an expression of frightened bewilderment on her face. She shakes her head sadly. A loud* "Mary Allen, *ahoy!*" *comes from above in* BARTLETT'S *voice, followed like an echo by the same hail from* NAT.

SUE *covers her face with her hands, shuddering.* NAT *comes down the companionway, his eyes wild and exulting)*

SUE. *(brokenly)* He's bad tonight, Nat. You're right to humor him. It's the best thing.

NAT. *(savagely)* Humor him? What in hell do you mean?

SUE *(pointing to the porthole)* There's nothing there, Nat. There's not a ship in harbor.

NAT. You're a fool—or blind! The Mary Allen's there in plain sight of anyone, with the red and the green signal-lights. Those fools lied about her being wrecked. And I've been a fool, too.

SUE. But, Nat, there's nothing. *(She goes over to the porthole again)* Not a ship. See.

NAT. I saw, I tell you! From above it's all plain. *(He turns from her and goes back to his seat by the table.* SUE *follows him, pleading frightenedly)*

SUE. Nat! You mustn't let this—— You're all excited and trembling, Nat. *(She puts a soothing hand on his forehead)*

NAT. *(pushing her away from him roughly)* You blind fool! *(Bartlett comes down the steps of the companionway. His face is transfigured with the ecstasy of a dream come true)*

BARTLETT. They've lowered a boat—the three—Horne and Cates and Jimmy Kanaka. They're a-rowin' ashore. I heard the oars in the locks. Listen! *(A pause)*

NAT. *(excitedly)* I hear!

SUE. *(who has taken the chair by her brother—in a warning whisper)* It's the wind and sea you hear, Nat. Please!

BARTLETT. *(suddenly)* Hark! They've landed. They're back on earth again as I swore they'd come back. They'll be a-comin' up the path now. *(He stands in an attitude of rigid attention.* NAT *strains forward in his chair. The sound of the wind and sea suddenly ceases and there is a heavy silence. A dense green glow floods slowly in rhythmic waves like a liquid into the room—as of great depths of the sea faintly penetrated by light*)

NAT. (*catching at his sister's hand—chokingly*) See how the light changes! Green and gold! (*He shivers*) Deep under the sea! I've been drowned for years! (*Hysterically*) Save me! Save me!

SUE. (*patting his hand comfortingly*) Only the moonlight, Nat. It hasn't changed. Be quiet, dear, it's nothing. (*The green light grows deeper and deeper*)

BARTLETT. (*in a crooning, monotonous tone*) They move slowly—slowly. They're heavy, I know, heavy—the two chests. Hark! They're below at the door. You hear?

NAT. (*starting to his feet*) I hear! I left the door open.

BARTLETT. For them?

NAT. For them.

SUE. (*shuddering*) Ssshh! (*The sound of a door being heavily slammed is heard from way down in the house*).

NAT. (*to his sister—excitedly*) There! You hear?

SUE. A shutter in the wind.

NAT. There is no wind.

BARTLETT. Up they come! Up, bullies! They're heavy—heavy! (*The padding of bare feet sounds from the floor below —then comes up the stairs*)

NAT. You hear them now?

SUE. Only the rats running about. It's nothing, Nat.

BARTLETT. (*rushing to the door and throwing it open*) Come

in, lads, come in!—and welcome home! (*The forms of* SILAS HORNE, CATES, *and* JIMMY KANAKA *rise noiselessly into the room from the stairs. The last two carry heavy inlaid chests.* HORNE *is a parrot-nosed, angular old man dressed in gray cotton trousers and a singlet torn open across his hairy chest.* JIMMY *is a tall, sinewy, bronzed young Kanaka. He wears only a breech-cloth.* CATES *is squat and stout and is dressed in dungaree pants and a shredded white sailor's blouse, stained with iron-rust. All are in their bare feet. Water drips from their soaked and rotten clothes. Their hair is matted, intertwined with slimy strands of seaweed. Their eyes, as they glide silently into the room, stare frightfully wide at nothing. Their flesh in the green light has the suggestion of decomposition. Their bodies sway limply, nervelessly, rhythmically as if to the pulse of long swells of the deep sea*)

NAT. (*making a step toward them*) See! (*Frenziedly*) Welcome home, boys.

SUE. (*grabbing his arm*) Sit down, Nat. It's nothing. There's no one there. Father—sit down!

BARTLETT. (*grinning at the three and putting his finger to his lips*) Not here, boys, not here—not before him. (*He points to his son*) He has no right, now. Come. The treasure is ours only. We'll go away with it together. Come. (*He goes to the companionway. The three follow. At the foot of it* HORNE *puts a swaying hand on his shoulder and with the other holds out a piece of paper to him.* BARTLETT *takes it and chuckles exultantly*) That's right—for him—that's right! (*He ascends. The figures sway up after him*)

NAT. (*frenziedly*) Wait! (*He struggles toward the companionway*)

SUE. *(trying to hold him back)* Nat—don't! Father—come back!

NAT. Father! *(He flings her away from him and rushes up the companionway. He pounds against the slide, which seems to have been shut down on him)*

SUE. *(hysterically—runs wildly to the door in rear)* Help! help! *(As she gets to the door* DOCTOR HIGGINS *appears, hurrying up the stairs)*

HIGGINS. *(excitedly)* Just a moment, Miss. What's the matter?

SUE. *(with a gasp)* My father—up there!

HIGGINS. I can't see—where's my flash? Ah. *(He flashes it on her terror-stricken face, then quickly around the room. The green glow disappears. The wind and sea are heard again. Clear moonlight floods through the portholes.* HIGGINS *springs to the companionway.* NAT *is still pounding)* Here, Bartlett. Let me try.

NAT. *(coming down—looking dully at the doctor)* They've locked it. I can't get up.

HIGGINS. *(looks up—in an astonished voice)* What's the matter, Bartlett? It's all open. *(He starts to ascend)*

NAT. *(in a voice of warning)* Look out, man. Look out for them!

HIGGINS. *(calls down from above)* Them? Who? There's no one here. *(Suddenly—in alarm)* Come up! Lend a hand here! He's fainted! *(*NAT *goes up slowly.* SUE *goes over and lights the lantern, then hurries back to the foot of the companionway with it. There is a scuffling noise from above. They reappear, carrying* CAPTAIN BARTLETT'S *body)*

HIGGINS. Easy now! *(They lay him on the couch in rear.*

SUE *sets the lantern down by the couch.* HIGGINS *bends and listens for a heart-beat. Then he rises, shaking his head*). I'm sorry——

SUE. (*dully*) Dead?

HIGGINS. (*nodding*) Heart failure, I should judge. (*With an attempt at consolation*) Perhaps it's better so, if——

NAT. (*as if in a trance*) There was something Horne handed him. Did you see?

SUE. (*wringing her hands*) Oh, Nat, be still! He's dead. (*To* HIGGINS *with pitiful appeal*) Please go—go——

HIGGINS. There's nothing I can do?

SUE. Go—please—— (HIGGINS *bows stiffly and goes out.* NAT *moves slowly to his father's body, as if attracted by some irresistible fascination*)

NAT. Didn't you see? Horne handed him something.

SUE. (*sobbing*) Nat! Nat! Come away! Don't touch him, Nat! Come away. (*But her brother does not heed her. His gaze is fixed on his father's right hand, which hangs downward over the side of the couch. He pounces on it and forcing the clenched fingers open with a great effort, secures a crumpled ball of paper*)

NAT. (*flourishing it above his head with a shout of triumph*) See! (*He bends down and spreads it out in the light of the lantern*) The map of the island! Look! It isn't lost for me after all! There's still a chance—*my* chance! (*With mad, solemn decision*) When the house is sold I'll go—and I'll find it! Look! It's written here in his handwriting: "The treasure is buried where the cross is made."

SUE. (*covering her face with her hands—brokenly*) Oh, God! Come away, Nat! Come away!

(*The Curtain Falls*)

THE ROPE

A Play in One Act

CHARACTERS

ABRAHAM BENTLEY

ANNIE, *his daughter*

PAT SWEENEY, *her husband*

MARY, *their child*

LUKE BENTLEY, *Abe's son by a second marriage*

THE ROPE

SCENE. *The interior of an old barn situated on top of a high headland of the seacoast. In the rear, to the left, a stall in which lumber is stacked up. To the right of it, an open double doorway looking out over the ocean. Outside the doorway, the faint trace of what was once a road leading to the barn. Beyond the road, the edge of a cliff which rises sheer from the sea below. On the right of the doorway, three stalls with mangers and hay-ricks. The first of these is used as a woodbin and is half full of piled-up cordwood. Near this bin, a chopping-block with an ax driven into the top of it.*

The left section of the barn contains the hayloft, which extends at a height of about twelve feet from the floor as far to the right as the middle of the doorway. The loft is bare except for a few scattered mounds of dank-looking hay. From the edge of the loft, half-way from the door, a rope about five feet long with an open running noose at the end is hanging. A rusty plow and various other farming implements, all giving evidence of long disuse, are lying on the floor near the left wall. Farther forward an old cane-bottomed chair is set back against the wall.

In front of the stalls on the right stands a long, roughly constructed carpenter's table, evidently home-made. Saws, a lathe, a hammer, chisel, a keg containing nails and other tools of the carpentry trade are on the table. Two benches are placed, one in front, one to the left of it.

The right side of the barn is a bare wall.

It is between six and half-past in the evening of a day in early spring. At the rising of the curtain some trailing clouds near the horizon, seen through the open doorway, are faintly tinged with gold by the first glow of the sunset. As the action progresses this reflected light gradually becomes brighter, and then slowly fades into a smoky crimson. The sea is a dark slate color. From the rocks below the headland sounds the muffled monotone of breaking waves.

As the curtain rises MARY *is discovered squatting cross-legged on the floor, her back propped against the right side of the doorway, her face in profile. She is a skinny, overgrown girl of ten, with thin, carroty hair worn in a pig-tail. She wears a shabby gingham dress. Her face is stupidly expressionless. Her hands flutter about aimlessly in relaxed, flabby gestures.*

She is staring fixedly at a rag doll which she has propped up against the doorway opposite her. She hums shrilly to herself.

At a sudden noise from outside she jumps to her feet, peeks out, and quickly snatches up the doll, which she hugs fiercely to her breast. Then, after a second's fearful hesitation, she runs to the carpenter's table and crawls under it.

As she does so ABRAHAM BENTLEY *appears in the doorway and stands, blinking into the shadowy barn. He is a tall, lean, stoop-shouldered old man of sixty-five. His thin legs, twisted by rheumatism, totter feebly under him as he shuffles slowly along by the aid of a thick cane. His face is gaunt, chalky-white, furrowed with wrinkles, surmounted by a shiny bald scalp fringed with scanty wisps of white hair. His eyes peer weakly from beneath bushy, black brows. His mouth is a sunken line drawn in under his large, beak-like nose. A two weeks' growth of stubby patches of beard covers his jaws and chin. He has on a threadbare brown overcoat but wears no hat.*

BENTLEY. (*comes slowly into the barn, peering around him suspiciously. As he reaches the table and leans one hand on it for support,* MARY *darts from underneath and dashes out through the doorway.* BENTLEY *is startled; then shakes his cane after her*) Out o' my sight, you Papist brat! Spawn o' Satan! Spyin' on me! They set her to it. Spyin' to watch me! (*He limps to the door and looks out cautiously. Satisfied, he turns back into the barn*) Spyin' to see—what they'll never know. (*He stands staring up at the rope and taps it testingly several times with his stick, talking to himself as he does so*) It's tied strong—strong as death—— (*He cackles with satisfaction*) They'll see, then! They'll see! (*He laboriously creeps over to the bench and sits down wearily. He looks toward the sea and his voice quavers in a doleful chant*) "Woe unto us! for the day goeth away, for the shadows of the evening are stretched out." (*He mumbles to himself for a moment—then speaks clearly*) Spyin' on me! Spawn o' the Pit! (*He renews his chant*) "They hunt our steps that we cannot go in our streets: our end is near, our days are fulfilled; for our end is come."

(*As he finishes* ANNIE *enters. She is a thin, slovenly, worn-out-looking woman of about forty with a drawn, pasty face. Her habitual expression is one of a dulled irritation. She talks in a high-pitched, sing-song whine. She wears a faded gingham dress and a torn sunbonnet*)

ANNIE. (*comes over to her father but warily keeps out of range of his stick*) Paw! (*He doesn't answer or appear to see her*) Paw! You ain't fergittin' what the doctor told you when he was here last, be you? He said you was to keep still and not go a-walkin' round. Come on back to the house, Paw. It's gittin' near supper-time and you got to take your medicine b'fore it, like he says.

BENTLEY. (*his eyes fixed in front of him*) "The punishment of thine iniquity is accomplished, O daughter of Zion: he will visit thine iniquity, O daughter of Edom; he will discover thy sins."

ANNIE. (*waiting resignedly until he has finished—wearily*) You better take watch on your health, Paw, and not be sneakin' up to this barn no more. Lord sakes, soon 's ever my back is turned you goes sneakin' off agen. It's enough to drive a body outa their right mind.

BENTLEY. "Behold, every one that useth proverbs shall use this proverb against thee, saying, As is the mother, so is her daughter!" (*He cackles to himself*) So is her daughter!

ANNIE. (*her face flushing with anger*) And if I am, I'm glad I take after her and not you, y'old wizard! (*Scornfully*) A fine one you be to be shoutin' Scripture in a body's ears all the live-long day—you that druv Maw to her death with your naggin', and pinchin', and miser stinginess. If you've a mind to pray, it's down in the medder you ought to go, and kneel down by her grave, and ask God to forgive you for the meanness you done to her all her life.

BENTLEY. (*mumbling*) "As is the mother, so is her daughter."

ANNIE. (*enraged by the repetition of this quotation*) *You* quotin' Scripture! Why, Maw wasn't cold in the earth b'fore you was down in the port courtin' agen—courtin' that harlot that was the talk o' the whole town! And then you disgraces yourself and me by marryin' her—*her*—and bringin' her back home with you; and me still goin' every day to put flowers on Maw's grave that you'd fergotten. (*She glares at him vindictively, pausing for breath*) And between you you'd have druv me into the grave like you done Maw if I hadn't married Pat Sweeney so's I could git away and live in peace. Then you took on so high and mighty 'cause he was a Cath'lic—*you* gittin' religion all of a moment just for spite on me 'cause I'd left—and b'cause she egged you on against me; *you* sayin' it was a sin to marry a Papist, after not bein' at Sunday meetin' yourself for more'n twenty years!

BENTLEY. (*loudly*) "He will visit thine iniquity——"

ANNIE. (*interrupting*) And the carryin's-on you had the six years at home after I'd left you—the shame of the whole county! Your wife, indeed, with a child she *claimed* was your'n, and her goin' with this farmer and that, and even men off the ships in the port, and you blind to it! And then when she got sick of you and ran away—only to meet her end at the hands of God a year after—she leaves you alone with that—*your* son, Luke, *she* called him—and him only five years old!

BENTLEY. (*babbling*) Luke? Luke?

ANNIE. (*tauntingly*) Yes, Luke! "As is the mother, so is her son"—that's what you ought to preach 'stead of puttin' curses on me. You was glad enough to git me back home agen, and Pat with me, to tend the place, and help bring up that brat of hers. (*Jealously*) You was fond enough of him all them years—and how did he pay you back? Stole your money and ran off and left you just when he was sixteen and old enough to help. Told you to your face he'd stolen and was leavin'. He only laughed when you was took crazy and cursed him; and he only laughed harder when you hung up that silly rope there (*she points*) and told him to hang himself on it when he ever came home agen.

BENTLEY. (*mumbling*) You'll see, then. You'll see!

ANNIE. (*wearily—her face becoming dull and emotionless again*) I s'pose I'm a bigger fool than you be to argy with a half-witted body. But I tell you agen that Luke of yours ain't comin' back; and if he does he ain't the kind to hang himself, more's the pity. He's like her. He'd hang *you* more likely if he s'pected you had any money. So you might 's well take down that ugly rope you've had tied there since he run off. He's probably dead anyway by this.

BENTLEY. (*frightened*) No! No!

ANNIE. Them as bad as him comes to a sudden end. (*Irritably*) Land sakes, Paw, here I am argyin' with your lunatic notions and the supper not ready. Come on and git your medicine. You can see no one ain't touched your old rope. Come on! You can sit 'n' read your Bible. (*He makes no movement. She comes closer to him and peers into his face—uncertainly*) Don't you hear me? I do hope you ain't off in one of your fits when you don't know nobody. D'you know who's talkin'? This is Annie—your Annie, Paw.

BENTLEY. (*bursting into senile rage*) None o' mine! Spawn o' the Pit! (*With a quick movement he hits her viciously over the arm with his stick. She gives a cry of pain and backs away from him, holding her arm*)

ANNIE. (*weeping angrily*) That's what I git for tryin' to be kind to you, you ugly old devil! (*The sound of a man's footsteps is heard from outside, and* SWEENEY *enters. He is a stocky, muscular, sandy-haired Irishman dressed in patched corduroy trousers shoved down into high laced boots, and a blue flannel shirt. The bony face of his bullet head has a pressed-in appearance except for his heavy jaw, which sticks out pugnaciously. There is an expression of mean cunning and cupidity about his mouth and his small, round, blue eyes. He has evidently been drinking and his face is flushed and set in an angry scowl*)

SWEENEY. Have ye no supper at all made, ye lazy slut? (*Seeing that she has been crying*) What're you blubberin' about?

ANNIE. It's all his fault. I was tryin' to git him home but he's that set I couldn't budge him; and he hit me on the arm with his cane when I went near him.

SWEENEY. He did, did he? I'll soon learn him better. (*He advances toward* BENTLEY *threateningly*)

ANNIE. (*grasping his arm*) Don't touch him, Pat. He's in one of his fits and you might kill him.

SWEENEY. An' good riddance!

BENTLEY. (*hissing*) Papist! (*Chants*) "Pour out thy fury upon the heathen that know thee not, and upon the families that call not on thy name: for they have eaten up Jacob, and devoured him, and consumed him, and made his habitation desolate."

SWEENEY. (*instinctively crosses himself—then scornfully*) Spit curses on me till ye choke. It's not likely the Lord God'll be listenin' to a wicked auld sinner the like of you. (*To* ANNIE) What's got into him to be roamin' up here? When I left for the town he looked too weak to lift a foot.

ANNIE. Oh, it's the same crazy notion he's had ever since Luke left. He wanted to make sure the rope was still here.

BENTLEY. (*pointing to the rope with his stick*) He-he! Luke'll come back. Then you'll see. You'll see!

SWEENEY. (*nervously*) Stop that mad cacklin', for the love of heaven! (*With a forced laugh*) It's great laughter I should be havin' at you, mad as you are, for thinkin' that thief of a son of yours would come back to hang himself on account of your curses. It's five years he's been gone, and not a sight of him; an' you cursin' an' callin' down the wrath o' God on him by day an' by night. That shows you what God thinks of your curses—an' Him deaf to you!

ANNIE. It's no use talkin' to him, Pat.

SWEENEY. I've small doubt but that Luke is hung long since—by the police. He's come to no good end, that lad. (*His eyes on the rope*) I'll be pullin' that thing down, so I will; an' the auld loon'll stay in the house, where he belongs, then, maybe. (*He reaches up for the rope as if to try and yank it down.* BENTLEY *waves his stick frantically in the air, and groans with rage*)

ANNIE. (*frightened*) Leave it alone, Pat. Look at him. He's liable to hurt himself. Leave his rope be. It don't do no harm.

SWEENEY. (*reluctantly moves away*) It looks ugly hangin' there open like a mouth. (*The old man sinks back into a relieved immobility.* SWEENEY *speaks to his wife in a low tone*) Where's the child? Get her to take him out o' this. I want a word with you he'll not be hearin'. (*She goes to the door and calls out*) Ma-ry! Ma-ry! (*A faint, answering cry is heard and a moment later* MARY *rushes breathlessly into the barn.* SWEENEY *grabs her roughly by the arm. She shrinks away, look-*

ing at him with terrified eyes) You're to take your grandfather back to the house—an' see to it he stays there.

ANNIE. And give him his medicine.

SWEENEY. *(as the child continues to stare at him silently with eyes stupid from fear, he shakes her impatiently)* D'you hear me, now? *(To his wife)* It's soft-minded she is, like I've always told you, an' stupid; and you're not too firm in the head yourself at times, God help you! An' look at him! It's the curse is in the wits of your family, not mine.

ANNIE. You've been drinkin' in town or you wouldn't talk that way.

MARY. *(whining)* Maw! I'm skeered!

SWEENEY. *(lets go of her arm and approaches* BENTLEY*)* Get up out o' this, ye auld loon, an' go with Mary. She'll take you to the house. (BENTLEY *tries to hit him with the cane)* Oho, ye would, would ye? *(He wrests the cane from the old man's hands)* Bad cess to ye, you're the treach'rous one! Get up, now! *(He jerks the old man to his feet)* Here, Mary, take his hand. Quick now! *(She does so tremblingly)* Lead him to the house.

ANNIE. Go on, Paw! I'll come and git your supper in a minute.

BENTLEY. *(stands stubbornly and begins to intone)* "O Lord, thou hast seen my wrong; judge thou my cause. Thou hast seen all their vengeance and all their imaginations against me——"

SWEENEY. *(pushing him toward the door.* BENTLEY *tries to resist.* MARY *pulls at his hand in a sudden fit of impish glee, and laughs shrilly)* Get on now an' stop your cursin'.

BENTLEY. "Render unto them a recompense, O Lord, according to the work of their hands."

SWEENEY. Shut your loud quackin'! Here's your cane. (*He gives it to the old man as they come to the doorway and quickly steps back out of reach*) An' mind you don't touch the child with it or I'll beat you to a jelly, old as ye are.

BENTLEY. (*resisting* MARY'S *efforts to pull him out, stands shaking his stick at* SWEENEY *and his wife*) "Give them sorrow of heart, thy curse unto them. Persecute and destroy them in anger from under the heavens of the Lord."

MARY. (*tugging at his hand and bursting again into shrill laughter*) Come on, gran'paw. (*He allows himself to be led off, right*)

SWEENEY. (*making the sign of the cross furtively—with a sigh of relief*) He's gone, thank God! What a snake's tongue he has in him! (*He sits down on the bench to the left of table*) Come here, Annie, till I speak to you. (*She sits down on the bench in front of table.* SWEENEY *winks mysteriously*) Well, I saw him, sure enough.

ANNIE. (*stupidly*) Who?

SWEENEY. (*sharply*) Who? Who but Dick Waller, the lawyer, that I went to see. (*Lowering his voice*) An' I've found out what we was wishin' to know. (*With a laugh*) Ye said I'd been drinkin'—which was true; but 'twas all in the plan I'd made. I've a head for strong drink, as ye know, but he hasn't. (*He winks cunningly*) An' the whiskey loosened his tongue till he'd told all he knew.

ANNIE. He told you—about Paw's will?

SWEENEY. He did. (*Disappointedly*) But for all the good it does us we might as well be no wiser than we was before.

(*He broods for a moment in silence—then hits the table furiously with his fist*) God's curse on the auld miser!

ANNIE. What did he tell you?

SWEENEY. Not much at the first. He's a cute one, an' he'd be askin' a fee to tell you your own name, if he could get it. His practice is all dribbled away from him lately on account of the drink. So I let on I was only payin' a friendly call, havin' known him for years. Then I asked him out to have a drop o' drink, knowin' his weakness; an' we had rashers of them, an' I payin' for it. Then I come out with it straight and asked him about the will—because the auld man was crazy an' on his last legs, I told him, an' he was the lawyer made out the will when Luke was gone. So he winked at me an' grinned—he was drunk by this—an' said: "It's no use, Pat. He left the farm to the boy." "To hell with the farm," I spoke back. "It's mortgaged to the teeth; but how about the money?" "The money?" an' he looks at me in surprise, "What money?" "The cash he has," I says. "You're crazy," he says. "There wasn't any cash—only the farm." "D'you mean to say he made no mention of money in his will?" I asked. You could have knocked me down with a feather. "He did not—on my oath," he says. (SWEENEY *leans over to his wife—indignantly*) Now what d'you make o' that? The auld divil!

ANNIE. Maybe Waller was lyin'.

SWEENEY. He was not. I could tell by his face. He was surprised to hear me talkin' of money.

ANNIE. But the thousand dollars Paw got for the mortgage just before that woman ran away——

SWEENEY. An' that I've been slavin' me hands off to pay the int'rist on!

ANNIE. What could he have done with that? He ain't spent it. It was in twenty-dollar gold pieces he got it, I remember Mr. Kellar of the bank tellin' me once.

SWEENEY. Divil a penny he's spent. Ye know as well as I do if it wasn't for my hammerin', an' sawin', an' nailin', he'd be in the poorhouse this minute—or the madhouse, more likely.

ANNIE. D'you suppose that harlot ran off with it?

SWEENEY. I do not; I know better—an' so do you. D'you not remember the letter she wrote tellin' him he could support Luke on the money he'd got on the mortgage she'd signed with him; for he'd made the farm over to her when he married her. An' where d'you suppose Luke got the hundred dollars he stole? The auld loon must have had cash with him then, an' it's only five years back.

ANNIE. He's got it hid some place in the house most likely.

SWEENEY. Maybe you're right. I'll dig in the cellar this night when he's sleepin'. He used to be down there a lot recitin' Scripture in his fits.

ANNIE. What else did Waller say?

SWEENEY. Nothin' much; except that we should put notices in the papers for Luke, an' if he didn't come back by sivin years from when he'd left—two years from now, that'd be—the courts would say he was dead an' give us the farm. Divil a lot of use it is to us now with no money to fix it up; an' himself ruinin' it years ago by sellin' everythin' to buy that slut new clothes.

ANNIE. Don't folks break wills like his'n in the courts?

SWEENEY. Waller said 'twas no use. The auld divil was plain in his full senses when he made it; an' the courts cost money.

ANNIE. (*resignedly*) There ain't nothin' we can do then.

SWEENEY. No—except wait an' pray that young thief is dead

an' won't come back; an' try an' find where it is the auld man has the gold hid, if he has it yet. I'd take him by the neck an' choke him till he told it, if he wasn't your father. (*He takes a full quart flask of whiskey from the pocket of his coat and has a big drink*) Aahh! If we'd on'y the thousand we'd stock the farm good an' I'd give up this dog's game (*he indicates the carpentry outfit scornfully*) an' we'd both work hard with a man or two to help, an' in a few years we'd be rich; for 'twas always a payin' place in the auld days.

ANNIE. Yes, yes, it was always a good farm then.

SWEENEY. He'll not last long in his senses, the doctor told me. His next attack will be very soon an' after it he'll be a real lunatic with no legal claims to anythin'. If we on'y had the money—— 'Twould be the divil an' all if the auld fool should forget where he put it, an' him takin' leave of his senses altogether. (*He takes another nip at the bottle and puts it back in his pocket—with a sigh*) Ah, well, I'll save what I can an' at the end of two years, with good luck in the trade, maybe we'll have enough. (*They are both startled by the heavy footsteps of someone approaching outside. A shrill burst of* MARY'S *laughter can be heard and the deep voice of a man talking to her*)

SWEENEY. (*uneasily*) It's Mary; but who could that be with her? It's not himself. (*As he finishes speaking* LUKE *appears in the doorway, holding the dancing* MARY *by the hand. He is a tall, strapping young fellow about twenty-five with a coarse-featured, rather handsome face bronzed by the sun. What his face lacks in intelligence is partly forgiven for his good-natured, half-foolish grin, his hearty laugh, his curly dark hair, a certain devil-may-care recklessness and irresponsible youth in voice and gesture. But his mouth is weak and characterless; his brown eyes are large but shifty and acquisitive. He wears a dark blue jersey, patched blue pants, rough sailor shoes, and a gray cap. He advances into the stable with a mocking smile on his lips until he stands directly under the rope. The man and woman stare at him in petrified amazement*)

ANNIE. Luke!

SWEENEY. (*crossing himself*) Glory be to God—it's him!

MARY. (*hopping up and down wildly*) It's Uncle Luke, Uncle Luke, Uncle Luke! (*She runs to her mother, who pushes her away angrily*)

LUKE. (*regarding them both with an amused grin*) Sure, it's Luke—back after five years of bummin' round the rotten old earth in ships and things. Paid off a week ago—had a bust-up—and then took a notion to come out here—bummed my way—and here I am. And you're both of you tickled to death to see me, ain't yuh?—like hell! (*He laughs and walks over to* ANNIE) Don't yuh even want to shake flippers with your dear, long-lost brother, Annie? I remember you and me used to git on so fine together—like hell!

ANNIE. (*giving him a venomous look of hatred*) Keep your hands to yourself.

LUKE. (*grinning*) You ain't changed, that's sure—on'y yuh're homelier'n ever. (*He turns to the scowling* SWEENEY) How about you, brother Pat?

SWEENEY. I'd not lower myself to take the hand of a——

LUKE. (*with a threat in his voice*) Easy goes with that talk! I'm not so soft to lick as I was when I was a kid; and don't forget it.

ANNIE. (*to* MARY, *who is playing catch with a silver dollar which she has had clutched in her hand—sharply)* Mary! What have you got there? Where did you get it? Bring it here to me this minute! (MARY *presses the dollar to her breast and remains standing by the doorway in stubborn silence)*

LUKE. Aw, let her alone! What's bitin' yuh? That's on'y a silver dollar I give her when I met her front of the house. She told me you was up here; and I give her that as a present to buy candy with. I got it in Frisco—cart-wheels, they call 'em. There ain't none of them in these parts I ever seen, so I brung it along on the voyage.

ANNIE. *(angrily)* I don't know or care where you got it—but I know you ain't come by it honest. Mary! Give that back to him this instant! *(As the child hesitates, she stamps her foot furiously)* D'you hear me? (MARY *starts to cry softly, but comes to* LUKE *and hands him the dollar)*

LUKE. *(taking it—with a look of disgust at his half-sister)* I was right when I said you ain't changed, Annie. You're as stinkin' mean as ever. *(To* MARY, *consolingly)* Quit bawlin', kid. You 'n' me'll go out on the edge of the cliff here and chuck some stones in the ocean same's we useter, remember? (MARY'*s tears immediately cease. She looks up at him with shining eyes, and claps her hands)*

MARY. *(pointing to the dollar he has in his hand)* Throw that! It's flat 'n' it'll skip.

LUKE. *(with a grin)* That's the talk, kid. That's all it's good for—to throw away; not buryin' it like your miser folks'd tell you. Here! You take it and chuck it away. It's your'n. *(He gives her the dollar and she hops to the doorway. He turns to* PAT *with a grin)* I'm learnin' your kid to be a sport, Tight-Wad. I hope you ain't got no objections.

MARY. (*impatiently*) Come on, Uncle Luke. Watch me throw it.

LUKE. Aw right. (*To* PAT) I'll step outside a second and give you two a chanct to git all the dirty things yuh're thinkin' about me off your chest. (*Threateningly*) And then I'm gointer come and talk turkey to you, see? I didn't come back here for fun, and the sooner you gets that in your beans, the better.

MARY. Come on and watch me!

LUKE. Aw right, I'm comin'. (*He walks out and stands, leaning his back against the doorway, left.* MARY *is about six feet beyond him on the other side of the road. She is leaning down, peering over the edge of the cliff and laughing excitedly*)

MARY. Can I throw it now? Can I?

LUKE. Don't git too near the edge, kid. The water's deep down there, and you'd be a drowned rat if you slipped. (*She shrinks back a step*) You chuck it when I say three. Ready, now! (*She draws back her arm*) One! Two! Three! (*She throws the dollar away and bends down to see it hit the water*)

MARY. (*clapping her hands and laughing*) I seen it! I seen it splash! It's deep down now, ain't it?

LUKE. Yuh betcher it is! Now watch how far I kin chuck rocks. (*He picks up a couple and goes to where she is standing. During the following conversation between* SWEENEY *and his wife he continues to play this way with* MARY. *Their voices can be heard but the words are indistinguishable*)

SWEENEY. (*glancing apprehensively toward the door—with a great sigh*) Speak of the divil an' here he is! (*Furiously*) Flingin' away dollars, the dirty thief, an' us without——

ANNIE. (*interrupting him*) Did you hear what he said? A thief like him ain't come back for no good. (*Lowering her voice*) D'you s'pose he knows about the farm bein' left to him?

SWEENEY. (*uneasily*) How could he? An' yet—I dunno—— (*With sudden decision*) You'd best lave him to me to watch out for. It's small sense you have to hide your hate from him. You're as looney as the rist of your breed. An' he needs to be blarneyed round to fool him an' find out what he's wantin'. I'll pritind to make friends with him, God roast his soul! An' do you run to the house an' break the news to the auld man; for if he seen him suddin it's likely the little wits he has left would leave him; an' the thief could take the farm from us tomorrow if himself turned a lunatic.

ANNIE. (*getting up*) I'll tell him a little at a time till he knows.

SWEENEY. Be careful, now, or we'll lose the farm this night. (*She starts towards the doorway.* SWEENEY *speaks suddenly in a strange, awed voice*) Did you see Luke when he first came in to us? He stood there with the noose of the rope almost touchin' his head. I was almost wishin'—— (*He hesitates*)

ANNIE. (*viciously*) I was wishin' it was round his neck chokin' him, that's what I was—hangin' him just as Paw says.

SWEENEY. Ssshh! He might hear ye. Go along, now. He's comin' back.

MARY. (*pulling at* LUKE's *arm as he comes back to the doorway*) Lemme throw 'nother! Lemme throw 'nother!

LUKE. (*enters just as* ANNIE *is going out and stops her*) Goin' to the house? Do we get any supper? I'm hungry.

ANNIE. (*glaring at him but restraining her rage*) Yes.

LUKE. (*jovially*) Good work! And tell the old man I'm

here and I'll see him in a while. He'll be glad to see me, too —like hell! (*He comes forward.* ANNIE *goes off, right*)

MARY. (*in an angry whine, tugging at his hand*) Lemme throw 'nother. Lemme——

LUKE. (*shaking her away*) There's lots of rocks, kid. Throw them. Dollars ain't so plentiful.

MARY. (*screaming*) No! No! I don' wanter throw rocks. Lemme throw 'nother o' them.

SWEENEY. (*severely*). Let your uncle in peace, ye brat! (*She commences to cry*) Run help your mother now or I'll give ye a good hidin'. (MARY *runs out of the door, whimpering.* PAT *turns to* LUKE *and holds out his hand*)

LUKE. (*looking at it in amazement*) Ahoy, there! What's this?

SWEENEY. (*with an ingratiating smile*) Let's let bygones be bygones. I'm harborin' no grudge agen you these past years. Ye was only a lad when ye ran away an' not to be blamed for it. I'd have taken your hand a while back, an' glad to, but for her bein' with us. She has the divil's own tongue, as ye know, an' she can't forget the rowin' you an' her used to be havin'.

LUKE. (*still looking at* SWEENEY'S *hand*) So that's how the wind blows! (*With a grin*) Well, I'll take a chanct. (*They shake hands and sit down by the table,* SWEENEY *on the front bench and* LUKE *on the left one*).

SWEENEY. (*pulls the bottle from his coat pocket—with a wink*) Will ye have a taste? It's real stuff.

LUKE. Yuh betcher I will! (*He takes a big gulp and hands the bottle back*)

SWEENEY. (*after taking a drink himself, puts bottle on table*) I wasn't wishin' herself to see it or I'd have asked ye sooner. (*There is a pause, during which each measures the other with his eyes*)

LUKE. Say, how's the old man now?

SWEENEY. (*cautiously*) Oh, the same as ivir—older an' uglier, maybe.

LUKE. I thought he might be in the bug-house by this time.

SWEENEY. (*hastily*) Indeed not; he's foxy to pritind he's looney, but he's his wits with him all the time.

LUKE. (*insinuatingly*) Is he as stingy with his coin as he used to be?

SWEENEY. If he owned the ocean he wouldn't give a fish a drink; but I doubt if he's any money left at all. Your mother got rid of it all I'm thinkin'. (LUKE *smiles a superior, knowing smile*) He has on'y the farm, an' that mortgaged. I've been payin' the int'rist an' supportin' himself an' his doctor's bills by the carpentryin' these five years past.

LUKE. (*with a grin*) Huh! Yuh're slow. Yuh oughter get wise to yourself.

SWEENEY. (*inquisitively*) What d'ye mean by that?

LUKE. (*aggravatingly*) Aw, nothin'. (*He turns around and his eyes fix themselves on the rope*) What the hell—— (*He is suddenly convulsed with laughter and slaps his thigh*) Haha! If that don't beat the Dutch! The old nut!

SWEENEY. What?

LUKE. That rope. Say, has he had that hangin' there ever since I skipped?

SWEENEY. (*smiling*) Sure; an' he thinks you'll be comin' home to hang yourself.

LUKE. Hahaha! Not this chicken! And you say he ain't crazy! Gee, that's too good to keep. I got to have a drink on that. (SWEENEY *pushes the bottle toward him. He raises it toward the rope*) Here's how, old chum! (*He drinks.* SWEENEY *does likewise*) Say, I'd almost forgotten about that. Remember how hot he was that day when he hung that rope up and cussed me for pinchin' the hundred? He was standin' there shakin' his stick at me, and I was laughin' 'cause he looked so funny with the spit dribblin' outa his mouth like he was a mad dog. And when I turned round and beat it he shouted after me: "Remember, when you come home again there's a rope waitin' for yuh to hang yourself on, yuh bastard!" (*He spits contemptuously*) What a swell chanct. (*His manner changes and he frowns*) The old slave-driver! That's a hell of a fine old man for a guy to have!

SWEENEY. (*pushing the bottle toward him*) Take a sup an' forgit it. 'Twas a long time past.

LUKE. But the rope's there yet, ain't it? And he keeps it there. (*He takes a large swallow.* SWEENEY *also drinks*) But I'll git back at him aw right, yuh wait 'n' see. I'll git every cent he's got this time.

SWEENEY. (*slyly*) If he has a cent. I'm not wishful to discourage ye, but—— (*He shakes his head doubtfully, at the same time fixing* LUKE *with a keen glance out of the corner of his eye*)

LUKE. (*with a cunning wink*) Aw, he's got it aw right. You watch me! (*He is beginning to show the effects of the drink he has had. He pulls out tobacco and a paper and rolls a cigarette and lights it. As he puffs he continues boastfully*) You country jays oughter wake up and see what's goin' on. Look at me. I was green as grass when I left here, but bummin' round the world, and bein' in cities, and meetin' all kinds, and keepin' your two eyes open—that's what'll learn yuh a cute trick or two.

SWEENEY. No doubt but you're right. Us country folks is stupid in most ways. We've no chance to learn the things a travelin' lad like you'd be knowin'.

LUKE. (*complacently*) Well, you watch me and I'll learn yuh. (*He snickers*) So yuh thinks the old man's flat broke, do yuh?

SWEENEY. I do so.

LUKE. Then yuh're simple; that's what—simple! You're lettin' him kid yuh.

SWEENEY. If he has any, it's well hid, I know that. He's a sly old bird.

LUKE. And I'm a slyer bird. D'yuh hear that? I c'n beat his game any time. You watch me! (*He reaches out his hand for the bottle. They both drink again.* SWEENEY *begins to show signs of getting drunk. He hiccoughs every now and then and his voice grows uncertain and husky*).

SWEENEY. It'd be a crafty one who'd find where he'd hidden it, sure enough.

LUKE. You watch me! I'll find it. I betcher anything yuh like I find it. You watch me! Just wait till he's asleep and I'll show yuh—ternight. (*There is a noise of shuffling footsteps outside and* ANNIE'S *whining voice raised in angry protest*)

SWEENEY. Ssshh! It's himself comin' now. (LUKE *rises to his feet and stands, waiting in a defensive attitude, a surly expression on his face. A moment later* BENTLEY *appears in the doorway, followed by* ANNIE. *He leans against the wall, in an extraordinary state of excitement, shaking all over, gasping for breath, his eyes devouring* LUKE *from head to foot*)

ANNIE. I couldn't do nothin' with him. When I told him *he'd* come back there was no holdin' him. He was a'most frothin' at the mouth till I let him out. (*Whiningly*) You got to see to him, Pat, if you want any supper. I can't——

SWEENEY. Shut your mouth! We'll look after him.

ANNIE. See that you do. I'm goin' back. (*She goes off, right.* LUKE *and his father stand looking at each other. The surly expression disappears from* LUKE'S *face, which gradually expands in a broad grin*)

LUKE. (*jovially*) Hello, old sport! I s'pose yuh're tickled to pieces to see me—like hell! (*The old man stutters and stammers incoherently as if the very intensity of his desire for speech had paralyzed all power of articulation.* LUKE *turns to* PAT) I see he ain't lost the old stick. Many a crack on the nut I used to get with that.

BENTLEY. (*suddenly finding his voice—chants*) "Bring forth the best robe, and put it on him; and put a ring on his hand, and shoes on his feet: And bring hither the fatted calf, and kill it; and let us eat and be merry: For this my son was dead, and is alive again; he was lost, and is found." (*He ends up with a convulsive sob*)

LUKE. (*disapprovingly*) Yuh're still spoutin' the rotten old Word o' God same's ever, eh? Say, give us a rest on that stuff, will yuh? Come on and shake hands like a good sport. (*He holds out his hand. The old man totters over to him, stretching out a trembling hand.* LUKE *seizes it and pumps it up and down*) That's the boy!

SWEENEY. (*genuinely amazed*) Look at that, would ye—the

two-faced auld liar. (BENTLEY *passes his trembling hand all over* LUKE, *feeling of his arms, his chest, his back. An expression of overwhelming joy suffuses his worn features*)

LUKE. (*grinning at* SWEENEY) Say, watch this. (*With tolerant good-humor*) On the level I b'lieve the old boy's glad to see me at that. He looks like he was tryin' to grin; and I never seen him grin in my life, I c'n remember. (*As* BENTLEY *attempts to feel of his face*) Hey, cut it out! (*He pushes his hand away, but not roughly*) I'm all here, yuh needn't worry. Yuh needn't be scared I'm a ghost. Come on and sit down before yuh fall down. Yuh ain't got your sea-legs workin' right. (*He guides the old man to the bench at left of table*) Squat here for a spell and git your wind. (BENTLEY *sinks down on the bench.* LUKE *reaches for the bottle*) Have a drink to my makin' port. It'll buck yuh up.

SWEENEY. (*alarmed*) Be careful, Luke. It might likely end him.

LUKE. (*holds the bottle up to the old man's mouth, supporting his head with the other hand.* BENTLEY *gulps, the whiskey drips over his chin, and he goes into a fit of convulsive coughing.* LUKE *laughs*) Hahaha! Went down the wrong way, did it? I'll show yuh the way to do it. (*He drinks*) There yuh are—smooth as silk. (*He hands the bottle to* SWEENEY, *who drinks and puts it back on the table*)

SWEENEY. He must be glad to see ye or he'd not drink. 'Tis dead against it he's been these five years past. (*Shaking his head*) An' him cursin' you day an' night! I can't put head or tail to it. Look out he ain't meanin' some bad to ye underneath. He's crafty at pretendin'.

LUKE. (*as the old man makes signs to him with his hand*)

What's he after now? He's lettin' on he's lost his voice again. What d'yuh want? (BENTLEY *points with his stick to the rope. His lips move convulsively as he makes a tremendous effort to utter words*)

BENTLEY. (*mumbling incoherently*) Luke—Luke—rope—Luke—hang.

SWEENEY. (*appalled*) There ye are! What did I tell you? It's to see you hang yourself he's wishin', the auld fiend!

BENTLEY. (*nodding*) Yes—Luke—hang.

LUKE. (*taking it as a joke—with a loud guffaw*) Hahaha! If that don't beat the Dutch! The old nanny-goat! Aw right, old sport. Anything to oblige. Hahaha! (*He takes the chair from left and places it under the rope. The old man watches him with eager eyes and seems to be trying to smile.* LUKE *stands on the chair*)

SWEENEY. Have a care, now! I'd not be foolin' with it in your place.

LUKE. All out for the big hangin' of Luke Bentley by hisself. (*He puts the noose about his neck with an air of drunken bravado and grins at his father. The latter makes violent motions for him to go on*) Look at him, Pat. By God, he's in a hurry. Hahaha! Well, old sport, here goes nothin'. (*He makes a movement as if he were going to jump and kick the chair from under him*)

SWEENEY. (*half starts to his feet—horrified*) Luke! Are ye gone mad?

LUKE. (*stands staring at his father, who is still making gestures for him to jump. A scowl slowly replaces his good-natured grin*) D'yuh really mean it—that yuh want to see me hangin' myself? (BENTLEY *nods vigorously in the affirmative.* LUKE *glares at him for a moment in silence*) Well, I'll be damned! (*To* PAT) An' I thought he was only kiddin'. (*He removes the rope gingerly from his neck. The old man stamps his foot and gesticulates wildly, groaning with disappointment.* LUKE *jumps to the floor and looks at his father for a second. Then his face grows white with a vicious fury*) I'll fix your hash, you stinkin' old murderer! (*He grabs the chair by its back and swings it over his head as if he were going to crush* BENTLEY'S *skull with it. The old man cowers on the bench in abject terror*)

SWEENEY. (*jumping to his feet with a cry of alarm*) Luke! For the love of God! (LUKE *hesitates; then hurls the chair in back of him under the loft, and stands menacingly in front of his father, his hands on his hips*)

LUKE. (*grabbing* BENTLEY'S *shoulder and shaking him—hoarsely*) Yuh wanted to see me hangin' there in real earnest, didn't yuh? You'd hang me yourself if yuh could, wouldn't yuh? And you my own father! Yuh damned son-of-a-gun! Yuh would, would yuh? I'd smash your brains out for a nickel! (*He shakes the old man more and more furiously*)

SWEENEY. Luke! Look out! You'll be killin' him next.

LUKE. (*giving his father one more shake, which sends him sprawling on the floor*) Git outa here! Git outa this b'fore I kill yuh dead! (SWEENEY *rushes over and picks the terrified old man up*) Take him outa here, Pat! (*His voice rises to a threatening roar*) Take him outa here or I'll break every bone in his body! (*He raises his clenched fists over his head in a frenzy of rage*)

SWEENEY. Ssshh! Don't be roarin'! I've got him. (*He

steers the whimpering, hysterical BENTLEY *to the doorway*) Come out o' this, now. Get down to the house! Hurry now! Ye've made enough trouble for one night! (*They disappear off right.* LUKE *flings himself on a bench, breathing heavily. He picks up the bottle and takes a long swallow.* SWEENEY *re-enters from rear. He comes over and sits down in his old place*) Thank God he's off down to the house, scurryin' like a frightened hare as if he'd never a kink in his legs in his life. He was moanin' out loud so you could hear him a long ways. (*With a sigh*) It's a murd'rous auld loon he is, sure enough.

LUKE. (*thickly*) The damned son-of-a-gun!

SWEENEY. I thought you'd be killin' him that time with the chair.

LUKE. (*violently*) Serve him damn right if I done it.

SWEENEY. An' you laughin' at him a moment sooner! I thought 'twas jokin' ye was.

LUKE. (*suddenly*) So I was kiddin'; but I thought he was tryin' to kid me, too. And then I seen by the way he acted he really meant it. (*Banging the table with his fist*) Ain't that a hell of a fine old man for yuh!

SWEENEY. He's a mean auld swine.

LUKE. He meant it aw right, too. Yuh shoulda seen him lookin' at me. (*With sudden lugubriousness*) Ain't he a hell of a nice old man for a guy to have? Ain't he?

SWEENEY. (*soothingly*) Hush! It's all over now. Don't be thinkin' about it.

LUKE. (*on the verge of drunken tears*) How kin I help thinkin'—and him my own father? After me bummin' and starvin' round the rotten earth, and workin' myself to death on ships and things—and when I come home he tries to make me bump off—wants to see me a corpse—my own father, too! Ain't he a hell of an old man to have? The rotten son-of-a-gun!

SWEENEY. It's past an' done. Forgit it. (*He slaps* LUKE *on the shoulder and pushes the bottle toward him*) Let's take a drop more. We'll be goin' to supper soon.

LUKE. (*takes a big drink—huskily*) Thanks. (*He wipes his mouth on his sleeve with a snuffle*) But I'll tell yuh something you can put in your pipe and smoke. It ain't past and done, and it ain't goin' to be! (*More and more aggressively*) And I ain't goin' to ferget it, either! Yuh kin betcher life on that, pal. And *he* ain't goin' to ferget it—not if he lives a million—not by a damned sight! (*With sudden fury*) I'll fix his hash! I'll git even with him, the old skunk! You watch me! And this very night, too!

SWEENEY. How'd you mean?

LUKE. You just watch me, I tell yuh! (*Banging the table*) I said I'd git even and I will git even—this same night, with no long waits, either! (*Frowning*) Say, you don't stand up for him, do yuh?

SWEENEY. (*spitting—vehemently*) That's child's talk. There's not a day passed I've not wished him in his grave.

LUKE. (*excitedly*) Then we'll both git even on him—you 'n' me. We're pals, ain't we?

SWEENEY. Sure.

LUKE. And yuh kin have half what we gits. That's the kinda feller I am! That's fair enough, ain't it?

SWEENEY. Surely.

LUKE. I don't want no truck with this rotten farm. You kin have my share of that. I ain't made to be no damned dirt-puncher—not me! And I ain't goin' to loaf round here more'n

I got to, and when I goes this time I ain't never comin' back. Not me! Not to punch dirt and milk cows. You kin have the rotten farm for all of me. What I wants is cash—regular coin yuh kin spend—not dirt. I want to show the gang a real time, and then ship away to sea agen or go bummin' agen. I want coin yuh kin throw away—same's your kid chucked that dollar of mine overboard, remember? A real dollar, too! She's a sport, aw right!

SWEENEY. (*anxious to bring him back to the subject*) But where d'you think to find his money?

LUKE. (*confidently*) Don't yuh fret. I'll show yuh. You watch me! I know his hidin' places. I useter spy on him when I was a kid—— Maw used to make me—and I seen him many a time at his sneakin'. (*Indignantly*) He used to hide stuff from the old lady. What d'yuh know about him—the mean skunk.

SWEENEY. That was a long time back. You don't know——

LUKE. (*assertively*) But I do know, see! He's got two places. One was where I swiped the hundred.

SWEENEY. It'll not be there, then.

LUKE. No; but there's the other place; and he never knew I was wise to that. I'd have left him clean on'y I was a kid and scared to pinch more. So you watch me! We'll git even on him, you 'n' me, and go halfs, and yuh kin start the rotten farm goin' agen and I'll beat it where there's some life.

SWEENEY. But if there's no money in that place, what'll you be doin' to find out where it is, then?

LUKE. Then you 'n' me 'ull make him tell!

SWEENEY. Oho, don't think it! 'Tis not him'd be tellin'.

LUKE. Aw, say, you're simple! You watch me! I know a

trick or two about makin' people tell what they don't wanter. (*He picks up the chisel from the table*) Yuh see this? Well, if he don't answer up nice and easy we'll show him! (*A ferocious grin settles over his face*) We'll git even on him, you 'n' me—and he'll tell where it's hid. We'll just shove this into the stove till it's red-hot and take off his shoes and socks and warm the bottoms of his feet for him. (*Savagely*) He'll tell then—anything we wants him to tell.

SWEENEY. But Annie?

LUKE. We'll shove a rag in her mouth so's she can't yell. That's easy.

SWEENEY. (*his head lolling drunkenly—with a cruel leer*) 'Twill serve him right to heat up his hoofs for him, the limpin' auld miser!—if ye don't hurt him too much.

LUKE. (*with a savage scowl*) We won't hurt him—more'n enough. (*Suddenly raging*) I'll pay him back aw right! He won't want no more people to hang themselves when I git through with him. I'll fix his hash! (*He sways to his feet, the chisel in his hand*) Come on! Let's git to work. Sooner we starts the sooner we're rich. (SWEENEY *rises. He is steadier on his feet than* LUKE. *At this moment* MARY *appears in the doorway*)

MARY. Maw says supper's ready. I had mine. (*She comes into the room and jumps up, trying to grab hold of the rope*) Lift me, Uncle Luke. I wanter swing.

LUKE. (*severely*) Don't yuh dare touch that rope, d'yuh hear?

MARY. (*whining*) I wanter swing.

LUKE. (*with a shiver*) It's bad, kid. Yuh leave it alone, take it from me.

SWEENEY. She'll get a good whalin' if I catch her jumpin' at it.

LUKE. Come on, pal. T'hell with supper. We got work to do first. (*They go to the doorway*)

SWEENEY. (*turning back to the sulking* MARY) And you stay here, d'you hear, ye brat, till we call ye—or I'll skin ye alive.

LUKE. And termorrer mornin', kid, I'll give yuh a whole handful of them shiny, bright things yuh chucked in the ocean —and yuh kin be a real sport.

MARY. (*eagerly*) Gimme 'em now! Gimme 'em now, Uncle Luke. (*As he shakes his head—whiningly*) Gimme one! Gimme one!

LUKE. Can't be done, kid. Termorrer. Me 'n' your old man is goin' to git even now—goin' to make him pay for——

SWEENEY. (*interrupting—harshly*) Hist with your noise! D'you think she's no ears? Don't be talkin' so much. Come on, now.

LUKE. (*permitting himself to be pulled out the doorway*) Aw right! I'm with yuh. We'll git even—you 'n' me. The damned son-of-a-gun! (*They lurch off to the right*)

(MARY *skips to the doorway and peeps after them for a moment. Then she comes back to the center of the floor and looks around her with an air of decision. She sees the chair in under the loft and runs over to it, pulling it back and setting it on its legs directly underneath the noose of the rope. She climbs and stands on the top of the chair and grasps the noose with both her upstretched hands. Then with a shriek of delight she kicks the chair from under her and launches herself for a swing. The rope seems to part where it is fixed to the beam. A dirty gray bag tied to the end of the rope falls to the floor with a muffled, metallic thud.* MARY *sprawls forward on her hands and knees, whimpering. Straggly wisps from the pile of rank hay fall silently to the floor in a mist of dust.* MARY, *discovering she is unhurt, glances quickly around and sees the bag. She pushes herself along the floor and, untying the string at the top, puts in her hand. She gives an exclamation of joy at what she feels and, turning the bag upside down, pours its contents in her lap. Giggling to herself, she gets to her feet and goes to the doorway, where she dumps what she has in her lap in a heap on the floor just inside the barn. They lie there in a glittering pile, shimmering in the faint sunset glow—fifty twenty-dollar gold pieces.* MARY *claps her hands and sings to herself: "Skip—skip—skip." Then she quickly picks up four or five and runs out to the edge of the cliff. She throws them one after another into the ocean as fast as she can and bends over to see them hit the water. Against the background of horizon clouds still tinted with blurred crimson she hops up and down in a sort of grotesque dance, clapping her hands and laughing shrilly. After the last one is thrown she rushes back into the barn to get more)*

MARY. (*picking up a handful—giggling ecstastically*) Skip! Skip! (*She turns and runs out to throw them as*

The Curtain Falls)

O'NEILL